IT'S **NOT** ALL IN YOUR HEAD

IT'S NOT
ALL IN YOUR HEAD

Now Women Can Discover
the Real Causes of Their Most
Commonly Misdiagnosed
Health Problems

**SUSAN SWEDO, M.D.,
HENRIETTA LEONARD, M.D.**

HarperSanFrancisco
An Imprint of HarperCollins*Publishers*

The opinions expressed herein are the views of the authors and do not necessarily reflect the official position of the National Institute of Mental Health or any other part of the U.S. Department of Health and Human Services.

All of the stories contained in this book are works of fiction. They are based on a combination of our experience and imagination, as well as known features of various psychiatric and medical conditions. Any resemblance to actual events or persons, living or dead, is entirely coincidental.

HarperCollins Web Site: http://www.harpercollins.com

HarperCollins®, ®, and HarperSanFrancisco™ are trademarks of HarperCollins Publishers, Inc.

FIRST EDITION

Library of Congress Cataloging-in-Publication Data
Swedo, Susan Anderson.
It's not all in your head : now women can discover the real causes of their most commonly misdiagnosed health problems / by Susan Anderson Swedo, Henrietta L. Leonard.
Includes bibliographical references.
ISBN 0–06–251286–2 (cloth)
ISBN 0–06–251287–0 (pbk.)
1. Biological psychiatry. 2. Women—Mental health. 3. Psychological manifestations of general diseases. I. Leonard, Henrietta L. II. Title.
RC455.4.B5S94 1996
616.89'0082—dc20   95–26602

96 97 98 99 00 ❖ RRD (H) 10 9 8 7 6 5 4 3 2 1

Dedicated to our families and friends

Contents

Acknowledgments

We are grateful to so many people for their help with *It's Not All In Your Head* and particularly to:

Our parents and grandparents for their love, faith, and constant support.

Our patients for teaching us to listen and helping us to understand that all symptoms have meaning and importance.

Phyllis Alexander, Edis Anderson, Holly Clement, Linda Dickson, Lucinda Dittmer, Dixie Jamison, Susan King, Ann Leonard, Susan Loughman, and Patty Mahafkey for their friendship and for encouraging us to "stop talking and start writing!"

Dr. Martha Manning for getting us started and for networking on our behalf.

Drs. Jane Gregoritch Baxter, Lewis Baxter, John Greist, Suzanne Griffin, Michael Jenike, Ellen Leibenluft, Martha Manning, Norman Rosenthal, Fuller Torrey, and Jerry Wiener for their letters of support.

Our colleagues at the National Institute of Mental Health for their many research contributions and for their continued efforts to find the cause and cure of mental illness.

Our mentor, Dr. Judith Rapoport, for all she has taught us.

Marsha Corbett, Billinda Dubbert, Beth Dyer, Elizabeth Gallup Spencer, and Drs. Marti Altemus, Lori Altshuler, F. Xavier Castellanos, Stephen Clement, Deborah Dauphinais, Carol Ann Dyer, Marjorie Garvey, Helene Emsellem, Ellen Leibenluft, John March, Barbara Mittleman, Katharine A. Phillips, Frank Putnam, Donna Randolph, Kenneth Rickler, and Sue Yanovski for their expertise and many helpful suggestions.

Cindy Anderson, Colleen Anderson, Leslie Armbruster, Lisa Bach, Diane Gnepp, Bunny Holliday, Marge Lenane, Edward Leonard,

Susan Leonard, Linda Randolph, Terry Rickler, Amy Rose, Kathy Ryan, Brenda Sandler, Lisa Miron Sidel, Jeanne Swedo, JoLynn Swedo, and Barb Tookey for their invaluable contributions.

Sara Dow and Maxine Steyer for the multitude of ways in which they made this book possible (and our lives easier!).

Elizabeth Swedo for editing early versions of the manuscript, Helen Goliash for her secretarial assistance, and Gregory Swedo for his computer help (without which, he says, the writing of this book would have taken much less time).

Arielle Eckstut, our agent, and Barbara Moulton, our editor, for all that they have done to turn a dream into reality.

Our wonderful children for letting their moms take on this task, and

Our beloved husbands for their love and patience.

Thank you all!

Introduction

Jewell, a forty-three-year-old mother of three, taught a special education class at the local elementary school, coached her daughter's soccer team, and was former president of the PTA. She was frequently described as a steadying force and a woman who had both feet firmly planted on the ground. She was as far from "attention seeking" as a woman could get, and no one would ever think of her as "flighty," much less label her as "a hysterical female." Yet it was exactly those words that the intern at the world-famous clinic used to describe Jewell as he spoke quietly to her husband about Jewell's "psychotic delusions."

Jewell had gone to the clinic with a variety of symptoms—fleeting periods of numbness in her hands and arms, small white patches on her skin that came and went, vague physical discomforts, and excruciating headaches that were accompanied by extreme fatigue, nausea, and vomiting. She had seen her doctor dozens of times for these symptoms before he finally made the referral. Until he saw the white patches with his own eyes, he had merely shaken his head and offered reassurances, but once he observed that her symptoms were real, he quickly referred her to the experts at the clinic. It had taken several more months to get an appointment, and Jewell's symptoms had continued to become worse. And now an impatient young intern listened to only half her story and performed a very cursory examination before concluding that Jewell's symptoms couldn't be real—they must be imagined. The intern's supervising physician spent even less time with Jewell before confirming the novice's diagnosis and recommending psychiatric treatment.

Jewell was both humiliated and furious. Why hadn't her doctor given the consultants the background information they needed in order to make the proper diagnosis? How could the so-called experts dismiss her symptoms before completing their evaluation? Why wouldn't anyone believe her?

Fortunately, Jewell was able to schedule a consultation with an immunologist at another hospital. There, the doctor took a complete history and performed a careful physical examination that revealed subtle changes in the skin and blood vessels. After asking some additional questions and listening thoughtfully to Jewell's answers, this doctor ordered laboratory studies that confirmed that Jewell had a connective tissue disease. The disease caused temporary spasms of the blood vessels—leading not only to the headaches but also to the numbness, tingling, and the white spots on her skin. Jewell faced a lifetime of therapy, but she knew that she could handle it. At last she was on the right track because someone had finally believed that her symptoms were not "all in her head"!

Jewell's physical illness was misdiagnosed partly because the doctors were faced with an uncommon illness and chose to dismiss her symptoms as imagined, rather than tracking down the true cause. Misdiagnoses are also made when doctors fail to recognize the psychiatric disorders underlying physical symptoms.

The paramedic spoke quickly to the doctor: "We've got a fifty-year-old female here with complaints of chest tightness, rapid pulse, and difficulty breathing. Respirations are 40 and labored, pulse is 110 but strong, and EKG monitor strip looks good. She's got four liters of oxygen running, and we started an IV with Lactated Ringers solution in the field. She's all yours; I've got another run to make." And with that, he left.

It was difficult for Lois to speak through the oxygen mask, so the emergency room physician asked her very few questions. He performed a quick physical exam, asked the nurse to run a cardiac rhythm strip, and ordered some blood work. Then he went off to see the next patient. Lois was left lying on the narrow bed, wondering if she was going to die. That was how this whole thing had started—with this terrible feeling that she was going to die.

Lois had been driving across a long bridge that morning on her way to work; traffic had been terrible and had come to a standstill right in the middle of the bridge. It was then that this terrible feeling of impending doom had come over her. Lois felt certain that she was about to die. Her chest felt heavy and tight, she could feel her pulse racing, and she couldn't breathe. No matter how hard she tried, Lois just couldn't get enough air. She stumbled out of her car and knocked on the window of the closest vehicle. Fortunately, the driver had a cellular phone and quickly called for help. The paramedics came within a few minutes, and by the time they arrived, Lois was feeling a little bit better. She tried to explain what had happened, but the paramedics advised her, "Keep still, ma'am, while we get you hooked up here," and "Shhh, save your strength, ma'am, looks like you're going to need it." So she rode silently to the hospital.

The emergency room physician returned and told Lois that she hadn't had a heart attack: "Your symptoms aren't really typical for a myocardial infarction—your physical exam is OK, and your rhythm strip looks perfect. I don't know what happened earlier this morning, but you're fine now. Follow up with your doctor in a few days to make sure your heart rate settles down."

Lois dressed and left, wondering whether she was really fine or whether her heart was about to stop. After all, the emergency room physician hadn't spent much time with her, and he might have missed something. The more she thought about it, the more concerned she became, so she drove straight to her doctor's office. When she reached Dr. Banks's office, she explained her problem to the nurse and was taken immediately to an examining room. Dr. Banks followed her in.

"What's wrong, Lois? Something with your heart?"

Lois explained what had happened on the bridge while Dr. Banks looked over the emergency room papers. Then he performed a brief examination and said, "Lois, it looks like you're going to be fine. I don't know what happened on the bridge this morning, but it wasn't a heart attack. Everything checks out on my exam now, but at your age, we can't be too careful, so let's get some more blood work and send you off for a stress test, an echocardiogram, and another rhythm strip. You have insurance, don't you?"

Lois told Dr. Banks that her husband's company had switched to a health maintenance organization (HMO) and that she wasn't covered yet because she had refused to switch doctors. Dr. Banks frowned and said, "Well, these tests are pretty expensive. Let's just hold off for a few days and check you again on Friday."

When Friday came, Dr. Banks seemed satisfied with her condition and told her he didn't need to see her again.

"You're fine. Looks like that little episode was nothing serious. You'll probably never know exactly what it was, but it's time to get on with your life. Tell your husband hello for me."

Lois nodded and left his office. But as she walked to her car she wondered, What did happen to me on that bridge? It wasn't nothing—it was real. I felt like I was going to die. I was almost certain that I was going to suffocate. I don't ever want to feel that way again—I couldn't bear it. Oh, my God, what if it happens again?

And it could. Because Lois had suffered her first panic attack on the bridge that morning. Panic attacks are a terrifying combination of physical and psychological symptoms. They occur suddenly and without warning—just like heart attacks do. But having a normal cardiac exam doesn't prevent panic attacks from recurring, and Lois left her doctor's office without any understanding of what was wrong with her and without adequate protection against future episodes. The more often panic attacks occur, the more debilitated the sufferers become. They live in terror that they will have another attack, afraid to go outside for fear they won't be able to get help, afraid to be in crowds for fear that they won't be able to escape, afraid to stay home alone because there is no one there to save them. And so they become prisoners of their illness. (Chapter Twelve offers a full description of panic attacks.)

Lois and Jewell are both victims of misdiagnosis. Jewell was told that her symptoms were "all in her head" when they weren't; Lois was told that she was "fine" when she wasn't. Their sagas served as inspiration for this book, because their experiences are far too common. Too many women have been sent home from the emergency room with the reassurance "you're fine" when they know that they are not. Or they are hospitalized or treated with drugs in order to eliminate the psychological causes of their "imagined" physical symptoms. But the treatments are not effective because the symptoms have not been diagnosed properly. In some unfortunate cases, the treatments induce side effects that leave the woman feeling tired and confused, or they have even more serious medical consequences. One purpose of this book is to provide information about the medical conditions that masquerade as psychiatric conditions, as well as the psychiatric conditions that mimic physical illnesses. With this information, it will be possible for you to help your doctor make the correct diagnosis.

Each set of symptoms that you bring to your doctor has an extensive "differential diagnosis." This means that there are multiple causes of most symptoms, and your physician must sort through these causes to determine the proper diagnosis and the proper treatment. This book will teach you about the common medical and psychiatric symptom complexes so that you can relay your history more precisely to your doctor.

It is important to use this book only as an aid to improving your relationship with your doctor rather than as a substitute for professional medical care. If a physical illness is the cause of your symptoms, then it should be diagnosed correctly and treated properly. If prescription medications or over-the-counter drugs are causing the symptoms, then they should be eliminated. If the symptoms are the result of a psychiatric disorder, then it too should be treated—without shame or stigmatization. This book will present you with information about when, how, and from whom to seek treatment and what to expect when you get it.

Unfortunately, it is often more difficult to seek treatment for psychiatric illnesses than for physical illnesses. A history of psychiatric treatment can make it more difficult to get certain kinds of insurance or to pass employment health exams. Thus, many people choose to suffer in silence. This is a tragedy. We will truly be free and empowered as women only when there is no more stigmatization of mental illness—when psychiatric disorders are considered to be medical conditions and, as such, on a par with other physical disorders.

Once we understand the cause of psychological disturbances, there will be no need to label its victims as weak or unbalanced. We hope that all of us will arrive at this understanding soon, and we take heart from the fact that it has already happened for many other illnesses. For example, epilepsy was once thought to represent demonic possession, but we now know that it is the result of abnormal electrical discharges in the brain. Patients with epilepsy are treated with medications and can lead a normal life. Tuberculosis was also originally considered to be the victim's fault. Before it was known that a bacteria causes tuberculosis, it was called "consumption"—a weakness that mainly afflicted young women of delicate constitutions. The illness had a mystical quality about it; it seemed to choose its victims by some unseen character flaw, skipping over some while taking others. We now know the reasons why some are afflicted and others are spared. We know the cause of tuberculosis and the cure, and this knowledge takes the mystery out of the illness. With mental illnesses, we now know the cause for some, we know the cure for a few, and for many we know the right treatments. The mystery is slowly disappearing. It is time for the stigmatization to disappear as well.

Advances in medical science in the past decade offer proof that all thoughts, feelings, and emotions are the result of chemical transmissions in individual nerve cells. This means that all psychological symptoms represent an alteration of a biochemical system in the brain, much as diabetes represents a malfunction of the glucose regulating system. If it sounds like human thoughts and feelings have been reduced to a mundane series of biochemical events, they have not. In fact, the recent scientific discoveries are revealing a process even more miraculous than we had dared to imagine before. It is a true miracle that the complex chemical transmissions occur in such a precise sequence and that the neurological processes result in such a wide variety of thoughts, feelings, behaviors, and emotions. It is awesome to contemplate that such complexity can be so carefully regulated by our bodies and frightening to think how subtle the alterations might be that cause the psychiatric disorders. Understanding the processes underlying mental health and mental illness is the challenge of psychiatric medicine in the next century.

For the present, we hope that this book will help you to understand that the mind is indistinguishable from the brain, that the brain is intimately connected to the body, and that if you suffer from depression or an anxiety disorder, you should feel no more shame than if you were diagnosed with diabetes or heart disease. For when the stigma is gone, women will finally receive both quality and equality in medical and psychiatric health care.

A Note to Our Readers

This book presents an approach to mental health that is subject to differences of opinion and interpretation. Although every effort has been made to ensure that all medical information presented here is accurate at the time of publication, therapeutic standards may change as medical research and practice advance. The authors and publisher expressly disclaim responsibility for any adverse effects resulting from the information contained herein.

In addition, this book is not intended as a substitute for the advice of a physician, and the reader should address any questions she may have to her own health care provider.

PART 1

EVOLUTIONS AND REVOLUTIONS

in Psychiatry

CHAPTER 1

From "Penis Envy" to Prozac:
The Revolution in Women's Psychiatry

Esther was a trichotillomaniac—a compulsive hair puller. She knew that she was because her psychiatrist had just told her so. Dr. Smith had pronounced his diagnosis with such great authority that Esther had no doubt that he was right. She was a trichotillomaniac. She wanted to ask about the diagnosis and what it meant, but instead, Dr. Smith was asking her the very same questions: "Why do you think that you pull out your hair, Esther? What does your hair pulling mean to you? Why do you think that you are choosing not to stop?"

With Dr. Smith's therapeutic prodding, Esther struggled to answer. But the answers didn't come quickly, and the pair met three times a week for over two months before Esther was able to come to any kind of self-awareness. Even then, it all seemed to come out in a mixed-up jumble. Dr. Smith had suggested so many possible explanations for her problem. She had started pulling her hair out when she was twelve years old—right around the time she got her first period. This might mean that she pulled her hair out because she didn't want to grow up or that she was ambivalent about her femininity. Perhaps she was rejecting her womanhood. Perhaps she had profound "penis envy" and pulled her hair out because it was long and thin, a phallic symbol representing her jealousy of men and her long-repressed childhood sexual fantasies.

Or maybe her hair pulling was a means of recapturing her happy childhood memories. Esther remembered that when she was a little girl, her mother had always held her tightly as she combed her hair out in the morning. Her mother had been very stiff and cold, and those interactions were the only times that her mother touched her. Maybe this meant that she pulled her hair out in order to recreate those moments, to experience her mother's love and affection once again. If only her mother had been more loving, maybe Esther wouldn't be nearly bald. Dr. Smith reflected that Esther seemed to be blaming her mother for her hair pulling and suggested that she explore the meaning of these feelings. Esther spent the next several months delving into the unsatisfactory relationship that she had had with her mother. It was hard work, but it was very helpful. Esther began to understand many things about herself and about the other failed relationships she'd had throughout her life. She began to feel happier and more at peace with herself. But she didn't stop pulling her hair.

After a while, it became clear that her relationship with her mother wasn't an adequate explanation for her symptoms. Esther was mainly concerned with the pain that she felt while pulling her hair and with the shame and humiliation that her baldness brought to her. She didn't want to keep pulling her hair, yet she couldn't stop. Why was she doing this to herself?

Dr. Smith answered Esther's question with a question. Could it be that her pain and self-mutilation were actually bringing her pleasure? Perhaps she had a deep-seated need to be hurt and humiliated. Perhaps she was actually enjoying the pain and embarrassment that her hair pulling caused and that was why she refused to "let go" of her hair-pulling symptom. Dr. Smith encouraged Esther to explore the origins of her masochism by bringing her unconscious conflicts into conscious awareness and resolving them there. Only then would she be free of her hair pulling.

It took several more months of therapy, but eventually, through free associations and dream interpretations, Esther was brought to the realization that her hair pulling was indeed a form of self-punishment—a means of seeking and gaining attention. Her bald spots drew attention; even though the strangers' stares were ones of disgust or pity, people noticed her. Otherwise she seemed to go through life as an invisible shadow. It was the same with the pain. Even though the hair pulling hurt, it was a "good" pain; she felt alive and connected to the world for the moment that she was experiencing it. At other times, she felt halfdead, cut off from herself and her experiences—just as she had when she was a child.

They were back to her mother again. Dr. Smith had helped Esther understand that her mother's lack of love and attention was the cause of it all—especially the masochism. Her mother had never provided her with the positive loving attention that every child deserves; she had only given negative attention in the form of punishment for bad behavior. As a young girl, Esther had learned to do naughty things so that her mother would hold her and talk to her, even if it was only to hold her still while she spanked her or to yell at her for being "stupid" or "lazy" or "bad." When Esther grew older, though, her mother just sent her to her room when she misbehaved. Even being naughty didn't make her mother notice her. But the bald spots did.

Her mother hated Esther's growing bald spots, and she spent a lot of time taking Esther to beauty parlors and doctor's offices and special clinics, seeking a cause and a cure for the hair loss. Her mother seemed so concerned about her, and they had such special times together as they traveled from one expert to another. It took months before the specialists figured out that Esther herself was the cause of the baldness, and even then it was OK, because her mother was still paying attention to her. She constantly nagged Esther to "stop pulling" and "stop touching your hair." Occasionally she'd say, "Here, let me fix your hair; you know the doctors said that it would help you stop pulling your hair out if you just took a little pride in your appearance." That was the best—her mother was making her look pretty. For a few short months, Esther had what she had always wanted and needed: her mother's attention and a small amount of care and concern.

Finally, Esther was beginning to see what Dr. Smith had wanted her to understand. It was all her own fault in a way. Even though the hair pulling hurt, it also helped; it served a purpose. She had brought it all on herself, and she could choose to stop it. Esther felt a sense of peace and contentment come over her. With Dr. Smith's help, she had finally figured it all out. Her hair pulling was a reflection of her masochism, which could be traced back to her mother's cold detachment. Esther turned to thank the therapist, but just as she did so, a thought struck her and she said, "But, Dr. Smith, if my relationship with my mother was the cause of all of this, why am I still pulling my hair out? My mother has been dead for over ten years."

"Ah, Esther . . . Let's try to understand your continuing need to redo your relationship with your mother through the hair pulling. What do you think it might mean? Why do you think that you continue to pull out *your hair, Esther? What does your hair pulling mean to you? Why do you think that you are still choosing not to stop?"*

With Dr. Smith's prodding, Esther struggled to answer these questions, and the therapy sessions continued.

Although Esther's story is fictionalized, it is not an exaggeration. We have seen dozens of patients who have spent ten years or longer in therapy for their hair pulling, without significant symptom improvement. Like Esther, they gain self-awareness and better self-understanding, but they never stop pulling their hair. This is because the hair pulling is usually a symptom of trichotillomania, rather than a symbol of masochism. Fortunately, we now know that trichotillomania is a biologically based disorder for which drug and behavior therapies are quite effective (see Chapter Fifteen). Unfortunately, this message isn't yet widespread. Women with trichotillomania and those with other psychiatric disorders, such as anorexia or anxiety or depression, are still being told that their symptoms arise from masochistic tendencies—that (at least unconsciously) their symptoms are "all their own fault."

Masochism—"It's All Your Own Fault"

Originally, the term *masochism* and its counterpart, *sadomasochism*, referred to men who achieved sexual arousal either through their own or through another's suffering. However, Dr. Sigmund Freud noted that masochism was not just related to men's sexual gratification but rather to all life circumstances. He proposed that women as a whole were masochistic by nature and that they "chose" to suffer in order to "gain" from the suffering.[1] Because the masochistic symptoms were of their own choosing (even if unconsciously), the masochism was their own fault. Freud believed that psychotherapy could help these women to understand their need for punishment and self-debasement and to replace these maladaptive responses with other, more positive patterns of behavior. But without such insight, the masochistic women were destined to seek pain and humiliation over and over again. Thus, Freud single-handedly rewrote psychiatric history: what had previously been a male sexual deviance became a female psychiatric disorder.

Over the next century, the diagnosis of masochism would continue to be used to criticize women for their "passivity" and victimization.

With the advent of a standardized diagnostic system, masochism was re-named "self-defeating personality disorder," but the meaning was the same: the woman is to blame for her own misfortune; she has set herself up to be victimized—"she has asked for it."

Judith Herman, in her book *Trauma and Recovery*, details how society continues to use the masochistic model to punish those who have been victimized.[2] She observes that a woman who has been raped is first traumatized by an individual, then by a system that strips the woman of her privacy and puts her reputation on trial. College students who attempt to charge acquaintances with date rape may find their prior sexual history a matter of public record. The implication is that if the young woman has had sexual intercourse previously, then she is somehow deserving of the assault—she asked for it. If that tactic fails, then she is labeled as having a "self-defeating personality disorder," with the implication being that her personality disorder caused her to invite the attack—she needed it. The label of self-defeating personality disorder has also been assigned to women who have filed sexual harassment or sexual discrimination suits. Their complaints have been completely discredited because the harassing males were, supposedly, merely responding to the women's need to be victimized—once again, it was the woman's fault.

Colette Dowling condemns such blame shifting in *The Cinderella Complex*.[3] She argues that women do not cause their own masochism and victimization but rather that society requires it of them by conditioning them to be subservient. Society has portrayed the ideal woman as patient, self-sacrificing, and obedient; she is taught to follow different rules than the ideal man, who is seen as self-sufficient, demanding of excellence, and assertive. In this societal model, the ideal man would reward the ideal woman's patience and self-sacrifice by taking care of her—riding in on his white horse and rescuing her from her travails.

The masochistic woman is thus merely a more vulnerable variant of the ideal woman. She is so dependent that she fears abandonment even more than she fears the harsh treatment that she receives. Because she is robbed of her self-esteem and feels powerless to effect meaningful improvements in her life, she acts in a manner that leads others to treat her as a dependent victim, creating a vicious cycle from which she cannot escape—until society and psychiatry stop blaming her and start helping her.[4]

Stigmatization

Treating someone with a mental illness differently or badly is called stigmatization, but it's really just plain old bigotry and discrimination. In many ways our understanding of mental illness hasn't really advanced at all beyond the notion of masochism—we still blame the victim. The blame serves to separate us from mental illness, to protect us in a way. If psychiatric disorders are the result of character flaws or poor parenting, then it couldn't happen to us, because we know that *we* aren't bad or weak. We would never *choose* to be mentally ill (even unconsciously), so we must be safe. It's their family member, not ours. It's her problem, not mine. The mentally ill must be held responsible for their symptoms, because if they're not, then it could happen to us or to someone we love.

In order for the separation and the "protection" of stigmatization to occur, the people who are suffering from a mental disorder must be identifiably different from yourself. This means that when you have a mental illness, you become that illness, just as Esther in our story becomes a trichotillomaniac. While women *get* cancer or *have* heart disease, they *are* anorexic or depressed. These labels serve to separate the mentally healthy from the mentally ill, to build even more protective barriers between us and them. People with mental illnesses quickly learn to stay behind the barriers because "coming out of the closet" leads to too many serious repercussions among friends and coworkers. When their illness is known, then they must carry all the baggage that others associate with their diagnosis. They are suddenly "weak" or "bad" or "unreliable." So instead, they lie and say that they missed two months of work recovering from abdominal surgery or a back injury instead of admitting that they were recovering from a life-threatening depressive episode. Or they check "no" on the employment form when it asks, "Have you ever had a mental illness?" because they fear that saying yes will cost them their job. And it does. Even medical licensing boards (which one might expect would be required to be free of discriminatory policies) may refuse licenses to physicians who have had a psychotic disorder, even if that psychosis was the result of a postpartum depression (which affects one in a thousand women giving birth, as described in Chapter Eleven).

But times are changing, and we hope that society's views of mental illness will soon change too. The National Alliance for the Mentally Ill

(NAMI) is launching a major campaign to fight discrimination against people with mental illness. Individual efforts are also beginning to gain attention. Tipper Gore used the tragic suicide of White House staff member Vince Foster as a means of educating the public about depression and its terrible consequences. The Clinton-Gore administration has continued to campaign strongly against stigmatization of the mentally ill because they know the impact that stigmatization has had on access to and payment for mental health care. They put their words into action in their hiring of a staff member with bipolar disorder and in their support of his public admission of his symptoms. When Sylvia Chase asked Tipper Gore about the staff member's "potential to embarrass the administration," Ms. Gore responded, "Well, let me put it this way. What if he had a heart attack? Would that embarrass us? No. Why should it embarrass us if he happens to have a manic-depressive episode?"[5]

With attitudes and efforts such as these, perhaps the public will finally recognize mental illness for what it is: a biological disorder that happens to affect the mind rather than the body. And with that recognition will come the realization that these disorders can affect any of us. They are tangible and real, not a matter of choice or a means of getting attention.

Hysteria—"It's All in Your Head"

The word *hysteria* is derived from the Greek word for womb and has always had uniquely feminine associations. *Hysteria* is used to describe any excessive physical or emotional reaction, such as fainting in response to bad news or becoming sick after ending a love affair. Women with hysteria are described as excessively emotional and attention seeking, inappropriately sexually seductive, and emotionally shallow and self-centered.

Anything that weakened a woman was thought to be capable of bringing on a hysterical attack. "Unfeminine activities [also] caused uterine derangement, which in turn caused mental illness," according to some practitioners in the latter half of the nineteenth century.[6] As with masochism, hysteria was used both to blame women for their symptoms and to restrict their potential. As recently as 1890, women were not allowed to attend college for fear that the mental strain would cause insanity and infertility. Even now, it is not uncommon to hear the opinion that a woman cannot be president of the United States because she might function at less than peak capacity (or worse!) for one week out of the month.

Until recent years, because women were thought to be inherently susceptible to hysteria, the term was used broadly to describe any mental disorder from which a woman suffered. Particularly in the first half of this century, the term was inappropriately applied as in the case of Charlotte Perkins Gilman, a writer whose career was stopped in the early 1900s because of her "hysterical depression." In her autobiography, *The Living of Charlotte Perkins Gilman*, she writes about feeling so weak and depressed that she could do "nothing other than to stay in bed."[7] She cried in "continuous pain" from her debilitating postpartum depression. Her local physician diagnosed her disorder as hysteria and told her that it was up to her when she got well—it was all in her head, so she could gain control of her symptoms at any time. But she knew that she couldn't, so she consulted the greatest nerve specialist in the United States. This doctor told her that "he could see there was nothing the matter with [her]." She was sent home with this prescription: "Live as domestic a life as possible. . . . Have but two hours' intellectual life a day. And never touch pen, brush, or pencil as long as you live."[8]

In its current, more narrow definition, hysteria is used to refer to neurological or behavioral symptoms that cannot be explained medically and that are not under the voluntary control of the patient; hysterical blindness and hysterical paralysis are examples. The symptoms have a psychological basis, but no medical causation. The symptoms that can result from hysteria are varied, bizarre, and sometimes contagious. During the Middle Ages, entire towns would become afflicted by hysterical seizure-like frenzies. The violent movements would cease only when the afflicted were able to pray at a holy shrine. Later, mass hysteria was attributed to demonic possession, as in the Salem witch trials. After watching a witch burning, the young, susceptible women would faint or have a seizure. This would lead in turn to their being charged with witchcraft, and their hysterical reactions to this charge would be used as further proof of their guilt. As more and more witches were discovered and punished, the terror increased, and so did the hysterical reactions.

If you think that mass hysteria is just a thing of the past, consider the new phenomenon of "sick building syndrome." An intriguing example is provided by a senior high school in northern Virginia, where in a single week, seven girls fainted during their math classes. Soon, there was an epidemic; curiously, only girls were affected, and they were only overcome during certain periods of the day, in a certain part of the building—the math wing. The concern was immediately raised that something about that part of the building was making the girls sick. Experts were called in and spent nearly six months trying to ascertain the cause of the infirmities. It was a puzzle, as the air-conditioning system serviced the entire school and the lighting and physical facilities in the math wing were identical to those in the rest of the school—yet the fainting spells kept occurring. After every conceivable explanation had been exhausted, it was determined that the fainting spells must have been the result of mass hysteria. Interestingly, after the parents and students were informed of the lack of scientific evidence for a sick building syndrome, the fainting spells stopped. Often, medical proof of the impossibility of a hysterical symptom is sufficient to cure it. Dee's case offers one example.

Dee reluctantly agreed to neurosurgery for the ruptured disk in her neck after the surgeon explained that further pressure from the disk could cause permanent nerve damage and possible paralysis of her arms. As a psychiatrist, Dee had studied neurology extensively and knew the urgent need for the surgery, but she also knew that recovery could be long and painful, and she had hoped to avoid the operation. When it became inevitable, Dee barely listened as the neurosurgeon, Dr. Charook, explained the potential risks and complications of the procedure, including the one-in-a-million chance of resultant paralysis. Dee trusted him completely and was confident that she would have a good outcome. After all, Dr. Charook was one of the world's premier surgeons and had done the operation hundreds of times, and has never had a complication.

At the time of the surgery, Dee felt no anxiety as she fell asleep from the anesthesia, but she awoke in a panic and found that she was completely paralyzed. Dr. Charook was quickly summoned and rushed to her side. At first the neurosurgeon was pale, fearing that there had been some disastrous event, but as he carefully examined her, he discovered that her paralysis was incompatible with any known neurological syndrome. Now relaxed, he smiled at Dee and said, "You really must have been more frightened than either you or I had realized. You've developed a hysterical paralysis. Good thing your pattern of paralysis is neurologically impossible, or it might have taken us a while to sort this out. Now that we know what this is, why don't you walk over here and help me write it up for your psychiatric journal!" With that, Dee breathed a sigh of relief and found that she could move her arms and legs. She smiled somewhat sheepishly, puzzled about how this could have happened. As a psychiatrist, how could she have succumbed to a hysterical paralysis? How could her unconscious fears about the surgery have been transformed into physical symptoms? How could her mind paralyze her body? How could symptoms so real have been "all in her head"?

The answers to these questions aren't yet known—it's not clear how psychological stressors can cause such profound neurological dysfunction. It is clear that the symptoms are real—the patients aren't making them up to get attention or "faking it." The paralysis is outside their voluntary control as much as if it were caused by a brain tumor or a stroke.

Of course, the opposite also happens—symptoms that are quite real can be falsely attributed to hysteria. A fascinating example of this occurred recently in California. Twelve emergency room staff members became ill after being exposed to a terrible ammonialike stench arising from a woman's body. When the woman's abdomen was opened during an emergency surgery, it emitted an unbelievably powerful odor. Some staff members ran from the room, retching and vomiting, while others passed out at the woman's bedside. All remained ill for several days or longer, and one physician developed severe complications that ultimately required three corrective surgeries. The Department of Health Services reported that the health care workers were suffering from "mass hysteria" in response to the noxious odor and denied all health insurance claims. After many months of investigation, scientists finally discovered that the odor was not only unpleasant but that it was a truly toxic substance; the health care workers' reactions had been chemically based. One of the doctors reported tremendous relief that at last "other people know it's not all in my head."[9]

This example demonstrates the problem with the diagnosis of hysteria. It is used whenever medicine or science is unable to explain the cause of a person's symptoms. Sometimes the symptoms are truly all in their heads, and sometimes we have simply failed to find the cause.

Hysteria as the Basis for Psychoanalysis

To understand how hysteria became so important to modern psychiatry, we must look, through Freud's eyes, at the work of Dr. Jean Martin Charcot (1835–93), one of the world's greatest neurologists. Dr. Charcot took a particular interest in hysteria and its unusual neurological symptoms. He used hypnosis to cure both male and female patients of their hysterical sensations and movements. In doing so, he demonstrated that the symptoms were not under conscious (voluntary) control and therefore were not due to imagination or simulation. Prior to this work, hysterics were thought to be manipulative pretenders who were using their symptoms to get attention or other rewards. Through his systematic studies, Dr. Charcot made hysteria a "respectable disease of the nervous system."[10] He thought that the symptoms were "legitimate" and of "medical" origin—the result of an unknown mental-neurological process.

Sigmund Freud's theories about the unconscious arose directly from his observations of Charcot's work with hysterical patients. Fascinated by the fact that physical symptoms could arise from the unconscious and were not in the patient's awareness or under voluntary control, Freud was determined to define the mental processes underlying hysteria. Based on Charcot's scientific observations, Freud postulated that part of a person's life goes on outside of awareness and that this unconscious part influences conscious experience and behavior. Once he determined the far-reaching effects of the unconscious, he developed a new treatment, psychoanalysis, which was designed to extend the therapeutic benefits of hypnosis. Unlike hypnosis, in which no attempt is made to connect the unconscious memories with conscious thought, psychoanalysis uses dream analysis and free association to raise these forgotten events to consciousness, where they can be understood and resolved through therapeutic interventions.

Freud believed that an individual's symptoms have a unique meaning, that this meaning originates in the person's childhood, and that the symptoms can be treated once this meaning has been uncovered and understood. Symptoms in adulthood were considered to be the product of an unconscious conflict, often resulting from unresolved childhood issues about aggression or sex. In psychoanalysis, dreams and free association could be used to access the forgotten feeling or trauma in order to bring the conflict to consciousness and resolve the symptom. During psychotherapy, several of Freud's female patients recalled having been sexually exploited during childhood. Freud theorized that the women's hysterical symptoms were caused by feelings arising from the traumatic events, feelings that had been repressed into the unconscious.[11] Subsequently, Freud determined that many of these episodes of childhood sexual abuse had not actually happened. He reconsidered his model and then proposed that the recollections represented forbidden childhood fantasies that had been repressed before they were resolved. The symptoms in adulthood were a means of working through these unresolved childhood conflicts.

Freud's writings on memories, fantasies, and dissociation have direct relevance to the contemporary debates raging about false memories syndrome. Patients, through the therapist's inappropriate and leading questions, are able to "recall" episodes of early childhood sexual abuse that never occurred—their "memories" are actually resurrections of repressed childhood fantasies. Therapists are becoming increasingly aware of this issue, and professional standards have been set for interviewing abuse victims. But it is often difficult to distinguish false memories from actual memories of abuse, as the origin and meaning of recalled memories of early childhood are still not well researched. Because false memories are in danger of damaging the credibility of true cases of abuse (which happen far too often and much more frequently than do false memories), it is imperative that this issue be resolved soon through scientific study. (See Chapter Ten for further discussion.)

Derivatives of Freud's various theories still play an important role in our lives and have meaning in modern society. In *Necessary Losses*, Judith Viorst writes, "I do unhesitatingly embrace Freud's conviction that our past, with all of its clamorous wishes and terrors and passions, inhabits our present, and his belief in the enormous power of our unconscious—of that region outside our awareness—to shape the events of our life."[12] There are pearls to be culled from Freud's work, for the impact of early experience on one's subsequent choices and destiny is clear. Many times we recreate patterns of earlier relationships in later ones and try to undo earlier mistakes by engaging in relationships that allow us to redo the process. This pattern has been used to explain why daughters of alcoholic fathers marry alcoholic men or why women who have witnessed their mother's abuse also become victims of battering relationships. Without therapy, however, these relationships are often merely a redoing rather than an undoing and a healing.

The Power of Penis Envy

Like the writings of his medical predecessors who thought that the womb was the source of all female mental illness, Freud's writings suggest a belief that women were predetermined, by virtue of their reproductive anatomy, to be deficient and, by virtue of their biology, to be passive, moody, and unsuccessful. He referred to girls as "the little crea-ture[s] without a penis" and believed that many of women's psychiatric symptoms were the result of "penis envy." He wrote that women "are more masochistic, narcissistic, jealous and envious than men, and also less moral . . . the inevitable consequences of the anatomical differ-ences between the sexes."[13]

Freud's writings were largely responsible for the subsequent treat-ment of women by the psychiatric community. His theories of penis envy, masochism, and hysteria were used to blame women for their mental illnesses. Subsequent generations of psychiatrists used these the-ories to blame women for their children's mental illnesses as well, since "schizophrenogenic mothers" were assumed to have been inadequate or cruel in raising their children and thus responsible for their children's psychosis.

Freud's writings seem to indicate that his was a pretty extreme case of misogyny, but his attitudes might be more appropriately attributed to his being Victorian and male. His beliefs and theories were shaped by his environment, as ours are today. Although his psychoanalytic theory is associated with psychology rather than with biology, he predicted that the biological contributions to psychiatry would one day be re-vealed. Freud had been trained as a neurologist and he struggled to find the physiological causes of mental processes. He did not succeed, but is credited with summarizing the main elements of the nature-versus-nurture debate.[14]

In this debate, "nature" referred to biological causes of personality and symptoms, while "nurture" referred to psychological determinants (environment or life experiences). Freud's writings crystallized the con-troversy over nature versus nurture and biology versus psychology. Per-haps the only difference between Freudian psychiatry and the new neuropsychiatry is that medicine has now advanced to the point where we are able to identify some of the physiological changes responsible for the effects of both nature and nurture; in other words, we are now able to establish more clearly what is and what is not all in our heads.

The Scientific Revolution Leading to the New Neuropsychiatry

Biological theories about the determinants of mood and temperament can be traced back at least to the time of the Greeks, when the body's fluids—phlegm, yellow bile, blood, and black bile—were held to be the causes of the phlegmatic (indifferent), choleric (angry), sanguine (cheerful), and melancholic (sad) temperaments, respectively. Throughout the early centuries, black bile was blamed for melancholic depression, and the mainstay of treatment for depression was bloodletting to rid the body of this bad fluid. The bloodletting did not help, but it is fascinating to see how accurately a two-thousand-year-old theory forecast our modern understanding of the role of dysfunctional body fluids (in the form of faulty brain chemicals) in depression and other psychiatric disorders.

The Greeks also foretold the future by the use of one word, *psyche*, to represent thought, feeling, and emotion. Through the ages, the psyche was eventually divided into two separate categories: the mind and the brain. The brain was a biological organ while the mind was a nebulous counterpart to the soul or the individual's spirit. The mind was the seat of thinking, feeling, and motivation, while the brain controlled the body's mechanical functions. The fields of psychology and neurology held fast to the separateness of the mind and brain (respectively), and when these fields first developed, this made sense.

Recently, however, this separation has been challenged. In the past few years, research has demonstrated that thoughts, emotions, and behaviors are all controlled by similar systems within the brain. Computerized brain scans have shown that emotions, such as happiness, anger, and sadness, cause the same kinds of brain activity as do muscle movements, speech, and problem solving. Even some personality traits, like shyness or excessive compulsiveness, appear to be biologically based, as they have predictable neurophysiological patterns and are altered by medications such as Prozac. The psychological processes are so similar to the neurological functions that they are indistinguishable by even our most sophisticated tests. The mind and brain are inseparable—once again joined as the psyche.

The term *neuropsychiatry* has been invoked to characterize the "indelible inseparability of brain and thought, of mind and body, and of mental and physical."[15] It is the understanding that human thoughts and behaviors are the result of both nature and nurture, of both biology and psychology. Although the term *neuropsychiatry* sounds technical and irrelevant to daily life, the reality is that it has tremendous meaning for everyone. Neuropsychiatric events shape every second of our lives; they are responsible for each and every thought, feeling, memory, and reaction. Scientists are beginning to explain how these neurochemical transmissions occur, but psychiatrists must attempt to understand *why* these events occur and what they mean for people in their daily lives.

This revolutionary change in the way we view the human mind has resulted in polarization within the field. Psychiatrists are divided between those who do and those who do not believe in the mind-brain and mind-body connections. As one might expect, some are resistant to the idea that those thoughts that make us uniquely human are the result of a common biochemical process. How can neurological connections and chemical messages be responsible for such diverse responses as the prose of Shakespeare, the rage of a jealous husband, or the calculating skill of a world-class bridge player?

Although few would dispute that an eye blink is the result of a simple biochemical event, many would argue that similar neurochemical transmissions could not possibly be responsible for the complex range of human experiences. Yet scientists are proving that thoughts, behaviors, and emotions are the result of the same type of neurochemical events that cause our muscles to move or our lips to speak; that the separation between mind and brain, between emotion and cognition, and between the mental and physical, is artificial. It has become clear that the mind and the brain are inherently intertwined in ways that we are just beginning to imagine.

This new understanding of the mind-brain connection has led to the development of the neuropsychiatric model. The model states that thoughts, feelings, and emotions are the direct result of biochemical events that are controlled not only by biology but also by life experiences. This interaction is so dynamic that there is really no cause and effect but rather a continuous circle of interactions, each of which feeds back on the others. The neuropsychiatric concept that mind and brain are neither separate nor distinguishable encapsulates the greatest change in psychiatry—a true revolution.

The neuropsychiatry revolution has dramatically changed the treatment of many psychiatric disorders. Take Esther's disorder, trichotillomania, for example. Trichotillomania was initially defined as a neurosis and later as a disorder of impulse control (see Chapter Fifteen). The women were thought to be unwilling, or unable, to resist the urge to pull their hair. Dynamically oriented psychiatrists, such as Dr. Smith, would help their patients to uncover the "meaning" of their symptom in the hopes that such understanding would lead to resolution of the hair pulling. However, the therapies were rarely successful.

In 1989 a landmark paper was published that showed that a specific drug, clomipramine, was more effective in reducing hair-pulling symptoms than was desipramine, another very similar drug. Brain-imaging scans were able to "predict" this therapeutic response, proving that the treatment was having a biological effect and that the symptoms had a biological basis. Trichotillomania was clearly a neuropsychiatric disorder.

Despite this strong evidence for a biological basis of trichotillomania, it is clear that environmental factors also play an important role in hair pulling. Stress, in its varying forms, has been shown to prevent a patient from receiving full benefit from treatment; it can even cause a sudden relapse. A woman taking a drug that blocks serotonin reuptake might be completely symptom free until her mother dies; then she suddenly begins to pull her hair again. The stress of her grief brings her trichotillomania back. In other instances, the women pull their hair only during periods of excessive stress. They may find that the anti-hair-pulling medications are completely ineffective but that psychological treatments are quite useful. Neuropsychiatrists recognize this diversity. They know that psychiatric disorders are affected by both psychology and neurology, and they consider all relevant symptoms before making a diagnosis and suggesting treatments.

Summary

Critics will claim that the outcome of the neuropsychiatric revolution is a new generation of "pill pushers"—that the biological basis of mental disorders is just an excuse to write prescriptions for toxic drugs. This is not true. The new neuropsychiatry is an integration of psychology and biology, of nurture and nature, and of mind and body. It is the logical conclusion of what both the Greeks and Freud were searching for. It requires clinicians to be skilled in both psychological and pharmacological treatments, for these "healers of the mind" must determine what single treatment or combination of treatments is most appropriate. Neuropsychiatry offers tremendous hope—hope that new, more effective treatments will be found; hope that by understanding the biological causes of these disorders, we will be able to prevent our daughters from suffering; and hope that patients soon will be told, "It's *not* all in your head."

Notes

1. Sigmund Freud. "The Economic Problem of Masochism," in *Collected Papers*, vol. 2 (New York: Basic Books, 1959).

2. Judith L. Herman. *Trauma and Recovery: The Aftermath of Violence—From Domestic Abuse to Political Terror* (New York: Basic Books, 1992), 66–68, 116–18.

3. Colette Dowling. *The Cinderella Complex* (New York: Pocket Books, 1982).

4. Herman, *Trauma and Recovery*, and Natalie Shainess. *Sweet Suffering: Woman as Victim.* (New York: Bobbs-Merrill, 1984).

5. Tipper Gore interviewed by Sylvia Chase, *Prime Time Live*, American Broadcasting Company, 19 July 1995.

6. Jeffrey L. Geller and Maxine Harris. *Women of the Asylum: Voices from Behind the Walls, 1840–1945* (New York: Anchor Books, Doubleday, 1994).

7. Gilman, Charlotte Perkins. *The Living of Charlotte Perkins Gilman* (New York: D. Appleton–Century Co., 1935), as cited in Geller and Harris, *Women of the Asylum*, 161–68.

8. Ibid., 166–67.

9. Elizabeth Gleick and Lorenzo Benet. "Solved: A Medical Puzzle," *People Weekly*, November 21, 1994, 107–8.

10. Ernest Jones. *The Life and Work of Sigmund Freud* (New York: Penguin Books, 1984). 204–5.

11. Sigmund Freud. "Studies on Hysteria" in *The Standard Edition of the Complete Psychological Works of Sigmund Freud*, vol. 2: 1893–95, trans. by James Strachey (London: Hogarth Press, 1955).

12. Judith Viorst. *Necessary Losses* (New York: Simon & Schuster, 1986), 17.

13. Sigmund Freud. "Some Psychical Consequences of the Anatomical Distinction Between the Sexes" and "Female Sexuality," in *The Standard Edition of the Complete Psychological Works of Sigmund Freud*, vol. 19 (1925) and 21 (1931), trans. by James Strachey (London: Hogarth Press, 1961).

14. Ernest Jones. *The Life and Work of Sigmund Freud.*

15. Stuart C. Yudofsky and Robert E. Hales. *The American Psychiatric Press Textbook of Neuropsychiatry*, 2nd ed. (Washington, DC: American Psychiatric Press, 1992).

CHAPTER 2

The Outcome of the Revolution:
What Psychiatry Offers Women Today

Cassandra was sick and tired of being sick and tired. It seemed as if she was always crabby and depressed. She had a constant headache, and was so worn out that she could barely function. Every morning, she woke up feeling more exhausted than when she had fallen into bed the night before. And no wonder—she slept only three to four hours each night before waking from a terrifying nightmare about being trapped in a dark cave. After awakening, Cassandra would lie in bed and worry—about the fight she'd had last week with her husband, their money problems, her daughter's failing grades, her son's poor choice in friends, her job, and her health. She was consumed with worry and guilt. She tried to meditate, as her friends had suggested, but she couldn't do it and just kept worrying until the sun came up. Then she would finally fall asleep for a few minutes before the alarm went off, reminding her that she must start another day. But getting through the day seemed impossible. She couldn't muster the energy to get out of bed, let alone work all day, cook dinner, spend time with her family, and make it through another PTA meeting. When the situation became unbearable, Cassandra finally scheduled an appointment with . . .

It would be a happy ending to this story and a lovely way to begin this chapter if Cassandra had found a physician right away who had the solution to her problems. Unfortunately, she didn't. It is often difficult to find a health care professional who understands that our symptoms have both a physical and a psychological basis. The dramatic developments and tremendous promise of neuropsychiatry have not been fully appreciated by the medical profession, so the options that neuropsychiatry provides are not always presented to the patients. By following Cassandra's story (which is actually a composite of many of our patients' stories), we will summarize the current state of psychiatric medicine and the problems frequently encountered in trying to get help.

Cassandra finally scheduled an appointment with her family physician. She had been a patient of Dr. Johnson's for years and knew that he was a good doctor. He listened to only half her story before reassuring her, "Oh, don't worry, Sandy, it's nothing. Your fatigue and insomnia are just symptoms of a mild depression. I see this kind of thing all the time in women your age. You're just trying to do too much. Cut back a little." Cassandra took his advice. She dropped out of the church choir, resigned as secretary of the PTA, and organized kitchen duty for her family so that she only had to cook once a week. It didn't help. In fact, the fatigue seemed to get worse. She talked to her sister, who suggested that she go see her gynecologist—"a fabulous woman doctor"—to get a second opinion.

Dr. Robb was a well-respected obstetrician and gynecologist who had a thriving practice. Her waiting room was always full, so Cassandra wasn't surprised that she was asked to disrobe before meeting the doctor for the first time. She was surprised, however, when Dr. Robb conducted the entire (albeit brief) interview while performing the physical examination—with Cassandra's feet up in the stirrups. Dr. Robb instructed her nurse to take some blood tests, told Cassandra to get dressed, and said (with her hand on the doorknob), "I'll call you Thursday with the test results. Everything looks fine on your physical."

On Thursday, Dr. Robb's nurse called and said that the test results were "all fine." When Cassandra insisted on speaking directly with the doctor, she was put on hold for ten minutes before Dr. Robb picked up the phone. Dr. Robb said, "I'm due in surgery, so I'll have to make this brief. My notes say that your physical examination was normal and your laboratory results were too. There is no evidence for early menopause as a cause for your symptoms. My workup suggests that there's no medical explanation for your fatigue, so it must be a psychological problem. I don't think you need a medical doctor, you need a psychiatrist. My nurse will give you some names." Then she handed the phone to her nurse, who read off three names, which Cassandra dutifully copied down. Cassandra had no intention of seeing any of the therapists, as she was much too upset by

Dr. Robb's tone and even more by the message "It's all in your head, and there's nothing medicine can do for you."

Cassandra was so discouraged by this message that she took to her bed for several days. Her family tried to convince her to see one of the doctors recommended by Dr. Robb, but Cassandra refused to go, saying, "I don't need a shrink. What I'm feeling has nothing to do with my head; it's my body that feels lousy. I'm tired and yet I can't sleep. This has to be a physical problem. It's not all in my head!"

Cassandra was right—her problem wasn't all in her head. Her symptoms suggested that she might have a physical illness, or a hormonal or vitamin deficiency, or perhaps a bad reaction to an over-the-counter medication. Until Dr. Robb had considered a variety of illnesses such as thyroid deficiency, mixed connective tissue disease, Lyme disease, and countless other medical problems that can cause symptoms similar to Cassandra's, she shouldn't have told her that her problems couldn't have a physical basis (see Chapter Five).

We made Dr. Robb a female physician intentionally, as too many patients are misled by the myth that seeing a woman doctor automatically guarantees that they will receive empathy and compassion. Dr. Robb was too harried to listen to Cassandra's complaints, and as an obstetrician-gynecologist, she didn't specialize in the kind of problems that Cassandra presented. She was right to send Cassandra to a psychiatrist, but her tone and manner implied that the referral was a brush-off and that Cassandra was being sent to a "shrink" because she was "crazy." It is no wonder that Cassandra wasn't willing to take her suggestion, and it is also not surprising that it is so difficult for so many women to seek psychiatric care. The stigmatization is too great, the barriers too high.

Certain that there must be a medical solution to her problems, Cassandra called her friend Ashley, who had been through something similar the year before. Ashley suggested that Cassandra see her doctor, Dr. Long, an alternative medicine practitioner who specialized in vitamin therapies. When she got to Dr. Long's office, Cassandra was impressed with the fact that she waited only a few minutes before being escorted into his spacious private office and offered a comfortable chair. Dr. Long listened attentively as Cassandra poured out her story and then said, "You poor thing. You've obviously been through a very rough period. Regular doctors never seem to understand about these kinds of symptoms, so I'm very glad that you came here to see me. I will need to analyze some samples of your hair in order to determine exactly which vitamins and minerals you lack, but meanwhile, take this specially prepared combination of vitamins and minerals." Cassandra felt better almost as soon as she took the first pills— her depression lifted and the fatigue even seemed to improve. For the first time in months, she had hope!

Cassandra was shocked when she received her bill a few days later— over $1,500 for the first appointment and the hair analysis—but since Dr. Long had seemed to understand her problems so well, she paid the bill without question. At her next visit, Dr. Long informed Cassandra that her vitamin deficiency was quite rare and that she could only correct the situation by taking a supplement especially formulated for her needs—at a cost of $30 a day or nearly $10,000 a year! Cassandra's health insurance wouldn't cover expenses for alternative treatments, but she was so desperate to feel better that she agreed to start the therapy.

After about six weeks of vitamin supplementation, Cassandra noticed she was still exhausted, and she was still having nightmares and insomnia every night. She really hadn't improved, after all. She consulted Dr. Long, who suggested doubling the dose. When Cassandra realized that this would cost her $350 a week, she decided that this wasn't the answer. She was angry and disappointed about the amount of time and money she had wasted. What was worse, she still felt lousy.

Alternative medicine is thought to be helpful for a variety of physical and psychological problems. For example, many people have had success with hypnosis therapy for anxiety disorders and with biofeedback for stress reduction and for lowering high blood pressure. Alternative therapies, such as hypnosis, acupuncture, and others, are being tested now for a variety of psychiatric disorders because they appear to benefit so many individuals. But none has yet been proved by scientific study to help the majority of people who receive them.

In the case of alternative treatments, such as vitamin therapy, one should be particularly cautious when any "special formulation" is required, particularly ones that are unreasonably expensive. Dr. Long was a quack, not a physician of alternative medicine as he claimed. Vitamins are vitamins, and even rare deficiencies can be corrected relatively inexpensively. Cassandra should have listened to her inner voice telling her that Dr. Long's promises were too grand and that $25 a day was too much money.

Cassandra finally scheduled an appointment with one of the doctors whom Dr. Robb had recommended. Dr. Freidman was on time for their appointment and quickly put Cassandra at ease. She said, "I'm a psychologist, not a psychiatrist, so I can't prescribe medications. If your problem is something that can be treated by psychotherapy, I can help you, but if it is more than that, I'll have to refer you to one of my psychiatric colleagues for medications." Cassandra was surprised to hear that there was a difference between psychologists and psychiatrists, particularly since Dr. Robb had implied that all "shrinks" were the same, giving Cassandra referrals to both psychologists and psychiatrists.*

Dr. Freidman listened attentively to Cassandra's history and then ordered a battery of psychological tests, including a standardized personality profile. On completion of the diagnostic assessment, Dr. Freidman informed Cassandra that she did indeed have a psychological problem. This conclusion was based on her symptoms, the fact that she had been told by two previous doctors that she had a normal medical workup, and the results of the psychological profile, which showed a high score on the hysterical scale. Dr. Freidman went on to explain that the pattern suggested that Cassandra overreacted to stressful situations and that her mind could cause her to feel sick—that is, her physical symptoms were frequently "all in her head" but certainly not under her control. Cassandra was disappointed to learn that the psychologist thought she was "a hysterical female," but when Dr. Freidman reassured Cassandra that she could be helpful to her, Cassandra no longer cared. She was finally going to get better.

After several months of twice-a-week therapy sessions, Cassandra felt like she had made terrific progress in understanding some of the causes of her long-standing unhappiness. She recalled that much of her childhood had been lonely and unhappy because her father had frequently been

---

*There is an important difference between psychologists and psychiatrists that is often not appreciated. Psychiatrists are physicians—medical doctors who not only have graduated from medical school but who also have completed an additional four years of training in psychiatry; they have studied first all medical illnesses and then, during residency training, the psychological and physical causes and treatments of neurological, emotional, and behavioral problems. Psychologists attend graduate school and have a doctoral degree in one of several psychological specialties; they typically do an internship in order to learn how to take care of patients, but they are not physicians and so cannot prescribe medications.

away on business trips and her mother had been critical, irritable, and aloof. Cassandra had always promised herself that she would be a better mother than hers had been, but she had found herself unwittingly treating her children in exactly the same way.

As Cassandra began to understand her sadness and disappointments in early life, she could identify her own negative patterns and work to change them. She came to realize that she was angry at her husband for leaving her with so many of the household responsibilities and had acted it out by distancing herself from him and the children. With her new understanding, she found that she was able to talk with him about her frustrations, and they reorganized the household obligations. Many other aspects of Cassandra's life also improved.

But her insomnia and fatigue continued. When she complained about this to Dr. Freidman, the psychologist suggested that Cassandra try to understand the meaning of the symptoms. What was she avoiding by being too tired? Did she feel that she needed to be taken care of? Cassandra addressed these issues in therapy for the next several weeks before becoming frustrated with the process. She knew that her remaining symptoms were not all in her head; after all, all the other symptoms had disappeared, and she desperately wanted to get better. So, reluctantly, she asked for a referral to a psychiatrist.

She was referred to Dr. Olde, a Swiss-trained psychiatrist. She told him about her symptoms, and after several diagnostic sessions, he told her that he agreed with Dr. Freidman's interpretation of her symptoms as psychologically based and told her that their meaning could be discovered by understanding her vivid nightmares. He saw her symptoms as resulting from the differences between her childhood experiences and the archetypal ideal. In order to get relief, she needed to work through her conflicts by understanding the metaphors within her dreams. Cassandra felt that she had already had enough of understanding her dreams and fantasies and did not believe for a second that channeling would be at all helpful to her, so she never went to see Dr. Olde again.

Perhaps you were surprised that when Cassandra saw Dr. Olde, she *still* didn't get the help she wanted. This is not a surprise at all, as there is tremendous variability in therapists' training, skills, schools of thought, clinical biases, and approaches. Sometimes the psychiatrist doesn't offer what you need; other times, there's a bad personality fit. Because the psychiatrist-patient relationship requires mutual trust and respect, it is important to find someone with whom you know you can work.

Cassandra's symptoms grew worse: she was sleeping only three hours each night and missed work every other day. In desperation, she called the local mental health clinic. She was seen immediately by the intake social worker, who took a brief history and then said, "It sounds to me like you're depressed. There are several therapists here who can be helpful to you. We believe that you must be an active participant in your own therapy, so I will provide you with several options, but you will be the one to choose whom you want to work with. You can choose from Dr. Mesmer, a hypnotist, or Dr. Freud (no relation), an insight-oriented dynamic psychotherapist, both of whom have had success in helping patients identify the unconscious basis for their symptoms. Of course, with Dr. Mesmer, you're in a hypnotic trance throughout the session, while with Dr. Freud, you're awake and utilizing free associations to make connections between past and present feelings. Then there is Dr. Ewert, who specializes in behavior therapy, in which you pick a symptom that you want to be desensitized from and he designs a behavior therapy plan to help you accomplish this. His colleague, Dr. Erick, utilizes cognitive therapy; with him, you will learn to identify and eliminate your negative and self-defeating thoughts. Both of these treatments target specific symptoms and employ homework. Our younger patients seem to prefer these methods. Or you might prefer relaxation therapy if anxiety and worries are your main complaints. If you're mainly tense and on edge, we offer biofeedback. The clinic also has a support group that meets every Wednesday evening and is led by a prominent psychotherapist. We do couples and family work as well, but it sounds as if you should start with individual treatment. Of course, if you'd like to try medication, you could choose to see Dr. Gilman, our expert on psychopharmacology. Typically, patients don't see him until they've tried several other therapies, but perhaps you're ready." At this point, Cassandra ran from the social worker's office in confusion.

Cassandra had too many choices and no information on which to base her decision. It sounded as if she would get a different treatment based on which clinician she saw. Which therapy was right for her symptoms? If even the experts couldn't agree, how was *she* supposed to make such an important decision? What guidelines should she use to ensure that she got the best care for her problem? Cassandra's questions are important ones that are shared by all women seeking psychiatric care.

Psychiatry Today

Student of Freud, analyst, shrink, quack, doctor, psychiatrist—the names given to psychiatrists reflect not only the diversity of the specialty but also various views of the role of psychiatrists. Psychiatry, a compound of the Greek words *psyche* and *iatra*, is literally defined as the "medical healing of the soul, spirit, and mind." By definition, psychiatrists are charged with guarding our sanity, restoring our mental health, and doctoring our spirits. The profession is devoted to healing the very essence of that which makes us human, and the stakes and expectations are very high. Is it any wonder that psychiatrists are always searching for new and better methods of treating mental disorders and so continue to create new psychiatric subspecialties?

The current field of psychiatry is so broad that you will find a wide variety of treatment recommendations for every disorder. Some psychiatrists might recommend insight-oriented psychotherapy, because they believe that current symptoms are the result of unresolved past conflicts. Biological psychiatrists might prescribe medications and nothing else—they feel that life issues are of little or no consequence to the psychiatric symptoms. Other therapists would also ignore life issues but would depend on relaxation therapy or cognitive-behavioral techniques to eradicate the problem symptoms. Neuropsychiatrists might utilize a combination of medication and psychotherapy, because they view psychiatric disorders as arising from an interaction of experience and biology. Obviously, it is our preference for you to see such a psychiatrist—one who appreciates the dual roles of biology and experience. However, neuropsychiatry is a relatively new subspecialty, and experienced therapists are not always available to you. What is most important is to find a psychiatrist or therapist whom you trust and with whom you feel you can work.

Choosing a Therapist

When researching the credentials of a psychiatrist or other mental health professional, you should ask what kind of training she has had, what her approach is to various symptoms, and what kind of therapies she utilizes. Often this process is difficult—it may feel too presumptuous or threatening to interview a potential therapist—but this is entirely appropriate and should be done. As physicians, we welcome such inquiries from our patients and feel that the interview process helps to establish a more therapeutic physician-patient relationship. It is this relationship that forms the basis for all the healing that takes place—even if the treatment is strictly pharmacological. For example, if the patient doesn't trust her physician's judgment, she might be unwilling to take the medications he prescribes. If the doctor is perfunctory or dismissive, the patient may be reluctant to discuss her true concerns—in which case he may never know that she has obsessive-compulsive symptoms in addition to her depression and she'll receive the wrong medication. If she feels that he doesn't have time for her, she might hesitate to raise concerns about the side effects she's experiencing and she might continue to suffer needlessly.

In order for you to receive optimal treatment, you must choose the right therapist. He or she should be compassionate, empathic, and interested in both the physical and the emotional problems that you need to discuss. He should seem truly to care about what happens to you and to be willing to expend the energy to ensure that you recover completely. The therapist should have enough time for you and make you feel welcome. You should be able to trust him enough to share your deepest secrets with him and know that he will keep them in strictest confidence. There should be an almost instinctual recognition that this is the right person to help you. In sum, you should "click." Trust your intuition. If the therapist doesn't feel quite right, he isn't quite right, so keep looking until you find someone who is.

How do you go about finding the therapists to interview? We do *not* recommend the Yellow Pages (although in some cities, the listings are quite complete). Your family physician is often a good starting point. He or she will know enough about you to suggest some potential "good fits." Make sure that you let your doctor know what kind of symptoms are troubling you. There may be particular therapists who specialize in treating your problems; for example, if you are having symptoms of anxiety and nervousness, your doctor might recommend a psychiatrist at the local anxiety disorders clinic, rather than a psychiatrist interested mainly in treating patients with depression.

Mental health clinics are also excellent sources for referrals. As in Cassandra's case, you might see an intake social worker first. Her job is to try to match you up with the proper therapist, so be clear about your needs and expectations. For example, if you have no intention of taking medication to treat your fear of flying, tell her this so that she can refer you to a therapist who specializes in behavioral treatments.

Other sources of referrals include medical schools, local psychiatric societies, and patient support group organizations, such as the Obsessive-Compulsive Foundation and the Depression and Manic-Depressive Association. These organizations are listed by symptom pattern in the "Resource" sections of Chapters Six through Fifteen.

When to Seek Mental Health Care

It is important to remember that not all emotional symptoms arise from psychiatric disorders. Some are caused by medical illnesses, others by toxic combinations of medications or over-the-counter drugs, and still others by stress or hormonal shifts. (The medical conditions that masquerade as psychiatric disorders are discussed in Chapters Three, Four, and Five.) Even if you have only psychological symptoms, such as anxiety or depression, you should still start with your family physician. Your doctor will probably ask detailed questions about your symptoms, do a physical examination, and may order blood tests. Depending on the results of this evaluation, you may receive treatment from your physician or be referred to a specialist qualified to care for your specific symptoms.

We believe that a woman should be able to seek mental health care whenever she thinks that it would be of benefit to her. This is not always possible, however, because of the time and expense involved and the fact that insurance benefits for psychological problems are often extremely limited. On a practical level, you might seek mental health care whenever you are experiencing *distress* from your symptoms and/ or they are causing *interference* in your life. Even with this restricted definition, nearly two-thirds of all women have, or have had, a psychiatric disorder of sufficient severity to warrant treatment. Yet only one in ten receives therapy. Perhaps as women (and their physicians) become aware of the dramatic advances that have been made in the treatment of neuropsychiatric symptoms, these numbers will increase.

We just mentioned distress and interference as the hallmarks for seeking treatment. They are also the keys to making the diagnosis of a psychiatric disorder. Throughout the later chapters of this book, you will see that psychiatric disorders are distinguished from other similar symptom patterns by the amount of accompanying distress and interference. If the symptoms aren't distressing and don't cause significant interference, the symptoms aren't diagnosed as a psychiatric disorder. So what is distress? What is interference?

Psychiatrists define distress as emotional pain or suffering. They use the term to describe symptoms that are persistent, disturbing, and troublesome—those that cause severe mental anguish. Obviously, in order for a woman to seek treatment, the distress does not have to be this profound. She might choose to seek treatment when her symptoms become upsetting or bothersome, or even merely annoying.

Interference is defined by psychiatrists as impairment or disability; they use the term to denote decreased functioning in one's personal and/or professional life. To the woman considering treatment, interference would include any intrusive symptoms—in other words, those symptoms that get in her way and prohibit her from doing something. If the symptoms are upsetting and create interference, the woman should definitely consider seeking treatment.

Distress and interference are very individualized. What is distressing to one woman may not be to another. Take for example, two coworkers, Alice and Betty, who are exposed to equal levels of job stress. Alice finds the stress overwhelming and begins to notice that she is more irritable than usual, that she's having trouble getting her work done, and that she feels tired all the time. Betty is equally stressed but doesn't notice its effects; even though she has slowed down in her productivity and appears tired to others, it doesn't bother her. She isn't distressed by her symptoms so she needn't seek therapy. Because Alice experiences both distress and interference, she might wish to seek treatment.

What to Expect When You Receive Mental Health Care

One of the most important things to realize before starting treatment is that there are no quick fixes. Qualified mental health professionals can't talk with you for five to ten minutes, make a diagnosis, and send you out the door with a prescription. This is a process, not a one-time intervention. Often the evaluation phase alone will take several sessions. The psychiatrist may need to contact your physician or receive the results of laboratory tests before completing the workup. She must find out a great deal of information about you and may ask you questions that seem irrelevant or intrusive. Usually they are neither, but if you feel that they are, ask the therapist why that particular piece of information is important to your care. If the therapist is right for you, this interchange will be easy and natural. She will welcome your questions, and you will be reassured by her answers.

Once the diagnostic evaluation is complete, your therapist will be ready to describe your symptom profile and suggest treatment options. In psychiatry, *symptoms* have frequently been confused with *syndromes*. Depression is a symptom, but it is also defined as a syndrome and classified as an "affective [mood] disorder" in the *Diagnostic and Statistical Manual of Mental Disorders* (the standard reference text for mental health professionals, usually abbreviated as *DSM-IV*).[1] Similarly, nonspecific anxiety (anxiety that is not associated with a specific object or thought) can be a symptom *or* a syndrome; so can panic, mania, inattention, hypochondriasis, insomnia, and so on. Experienced therapists recognize this distinction and consider the entirety of your symptom profile. You may have the symptom of depression, for example, but discover with your therapist that it is actually part of the syndrome of obsessive-compulsive disorder; the sadness in this case is a result of the difficulties you face in coping with distressing thoughts (obsessions) and time-consuming rituals (compulsions)—it is not a symptom of an affective disorder.

Even when the symptom of depression falls within the syndrome of depression, it is necessary to define it further (in terms of cause, severity, and accompanying symptoms) before initiating treatment. Depression is a very broad diagnostic category, and the treatments of the various subtypes of depression vary widely (as discussed in Chapter Nine). Yet all are referred to as affective (or depressive) disorders. The majority of psychiatric syndromes are equally broad—they derive their names from the primary symptom (for example, anorexia, depression, anxiety disorder, and so on), but this tells you nothing about the severity of the symptoms, the possible causes, or the likely treatments.

We can draw an analogy between the diagnostic confusion of these psychiatric disorders and those of certain medical conditions, such as cancer. Many years ago, doctors thought that all cancers were the same; the patient developed a cancerous lump and within a few months, she was dead. She had cancer and it (like all cancers) was fatal. Now we know that there are dozens of different kinds of cancer, each of which has a different outcome and a different optimum treatment regimen. For a physician to say that a woman has cancer is no longer sufficient;

the doctor must specify which type. Perhaps one day soon, we will be able to have the same diagnostic specificity for psychiatric disorders, and this in turn will lead to the same level of understanding of expected outcome and preferred treatments.

Treatment of Psychiatric Disorders

The most effective treatments for each of the psychiatric disorders are discussed in specific detail in the individual chapters. In general, these treatments fall into three major categories: psychotherapy, medication, and behavior therapy. Few head-to-head comparative studies have been made—where psychotherapy is used to treat half of the patients while the other half receives medications and then the outcomes of the two groups are compared—but it appears that the treatments may all be equally effective (with some important exceptions). It also appears that the effects are additive, so that a woman taking medication may see additional benefits if she also participates in behavior therapy or psychotherapy.

In Chapter One, Esther's dynamic psychotherapy was so ineffective for her hair pulling that you might have been surprised to see psychotherapy listed as a mainstay of psychiatric treatment. For some disorders, such as obsessive-compulsive disorder and trichotillomania, psychotherapy isn't very helpful. For others, including anxiety disorders and depression, it can be curative. As with medications and behavior therapy, appropriate psychotherapy depends both on the patient and on her symptoms. The treatments must always be individualized. That is why it is essential to find an experienced therapist who is knowledgeable about the advantages and disadvantages of each of the therapies.

Psychotherapy. Psychotherapy is the name given to a varied group of treatments that range from insight-oriented (or dynamic) psychotherapy to cognitive therapy. These therapies have a common basis in that they all attribute the patient's current symptoms to internal (usually unconscious) conflicts. Cognitive therapy focuses mainly on the present, and the patient is encouraged to identify patterns of learned behaviors and to understand her feelings and reactions in terms of the current situation in which they occur. Coping strategies are practiced, and she learns to reframe her negative responses as positive ones. For example, "I'm worthless because I don't have a date tonight" might become "I'm alone tonight because I don't have a date, but I'm a worthwhile person and I can enjoy my own company."

Dynamic psychotherapy views the current symptoms as arising from long-repressed childhood conflicts. The therapist helps the patient to recall these conflicts through free associations and dream interpretations. By bringing the repressed memories to the surface, the patient is able to gain understanding of the nature of the symptoms, and this alone brings significant symptom relief. Further, she can often resolve the conflict by reinterpreting the feelings within the context of a therapeutic relationship. Having an empathic therapist may help the woman to redo and relearn certain response patterns. These insights are then used to help the patient gain understanding and mastery of her interpersonal relationships.

Behavior Therapy. There are numerous types of behavioral therapy techniques as well. The principle underlying behavior therapy is that negative responses can be eliminated and replaced with positive reactions. These therapies are more action oriented than are the psychotherapies. Little or no attempt is made to understand the meaning of the symptom (although the context in which the symptoms occurs is considered part of the scheme for eliminating them). Rather, the therapist helps the patient to practice positive or neutral responses to stressful situations and to avoid negative responses. For example, a patient with obsessive-compulsive disorder might exhibit excessive hand washing in response to obsessive fears about dirt and germs on her hands. The aim of the behavior therapy would be to eliminate the compulsive hand washing. With the therapist's support, the patient would purposefully make her hands "dirty" and then avoid excessive washing. Eventually, the anxiety associated with having dirty hands would disappear (see Chapters Twelve and Thirteen for more in-depth discussions of behavior therapy).

Medications. Medications have revolutionized the treatment of psychiatric disorders. Antipsychotic drugs (used to treat schizophrenia and other serious mental illnesses) were the first psychiatric drugs used in the United States and became available in the mid 1950s. Tricyclic antidepressants followed soon after, although lithium, a medication widely used to stabilize patients with bipolar disorder, wasn't available until the mid 1970s. Antianxiety medications, newer antidepressants, and other medications soon followed.

Thus, the treatment of psychiatric disorders with medications has followed a parallel course to that of treatment of infections with antibiotics: both psychiatric drugs and antibiotics first became available during the Korean War and have been rapidly improved to deliver greater therapeutic benefits with fewer side effects. In the past five years alone, we have seen the introduction of dozens of medications, such as the drugs that block serotonin reuptake (Prozac is one example); these new drugs promise greater symptom relief for a wider variety of psychiatric disorders.

Drug treatment is not suitable for every condition or every individual, however. In some patients, the benefits of drug treatment are outweighed by the potential risks of such therapy, so medications should be avoided. But in most patients, drug treatment offers benefits far in excess of any adverse side effects. At present, medications are helpful to nearly three-fourths of the patients for whom they are prescribed and are available for almost all of the psychiatric disorders considered in this text. The specific guidelines for medication use are discussed in the context of each of these disorders (Chapters Six through Fifteen).

There is an additional point worth mentioning about medication treatment. That is the concept of the "placebo effect." Perhaps you noticed that Cassandra felt better for a little while after Dr. Long told her that he could help her and prescribed the vitamins. This was due to a placebo effect. The placebo effect refers to the situation where symptoms improve due to something other than the actual treatment being prescribed. For example, people might get better on placebos because they are receiving care, or because they are more hopeful, or because they believe that the pills should work. This improvement is a very real response, with observable physical changes. Placebo responses are seen in over one-third of depressed patients participating in scientific studies. They are also observed in patients with high blood pressure and diabetes and many other medical conditions, but the improvement appears to have nothing to do with the therapy administered, only with the administration of the therapy. With some disorders, placebos are all that is required, leading skeptics to claim that this is proof that the disorder is "all in the patient's head," but it is important to note that just as many medical conditions fall into this category as do psychiatric disorders. Furthermore, scientific research is showing that placebo responses are actually biological events—they can cause as dramatic and significant a change in brain chemistry as do active medications. We believe that in many ways the placebo effect strengthens (rather than weakens) the argument that symptoms are a complex interrelationship of our physical and emotional states and of our biology and psychology.

After fleeing in confusion from the social worker's office, Cassandra called her family physician again. This time, she asked that she be given an extra fifteen minutes with Dr. Johnson for a consultative session. The receptionist agreed and suggested that Cassandra come in the next afternoon for the last appointment slot. As soon as she saw him, Cassandra remembered why she liked Dr. Johnson so much. He was warm, affable, and empathic. And with sufficient time allotted, he was interested in hearing her entire history. Cassandra described her travails over the past year and her current symptoms. She told him that although her mood was generally improved, she was still more irritable than she wanted to be and that she continued to have a great deal of difficulty with fatigue and insomnia. Dr. Johnson asked several questions that helped Cassandra to describe her symptoms more fully. After he performed a careful physical examination, he asked her to dress and join him in his consultative office.

There, Dr. Johnson told Cassandra that he had just returned from a course in neuropsychiatric disorders and that he thought he knew what was wrong with her: she had a sleep-phase disorder. However, because he didn't consider himself to be an expert in these disorders, he would refer her to one of the physicians who had taught the neuropsychiatric course. "You'll like Dr. Newton, Cassandra. She really knows her stuff. I'm sure that she'll want some blood work and an EKG, so let's get those done before your first appointment." Cassandra left his office feeling incredulous—why couldn't this have happened a year ago?

When Cassandra saw Dr. Newton, she was everything that Dr. Johnson had promised that she would be—smart, compassionate, and insightful. Dr. Newton explained that the diagnostic workup would take a few sessions to complete and that at the end of that time, there would be an additional delay before the therapy that she prescribed would become effective. Cassandra was disappointed that she would have to wait even longer to begin feeling better, but she was pleased with Dr. Newton's thoroughness and her honesty. She agreed to return for a complete diagnostic evaluation. After the workup was completed, Cassandra sat in Dr. Newton's office nervously awaiting the results. What was wrong with her? Was it treatable? Curable? Did Dr. Newton really have the solution to her problems, or would she turn out to be just another disappointment?

Dr. Newton entered the room and spoke softly to Cassandra: "Ms. Jones, I think that I can be helpful to you. Your disorder is easily treated with a combination of medication and behavior therapy. It's called . . ."

Cassandra might have had a medical disorder that was masquerading as a psychiatric condition (Chapter Five), or perhaps a sleep/wake-cycle disorder (Chapter Seven), or perhaps she had a depressive disorder (Chapter Nine). It doesn't really matter what diagnosis Dr. Newton gave Cassandra. What matters is that she was finally taken seriously and that she received a complete diagnostic workup that revealed the true nature of her symptoms. She was finally going to get treatment. At last, she knew for certain that her symptoms were not all in her head!

Summary

The revolution in psychiatric health care has brought more accurate diagnoses and improved treatments—offering real solutions to the psychological problems faced by thousands of women on a daily basis. If you are having symptoms that distress you in some way or that interfere with your abilities, then you should seek treatment from an experienced mental health professional. Choose a therapist who specializes in the kind of problems that you're having and that you feel comfortable working with; one who understands that the new psychiatry means your symptoms are *not* all in your head.

Resources

Office of Scientific Information
National Institute of Mental Health
5600 Fishers Lane, Room 7C–02
Rockville, Maryland 20857
301–443–4513

Further Reading

American Psychiatric Association. *Diagnostic and Statistical Manual of Mental Disorders.* 4th ed. Washington, DC: American Psychiatric Press, 1994.
Engler, Jack, and Daniel Goleman. *The Consumer's Guide to Psychotherapy.* New York: Simon & Schuster, 1992.
Gorman, Jack M. *The Essential Guide to Psychiatric Drugs.* New York: St. Martin's Press, 1995.

Notes

1. American Psychiatric Association. *Diagnostic and Statistical Manual of Mental Disorders*, 4th ed. (Washington, DC: American Psychiatric Press), 1994.

PART 2

THE MIND-BODY CONNECTION:

Physical Causes

CHAPTER 3

"All This Stress Is Driving Me Crazy"

4:16 A.M. *Amy is awakened by her four-year-old, Timmy, as he climbs into bed with her. He has had a bad dream and needs some reassurance before going back to sleep. Amy is too tired to get up and put him back into his bed, so she lets him stay in bed with her. Unfortunately, his presence keeps her from falling back to sleep—just like it has for the last three nights in a row.*

5:26 A.M. *Amy is still awake and struggling with a variety of issues: the overdue bills, the never-ending problem of child care (her latest sitter walked out in a huff the previous evening and announced she wouldn't be back), the mountain of work waiting to be tackled at the office in the morning, and the constant demands of being a single mother.*

6:35 A.M. *Amy falls asleep shortly before the alarm goes off. She hits the snooze bar twice and finally gets up at . . .*

7:10 A.M. *"We're late! Get up, honey, we're late!" Amy arouses her son and his older brother, George, and tries to get everybody back on track. She fears that she will miss the 7:50 bus and will be at least fifteen minutes late to work. She can't afford to be late today—she has an important presentation to make. Of course, as with most Mondays, the school lunches haven't been made and the backpacks can't be found. Amy decides to skip breakfast so that she can iron her skirt and go over her presentation one last time. Just as she goes to pick it up off the kitchen table, Timmy spills* his milk all over it. Amy flies into a rage and screams at him that he will never learn to be careful and that he has ruined her life.

Leaving Timmy in tears, Amy goes into the study to print out a new draft and decides that she will have to drive into work this morning. Amy hates to drive into the city; the traffic is so frightening and leaves her feeling shaken and exhausted by the time she gets to work.

9:17 A.M. Amy finally arrives at the office and is immediately greeted by her assistant, who informs her that the presentation has been moved up to 9:30 and that her boss is waiting for her to do a quick run-through. Amy had hoped to grab something to eat in order to settle the queasy feeling in her stomach, but now there's no time. Throwing down her briefcase, she picks up her presentation and hurries into her boss's office.

Mr. Smith greets her with a growl: "I've been waiting for you—I would have thought you would have come in on time this morning. Sure hope you've got a new draft ready. The one you showed me on Friday was totally unacceptable." Amy quietly listens to his criticism and then goes over her presentation. She is relieved when he pronounces it "passable."

9:31 A.M. Mr. Smith and Amy enter the conference room where the team of twenty executives waits to hear her presentation. Amy begins nervously and, just as she is about to relax, discovers that she doesn't have the appropriate charts. Desperately, she tries to signal to her assistant, but the woman remains remarkably oblivious to the situation. So Amy has to admit that she has come unprepared and sends her assistant back to her office for the visual aids.

9:57 A.M. The young woman returns after a very long and embarrassing silence—without the materials. She tells Amy in a loud voice, "I can't find them; maybe you didn't bring them into work this morning." Totally humiliated, Amy dashes from the room and into her office. Of course, the visual aids are lying in plain sight right on top of the credenza just as she had told her assistant. She grabs the materials and races back to the conference room—mentally cursing both her own stupidity and her assistant's treachery as she runs.

10:46 A.M. Amy's presentation finally comes to a close, and she feels a moment of relief before the group starts its critique. The relief is short-lived. Every single one of the twenty or so executives has something negative to say about the project, and it's all Amy can do to hold back the tears of frustration.

11:37 A.M. *The meeting is finally over. Its outcome: redo the entire port-folio—by Wednesday morning. Amy can't think about that hurdle quite yet, so she goes to her office and opens her E-mail. It's just as bad. She has forty-six messages, each one marked "priority."*

It isn't even noon yet, and Amy is exhausted and sick. No time for lunch, either, so she downs a few antacids and gets to work on the corre-spondence.

12:48 P.M. *Amy receives a call from her son's day-care teacher who asks her to have someone come pick him up. Timmy has a temperature of 99.3 degrees and is complaining of feeling sick. Because she has no sitter, Amy has to go. She throws a few papers in her bag, asks her secretary to cancel the rest of her day's appointments, and flies out the door.*

As she drives the forty-five minutes back home, she berates herself for making poor Timmy sick. Amy constantly struggles with the guilt of not being home with her sons, and she accepts Timmy's illness as fitting pun-ishment for her crabbiness that morning. As she drives, she uses the car phone to schedule a doctor's appointment for Timmy and calls George's school, arranging to pick him up early so that he won't have to come home to an empty house.

5:37 P.M. *Amy and the boys are finally home from the doctor's office. It seemed to take an eternity to be seen and to pick up the prescription at the pharmacy. After giving Timmy his medicine, Amy tucks him into bed for a quick nap while she makes dinner. As she prepares their evening meal, she also does a load of laundry, picks up and vacuums the family room, and sorts through the mail. She really has to pay bills tonight—it's already the ninth of the month and everything was due on the first. Maybe after dinner . . .*

6:45 P.M. *Dinner is over. Time for Amy to clean up the kitchen, do an-other load of laundry, and get the kids ready for bed. First, she has to go over George's homework and his big science project (which of course has to be totally redone, so that he gets to bed an hour late).*

9:40 P.M. *Amy digs into her briefcase and works solidly for the next two hours on the five different projects that she's been assigned. As she works, she begins to have a terrible pain underneath her breastbone; it's so in-tense that it feels like she's being sawed in half. She swallows a few more antacids and they help a little, but only a little and only for a short while.*

12:18 A.M. *Totally exhausted, Amy decides to go to bed, even though she has only gotten halfway through her briefcase. But as she starts up the stairs to bed, she remembers THE BILLS! and settles down at the kitchen table with her checkbook, the calculator, and a mountain of bills to pay.*

1:10 A.M. *Amy takes two more antacids and collapses into bed.*

2:53 A.M. *Awakened by a gnawing pain that pierces through from her stomach to her back, Amy gets up to take some more antacids and decides that she will have to see the doctor for this pain after all.*

When she visits her physician later that day, he informs her that she may be "lucky and just have a stress-induced gastritis," but he suspects that she has a full-blown ulcer and schedules her for an endoscopy and a set of X rays. The tests reveal that she does indeed have an ulcer, and she is started on a variety of medications. Before Amy leaves the office, her doctor gives her a strict lecture about the bad effects of stress. He closes by saying, "Amy, if you don't get control of this, you are going to make yourself really sick."

Stress is defined as the physical and psychological reaction to a threat, an emergency, or pressure. It comes in two forms: *acute stress* is caused by major life events, such as losing your job, a divorce, or the death of a spouse, while *chronic stress* is caused by multiple repeated stressors, such as those experienced by Amy and so many others of us. It's sometimes quite difficult to step back and realize just how much stress you're under, but it is essential to do so. Chronic stress is more subtle than acute stress, but the effects can be just as dramatic and damaging as those of acute stress.

Nearly thirty years ago, Drs. Holmes and Rahe developed a life stress scale that measures the degree of impact that any particular stress has on your body and mind.[1] Major events, such as the death of a spouse or a close family member, divorce, loss of your job, or serious injury or illness, give you many more points than do minor things, such as change in social activities, change in sleeping habits, failed job assignments, vacations, and others. However, it is the sum of the life changes (the total number of points) that influences the degree of stress felt, so the accumulation of many small stressors can quickly exceed the tolerable limits.

An interesting outcome of the research done by Holmes and Rahe is that they found that positive stressors, such as vacations or promotions, can have as much negative impact on your body as can negative stressors, like fights and foreclosures. The positive stressors appear to cause the same physiological changes as do the negative stressors. This may explain why people tend to get sick during (or immediately after) their vacations or why brides lose weight as they're planning their weddings.

Dr. Susan Lark has published a daily stress evaluation that assesses stress within three general areas: work, relationships, and emotional state.[2] She defines stressors within the work arena as having too much responsibility or a sense of time urgency, job instability, poor job performance, difficulty getting along with your coworkers or your boss, understimulation, and uncomfortable physical conditions. Relationship stressors are mainly related to the relationship between you and your spouse (or significant other); they include hostility, lack of communication or discrepancy in communication, lack of affection, and disagreements about sex, children, organization, money, time, and responsibilities. The final category, emotional state, includes such things as poor self-image, being too critical, having an inability to relax, too much anxiety, not enough time for self-renewal, and being too angry. Managing these chronic daily stressors is key to physical and psychological health, for as you will see in this chapter, chronic stress can have a cumulative effect as powerful as that of any major, acute stress.

Psychological Effects of Stress

The everyday results of stress are well known, and each of us has experienced them at one time or another: feeling tired, sad, or depressed; feeling overwhelmed; or being nervous, tense, or jittery. Although these sensations are unpleasant, the long-term psychological effects of stress are even worse. The psychological disorders associated with stress include depression, anxiety disorders and panic, and cognitive (thinking) changes, such as memory loss and concentration difficulties.

Depression is a common result of stress. Acute stress, such as the loss of a loved one or being fired from a job, is often associated with a grief reaction or a reactive depression. Chronic stress can also cause depressive symptoms, including dysthymia (a chronic low-grade depression). Dysthymia may result when the stressors are less intense but more chronic, as in Amy's case. Sometimes, even low-grade stress can tip the balance enough to cause full-blown depression. In such cases, antidepressant medications and psychotherapy may be necessary, although the "cure" for stress-induced depression is actually stress management. (See Chapter Nine for a complete description of depression and dysthymia.)

Anxiety disorders may also result from chronic stress. Each time your body is exposed to a stressor—whether emotional, psychological, or physical—it produces a hormonal response, known as the "fight-or-flee" response (literally, the preparation of your body to fight an enemy or flee from the stressful situation). Adrenaline, the major hormone involved in the reaction, turns up the necessary functions (such as breathing, oxygen delivery to the muscles, and vigilance, among others) while turning down the irrelevant body functions (such as digestion and the reproductive and immune systems). Thus, adrenaline causes your heart to race and blood pressure to rise, your face to flush, and your senses to become more aware. This increased state of arousal leaves you feeling jittery, anxious, or keyed up. When these effects are prolonged by chronic stress, they can cause symptoms of the anxiety disorders. Anxiety disorders are characterized by feelings of being chronically on edge and overly aware of external stimuli. This hyperarousal contributes to the chronic nature of the symptoms: once our responses have been turned up, we are even more susceptible to the little stressors, which set off the responses all over again. This becomes a vicious cycle in which stress begets more stress. The cure for stress-induced anxiety disorders is stress reduction. When that is not possible, it may be necessary to treat the anxiety disorders that have resulted. (See Chapter Twelve for a complete discussion of the anxiety disorders and panic disorder.)

Cognitive (brain) changes, such as memory loss, can also result from chronic stress. Each of us has experienced the frustration of being unable to recall a name or phone number in a stressful situation; even worse, as soon as we become frustrated by the situation, our stress level goes up even further and retrieval of the information becomes impossible. If you multiply the effect of that single stressful event several thousand times, you begin to understand the effects of chronic stress on cognitive functions.

Stress has been shown to cause difficulties with both memory and concentration. These difficulties show themselves in forgetfulness, memory lapses, trouble concentrating, easy distractibility, and difficulty learning new things. (See Chapters Six and Eleven for a complete discussion of the cognitive disorders.) As with the other psychological manifestations of stress, treatment of the cognitive disorders must be aimed at both reducing the stress and ameliorating its effects.

Physical Effects of Stress

Stress has an impact on every system of the body. Physical symptoms associated with excess stress include stomach problems, high blood pressure, dysfunction of the immune system, fatigue, and headaches.

Stomach Problems

Stress can cause excess stomach acid production and result in *heartburn*, *gas*, and eventually, *gastritis* (inflammation of the stomach lining). In each case, if the stomach problems are the result of stress, then decreasing or eliminating stress is an important part of the prescription for health.

Ulcers were thought to be the ultimate complication of stress until scientists recently discovered that many ulcers are the result of bacterial infections. Now, ulcer patients are likely to be given a prescription for antibiotics, as well as antacids and antiacid medications such as Zantac or Tagamet. Even in cases where the ulcer is caused by an infection, stress reduction is important, as stress clearly contributes to the severity of the ulcer condition.

High Blood Pressure

Acute stressors cause an *increase in blood pressure* as part of the fight-or-flee response. Chronic stress also causes increased blood pressure by increasing adrenaline levels; if the stress is prolonged, high blood pressure (hypertension) can result. Antihypertensive (blood-pressure-lowering) medicines can be helpful, but lifestyle changes are usually required for true control of blood pressure. These lifestyle changes include stress reduction, improved nutrition (limiting salt intake, among other things), and increased exercise. Exercise alone is often able to decrease high blood pressure, and it also counteracts many of the other destructive effects of chronic stress.

Immune System Problems

Both chronic stress and acute stress can alter the body's *immune response*. At present we don't know quite how this occurs, but one possible explanation is that the stress hormone, adrenaline, causes some parts of the immune system to be suppressed in order to conserve vital energy for the fight-or-flee reaction. For some women with allergic disorders, this is an advantage: when they are under excessive stress at work or at home, their allergies are less problematic (perhaps because allergies represent an overactivity of the immune system, and stress has reduced the functioning of the immune system to normal levels). However, for most women, decreased immune function is a problem. It leads to increased vulnerability to infections, and the woman can become sick more easily and recover more slowly from colds, flu, and the like.

Stress can also cause or worsen autoimmune disorders, like systemic lupus erythematosus (lupus) or rheumatoid arthritis. When stress suppresses the immune function, the body tries to fix itself by turning up the reactivity of the immune system. Then, when the external stressors disappear, the thermostat is too high, and the excess immune function can turn against the woman's own body, resulting in autoimmune disorders like lupus and rheumatoid arthritis. Thus, stress can decrease immune function and leave a woman vulnerable to infections, or it can increase immune function to excessive levels that result in autoimmune disorders. In both cases, the "cure" is stress reduction—but it must be done before stress has a chance to alter immune function.

Fatigue

Fatigue is probably the most common symptom of excess stress. It comes not only from poor sleep but also from the energy drain produced by the stress reaction. The stress-induced adrenaline response consumes a tremendous amount of physical energy and leaves little in reserve to handle physical stressors, such as infection, hormone changes, and allergies. Stress is just one of many causes of fatigue; others include chronic fatigue syndrome (discussed in detail in Chapter Five), sleep disorders (Chapter Seven), and depression (Chapters Eight and Nine). Fatigue can be caused by a number of physical problems as well, and before assigning your tiredness to excess stress or a psychological problem, you (and your doctor) should consider the following possibilities:

1. **Chronic anemia.** Women who are anemic may be pale, dizzy, weak, and/or worn out by simple exertions such as walking up the stairs. They are equally likely to have fatigue as their only symptom. A simple blood test is usually sufficient to diagnose anemia, but there are multiple causes for a low red blood cell count, and it is important to know whether or not your anemia is the result of iron or zinc deficiency, deficiency in the B vitamins, or the result of a hereditary form of anemia requiring special treatment.

2. **Diabetes mellitus.** Diabetes is a less common cause of fatigue but is more serious if left untreated. The physical signs of diabetes include frequent urination, excessive thirst, fatigue, blurry vision, dizziness, and prolonged healing of cuts or sores. You are at greater risk for diabetes if you have a family history of the disease, seem to crave sweets, or are very overweight. Although diabetes can frequently be diagnosed by examining the urine for sugar, it is sometimes necessary to do a glucose tolerance test to make an accurate diagnosis.

3. **Hypoglycemia.** Hypoglycemia is another great "mimicker." It may show up with any number of physical and psychological symptoms. Fatigue is a frequent complaint because the low blood sugar causes decreased energy levels, particularly before meals when the blood sugar is at its lowest level. A special blood test (the glucose tolerance test, among others) can help determine whether or not a woman is suffering from hypoglycemia. If so, she should follow her doctor's instructions closely; most hypoglycemia can be managed by eating small meals and avoiding large carbohydrate loads (which cause increased insulin production and then a "crash" of blood sugar levels).

   The diagnosis of hypoglycemia is probably made much too frequently in the United States. The condition is relatively rare, yet millions of American women have been told that they are "a little bit hypoglycemic." There is no such disease. If your blood sugar levels are in the low range of normal, they are still normal and do not require treatment. Following a hypoglycemia diet will probably not hurt you and may even be helpful if it forces you to eat a healthier combination of foods, but the dietary restrictions are not necessary for "treatment" of low-normal blood sugar levels. Before accepting the diagnosis of hypoglycemia, you should find out whether you are truly suffering from the disorder. If not, the medical evaluation should continue until the true cause of your fatigue is found.

4. **Hypothyroidism.** Decreased thyroid hormone levels (hypothyroidism) are a common cause of fatigue in women, particularly during their late twenties to early forties. If you have hypothyroidism, you might have noticed decreased hair thickness and an inability to tolerate cold temperatures, as well as physical symptoms such as weakness, fatigue, weight gain, and constipation. A

physical examination and a simple blood test are usually sufficient to diagnose hypothyroidism. (See Chapter Five for a complete discussion of the thyroid disorders.)

5. **Acute infections.** Infectious diseases, such as walking pneumonia or Lyme disease, usually have other symptoms in addition to fatigue. For example, in Lyme disease, a tick bite, joint pains, rash, and neurological symptoms typically occur. But the disease can be tricky to diagnose because the symptom patterns vary from one individual to the next, and there is often a long delay between the tick bite and the onset of symptoms. Usually the diagnosis is made by doing a blood test, which shows whether the woman has been infected. In Lyme disease, it is very important that your blood be tested by the most reliable method possible. Some tests are not very accurate, and it may be necessary for your doctor to send your blood to a special laboratory. Because there can be a long delay in getting the results back, some physicians will begin treatment without having proof of Lyme infection.

6. **Chronic infections.** Chronic infections, such as AIDS, infectious mononucleosis, and chronic Epstein-Barr viral (EBV) infections, can all cause fatigue, sometimes as the only symptom. Infectious mononucleosis and chronic EBV infections are discussed in Chapter Five under "Chronic Fatigue Syndrome." The fatigue of AIDS is usually accompanied by other symptoms, including signs of immune system dysfunction—chronic infections, diarrhea, or skin lesions. The AIDS and Epstein-Barr viruses are easily detected with routine physical examination and reliable blood tests.

   AIDS deserves special mention as a cause of fatigue because it is becoming an increasing problem for American women. AIDS is caused by an infection with HIV. The virus is spread through blood, semen, and other secretions. The risk factors for HIV infection are blood transfusion between 1980 and 1986, recreational drug use, intravenous drug use, and unprotected sexual intercourse (anal, oral, and vaginal). Anytime you have unprotected sex, you are taking a risk of getting AIDS or another sexually transmitted disease—it's not worth the risk: use protection!

Even Headaches Aren't All in Your Head

Penny was having a great day! She had finished the stack of correspondence on her desk by noon, and then she and her coworkers had toasted the closing of the Bottomley account with a lovely lunch at Jean-Pierre's—even the bottle of burgundy was on the company's expense account! Now she was making good progress on the latest spreadsheet. If she kept up the pace, she might even get out on time, for a change.

Penny worked a little while longer before getting up to check a reference. When she stood up, she felt dizzy for a few seconds and her vision seemed slightly blurry. "Whew!" she thought. "Guess I've been sitting still too long. Maybe I'll get a quick drink of water and stretch my legs." Before she reached the watercooler, Penny was overcome by a wave of nausea and an incredibly sharp headache; the throbbing pain nearly blinded her. Afraid that she was about to pass out, Penny quickly sat back down and rested her head on the cool Formica of the desktop.

"Oh, no, not another one—I've already had two this month. I really don't have time for a migraine today." But whether she had time or not, Penny was having a migraine and it promised to be a doozy, given how quickly it had started and how awful the pain already felt.

Penny arranged for a ride home and went straight to bed. Sometimes if she took some aspirin and got to sleep right away, she could limit the headache to twelve hours or so. Otherwise, she was in for a two-day siege. She had had migraines for years, but lately they seemed to be more severe and were happening much more often. She had seen her doctor after her last headache, and he had referred her to a neurologist, but her appointment with Dr. Franklin wasn't until next week. Meanwhile, she'd just have to hope and pray that this wasn't one that would send her to the emergency room.

Fortunately, it wasn't. Penny's migraine was much better when she woke up later that evening. Her head still throbbed, but the nausea and dizziness were gone—she knew that meant that she'd be feeling well enough to go to work in the morning. Good thing, too, since she'd used up almost all of her sick leave.

The next week, Dr. Franklin took a lengthy history and performed a neurological examination before confirming Penny's suspicions that she had migraine headaches. He gave her a prescription for a new drug that should help prevent her migraines, as well as provide much better pain relief than aspirin could. He also gave her a pamphlet with information about the cause and treatment of migraines, including advice about how to prevent future headaches. (Who would have believed that migraines could be triggered by Chinese food, chocolate, and red wine?) Dr. Franklin gave Penny something else—hope, the hope that there might be a way to prevent future migraines.

Headaches are the most common and one of the most immediate responses to excessive stress. Apparently, headaches result because stress causes the body to release hormones and neurochemicals that affect the contraction of the blood vessels in the brain.

The most common type of stress-related headache is known as the *tension headache,* which causes pain over the eyes and at the base of the neck. Tension headaches are more frequent in the late afternoon and evening hours, and they often feel like a band or vise has been clamped around your head. Tightness and tension characterize these headaches. They are frequently relieved by rest and over-the-counter pain medications, such as aspirin or Tylenol.

Temporomandibular joint dysfunction causes what are known as *TMJ headaches.* The temporomandibular joint is the hinge joint with which you open and shut your mouth, and the temporalis muscles overlay the area in front of your ears and your jaws, so TMJ headaches occur most frequently at the front and sides of your head. These headaches are frequently confused with tension headaches, but the cause and treatment are quite different. TMJ headaches can occur in the absence of stress, but stress, which increases teeth clenching and teeth grinding, often aggravates TMJ dysfunction, especially in women who have poorly aligned teeth or misaligned temporomandibular joints. The TMJ dysfunction causes spasm of the temporalis muscles, which in turn causes headache and/or pain behind the eyes, in the jaw region, or over the sinuses.

Women with TMJ dysfunction may awaken with a headache on one or both sides of their head, feelings of tiredness because they have not slept well, or a vague sense of discomfort and irritability. The distinguishing feature of TMJ headaches is that they are often present upon awakening, while tension headaches are infrequently present then. Because TMJ is a relatively new disorder, it may be necessary to bring it to your doctor's attention. Often, your doctor will refer you to an orofacial pain specialist or an orthodontist who specializes in TMJ treatment. Treatment varies by individual, but often a night guard or other device that splints the jaw in proper position will provide sufficient pain relief. In some extreme cases, surgery may be necessary, but this should be reserved for those patients who don't respond to more conservative medical therapies. We recommend that you get a second opinion confirming the need for surgery before proceeding with an operation to correct TMJ dysfunction. A second opinion may be advisable before beginning orthodontic treatment, as well.

Migraine headaches are quite common, especially among women in their twenties, thirties, and forties. These headaches can often be excruciatingly painful and are frequently accompanied by nausea, vomiting, dizziness, and other symptoms. Unlike tension headaches, which follow the triggering stress fairly closely, stress-triggered migraines tend to lag behind the stressor by at least a few hours. For example, a woman who had a very stressful day at work on Friday might spend Saturday in bed with a severe migraine.

Migraines are thought to be caused by a brief constriction and then dilation of the blood vessels in the brain. This process appears to be under the control of serotonin, one of the primary brain messenger chemicals. Migraines may result from a genetic defect in serotonin regulation, since the headaches tend to run in families. Because of the proposed defect in serotonin metabolism, one would also expect to see an increased frequency of other serotonin-based disorders, such as depression, eating disorders, and obsessive-compulsive disorder. Although scientific data are not yet available to support such a theory, case reports suggest that the rates of these psychiatric disorders are indeed higher among migraine sufferers.

Migraines are more common in women than in men, and they have a close connection to the female hormones of estrogen and progesterone. The headaches often start with the first menstrual period and may be triggered by ovulation or menstruation. They may be aggravated by taking oral contraceptives (birth control pills), so women with migraines or a family history of migraine headaches should be cautious about taking contraceptive medications (particularly since they are more likely to have serious complications from the pill). Menstrual migraines are those that occur immediately (within two days) before, during, or right after the woman's menstrual periods and at no other time during her cycle. Menstrual migraines can be more difficult to treat than other forms of migraine headaches and may require ongoing therapy.

Migraines and other types of vascular headaches have been reported to occur in response to food additives, such as monosodium glutamate (MSG). The so-called Chinese restaurant syndrome is characterized by a severe headache that comes on within a few hours of consuming Chinese food. The binitrates found in hot dogs and the sulfites found in some salad bars can also cause these headaches. The mechanism is believed to be the same as for a typical migraine: the food additives cause constriction and dilation of the brain's blood vessels, and this results in a headache. Red wines, aged cheeses, some beers, chocolate, and caffeine can also trigger vascular headaches. Other triggers include hypoglycemia and missed meals, alcohol, stress, and changes in sleep. Migraine-like headaches can even occur in association with sexual intercourse (the term for this is coitalcephalgia—or a sex headache). In such instances, a careful workup and an accurate diagnosis may help save a relationship.

In the classic variety of migraine headaches (which actually occur in only about 20 percent of the patients), the headache is preceded by an aura. Often the aura involves changes in vision, such as a partial loss of vision or seeing colored flashes of light, zigzagging lines, or lightning-like streaks. In some cases, the woman will have tubular vision—she will feel like she is looking out at the world through a tube. Even in the absence of an aura, migraines are frequently associated with visual changes, such as increased sensitivity to light or the presence of pinpoint "floaters." Abdominal pain, nausea, and vomiting are also common with migraine headaches. Migraine headaches themselves are often severe and unremitting, lasting as long as twenty-four to forty-eight hours. They may require treatment in an emergency room, and sometimes narcotics will be administered for pain control.

Tremendous progress has been made in the past few years in the treatment of migraine headaches. There are four main drugs that have proved effective for the treatment of acute migraines: ergotamine tartrate (Cafergot, Wigraine); isometheptene mucate combinations (Midrin, Isocom); dihydroergotamine (DHE–45); and sumatriptan (Imitrex). Sumatriptan was recently released in oral form. It was eagerly anticipated because it was specifically designed to treat migraine headaches. Sumatriptan and the other medications work on the serotonin system and/or the dilated blood vessels to bring constriction of the blood vessels and pain relief. Some of these medications have unpleasant side effects, including nausea, fatigue, body aches, flushing of the face, dizziness, numbness, tingling, and occasional chest pain. Ergotamine is of particular concern because it can cause physical and psychological dependency; the migraine sufferer may feel rebound pain when stopping the ergotamine, so she continues its use beyond the recommended period. Use of these drugs must be carefully monitored by an experienced physician.

Prevention of migraine headaches includes not only dietary restrictions and stress management but also use of medications that block the changes in the blood vessels of the brain that lead to the headaches. The variety of compounds used include the following:

- Beta-blockers—propranolol (Inderal), atenolol (Tenormin), and metoprolol (Lopressor)
- Calcium channel blockers—such as verapamil (Calan, Isoptin)
- Serotonin regulatory agents—methysergide (Sansert), cyproheptadine (Periactin), and methylergonovine maleate (Methergine)
- Antidepressants—particularly the tricyclic antidepressants and selective serotonin reuptake inhibitors, or SSRIs (see Chapter Nine)
- Anticonvulsants such as valproic acid (Depakote) and other drugs.

Because progress is being made so rapidly in the treatment and prevention of migraine headaches, you should consult a specialist if you think that you might have migraines; usually this specialist will be a neurologist who focuses on headache management.

Summary

The message for this chapter is simple: excess stress is not good for you, whether it is chronic or acute. While both acute and chronic stressors have negative effects, the chronicity and pervasiveness of chronic stress mean that the effects are often more severe. It might be said that acute stress can make you tongue-tied and give you butterflies in your stomach, but chronic stress makes you brain-tied and gives you ulcers in your stomach. Although stress cannot be eliminated, it should be reduced whenever possible, and its negative effects should be recognized and treated.

Resources

Headaches

American Council for Headache Education (ACHE)
875 Kings Highway, Suite 200
Woodbury, New Jersey 08096
In New Jersey: 609–845–0322
Outside New Jersey: 800–255–ACHE

National Headache Foundation
5252 North Western Avenue
Chicago, Illinois 60625
In Illinois: 800–523–8858
Outside Illinois: 800–843–2256

Further Reading

Burks, Susan L. *Managing Your Migraine: A Migraine Sufferer's Practical Guide.* Totowa, NJ: Humana Press, 1994.

Constantine, Lynne M., and Suzanne Scott. *Migraine: The Complete Guide.* New York: Dell Publishing, 1994.

Rapoport, Alan M., and Fred D. Sheftell. *Headache Relief: A Comprehensive, Up-to-Date, Medically Proven Program That Can Control and Ease Headache Pain.* New York: Simon & Schuster, 1990.

Notes

1. T. H. Holmes and R. H. Rahe. "Social Readjustment Ratings Scale," *Journal of Psychosomatic Research*, vol. 2 (1967), 213–18.
2. Susan M. Lark. *Chronic Fatigue and Tiredness: A Self-Help Program.* The Women's Health Series (Los Altos, CA: Westchester Publishing Company, 1993). 38–41.

CHAPTER 4

"My Hormones
Are Driving Me Crazy"

"You stupid idiot! Why can't you be more careful?" shouted Anita, as her daughter Judy wiped up the milk she had just spilled. "I've told you and told you to be careful, but you never listen. You're just so clumsy." At this point, Judy ran from the room in tears, and Anita was left to clean up the rest of the mess.

Nothing was going right today. Anita felt bloated and achy all over, and she had slept poorly for the third night in a row. She had a terrible headache too. It felt like a giant's hand was squeezing her temples as hard as it could. Although she had taken both Tylenol and aspirin, her headache had not improved, while the medicines had left her stomach upset. Compounding all of this was her bad mood. Anita felt depressed, crabby, irritable, and sad—all at the same time and all for no good reason.

Every month it was the same: Anita felt absolutely miserable for five to seven days before her period began. Her husband and children called her the "Witch from the Black Lagoon" during this time. They were only half-joking when they said this, because her irritability, sour moods, and snappish remarks really upset them. They upset Anita too. She hated being such a grouch, and she worried about the emotional scars she was inflicting on her children.

At her annual gynecological exam, Anita had mentioned the symptoms to her gynecologist, who said, "Of course you have PMS. You're in your thirties, a mother of two, and working outside the home. Every woman in that situation has PMS." Anita wasn't quite sure whether this was true, as many of her friends reported that they sailed through their monthly cycles without problems, but at least her doctor had taken her seriously enough to recommend that she keep a journal for the next few months and note the days when she was symptom free and the days in which she had her worst three symptoms—headache, irritability, and bad moods. The doctor also scheduled a follow-up appointment for her in three months' time so that he could examine the journals and determine whether or not there was a problem.

When Anita went back to her gynecologist, the daily log clearly showed a relationship between her troublesome symptoms and her menstrual cycle. For each of the three months, five to seven days before she began her period, she had noted headache, irritability, and depression. She also noted that she had problems with aching joints, swelling, bloating, and pains in her wrists and hands. Her gynecologist said that he was able to treat the physical symptoms with ibuprofen and diuretics (water pills) but recommended that she see a psychiatrist for treatment of the psychological problems.

Anita consulted Dr. Solomon, who examined her journal and asked many additional questions. After completing the careful history, he informed her that her symptoms were severe enough to be characterized as premenstrual dysphoric disorder or PMDD. Anita was a little confused. She had come to Dr. Solomon thinking that she had plain old PMS, but now she was being told that she had a psychiatric disorder. Dr. Solomon explained that PMDD was a form of PMS but that it was at the far end of the spectrum of symptoms; as such, it required more intensive treatment. He recommended that Anita try a medication that would block serotonin reuptake (fluoxetine) and suggested that she use it daily, rather than just during the premenstrual period. The pair discussed the pros and cons of drug treatment, and Anita decided to try the fluoxetine. Dr. Solomon also recommended oral contraceptives as a means of lessening her hormonal shifts.

Anita started the medications right away and, at her next period, noticed that her symptoms were less troublesome. By the third month of treatment, she found that her PMDD was "cured": her headaches were gone, her moodiness was gone, and even her irritability had disappeared. Anita stayed on her medications, and the Witch from the Black Lagoon retired for good!

Premenstrual Syndrome (PMS)

Premenstrual syndrome (PMS) can be annoying and even quite troublesome but should not cause serious difficulties. The most common emotional symptoms associated with PMS include anxiety, irritability, nervous tension, excessive mood swings, depression, anger, sadness, crying easily, and being overly sensitive. There appear to be different patterns of PMS. One group of patients complains mainly of nervous tension, excessive mood swings, irritability, and anxiety, while another complains more of physical changes such as weight gain, swelling of the legs and hands, breast tenderness, and abdominal bloating. A third group has depression or low mood, increased crying, mental confusion, and insomnia, while a fourth group has physiological changes such as increased appetite and cravings for sweets, heart palpitations (fast, pounding heart), headache, fatigue, and dizziness. Although these categories hold generally true, any individual woman may have symptoms from two or more categories.

The physical changes of PMS will not be described in detail in this text, but interested readers might wish to consult one of the references at the end of the chapter. The most common physical complaints include breast tenderness and swelling, bloating, fatigue, difficulty sleeping, abdominal cramps, aches and pains, weight gain, skin problems, dizziness, heart palpitations, and swelling of the hands, legs, and feet. Headache is a particularly troublesome symptom, and there appear to be three kinds of headaches associated with PMS. The first is a variant of a sinus headache and is thought to be caused by excessive fluid retention in the sinus area. The second is a tension headache (such as that experienced by Anita in the preceding case), and the third is a migraine headache, which is the result of the vascular changes associated with the hormonal shifts (see Chapter Three).

The behavioral changes associated with PMS follow naturally from the physical and emotional changes and include social isolation, quarrelsomeness, a decrease in motivation and efficiency, change in sex drive (usually a decrease), poor concentration, forgetfulness, and trouble thinking coherently. Women may also experience increased alcohol intake, increased appetite, and unusual food cravings. This is of particular concern for patients with a tendency toward alcohol abuse, obesity, or other eating disorders. Psychiatric disorders, including anxiety disorders, depression, and obsessive-compulsive disorder, have also been noted to grow worse during the premenstrual period. Although the mechanism for this effect is unknown, it may be related to the close association between the female hormones (estrogen and progesterone) and the brain's messenger chemicals. Any pattern of symptoms that worsen during the premenstrual period should be brought to your doctor's attention; he may choose a different medication that can treat the primary psychiatric disorder and the PMS symptoms simultaneously.

The diagnosis of PMS depends totally on the temporal relationship between the symptoms and the menstrual cycle. Premenstrual syndrome is often blamed for recurrent problems that have nothing to do with the hormone shifts occurring before menstruation. Daily diaries (such as the one kept by Anita) provide invaluable information that will help make the determination of whether or not the symptoms are related to PMS. For example, a woman might blame her monthly headaches or recurrent irritability on PMS, but if her diary shows that the symptoms occur only during the first two weeks of her cycle, then they clearly are not related to PMS, so she and her doctor must look for other causes.

In order to determine whether your symptoms are menstrually related, you need to keep a symptom diary. As you fill out your diary, remember that a menstrual cycle is timed from the first day of one period to the first day of the next period. Some women count their periods from the end of menstrual bleeding to the onset of the next menstrual bleeding, but that is not correct. It is always the first day of one menstrual period to the first day of the next menstrual period. The average length of a menstrual cycle is twenty-eight days, although anywhere between twenty-one and thirty-five days is considered normal. The following is an example of a symptom diary:

Day/Date:	Symptoms:
1 (9/22)	Started period—moderate cramps and heavy flow. Feel sad and tired. Tummy bloated.
2	No cramps. Flow moderate. Less tired but still cranky.
3	Moderate flow. Headache today, better mood though.
4	Light flow—no problems.
5	Light flow.
6	Period over. Feel great!!

7	Good day—no news.
8 —	. . .
15	Pain in lower abdomen this morning—sharp. Aching joints.
16	No pain in abdomen, but severe headache tonight.
17	Good day, except felt cranky all afternoon.
18 —	. . .
23	Good day—no problems.
24	Gained one and a half pounds! Bad mood today. Tired.
25	Headache and swollen fingers. Terrible mood today.
26	Didn't feel good this A.M. and should have stayed home—big fight with Jane and Terry. Feel depressed.
27	Feeling gross—fat, crabby, and aching all over. Very depressed—getting very far behind at work.
1 (10/20)	Started period—heavy flow and cramps. Here we go again!

PMS versus PMDD

In the late 1980s, some of the emotional and behavioral symptoms that had been included in premenstrual syndrome (PMS) were reclassified as late luteal phase dysphoric disorder (LLPDD)—a psychiatric disorder. When the change was made, there was a storm of controversy from a number of women's groups. The women insisted that it was discriminatory to classify such common female symptoms as a psychiatric disorder. In the latest diagnostic manual *(DSM-IV)*, LLPDD was renamed premenstrual dysphoric disorder (PMDD), but it was still considered a psychiatric disorder because psychiatrists know that the symptoms of PMDD are quite different from PMS; they cause significantly greater distress and impairment. Although the statistics vary widely, it is estimated that only about 15 percent of women seeking treatment for premenstrual symptoms will meet criteria for PMDD. That means that the majority of women seeking treatment for PMS (already a more seriously affected group than the typical woman with premenstrual symptoms) do *not* have a psychiatric disorder. Those who do have PMDD, however, deserve accurate diagnosis and effective treatment—again, without shame or blame.

Premenstrual Dysphoric Disorder (PMDD)

Premenstrual dysphoric disorder (PMDD) is a syndrome of regularly occurring emotional symptoms. The symptoms occur only during the late luteal phase of the menstrual cycle (the last week before menstrual bleeding occurs or, in women who have had hysterectomies, the second week after ovulation). Thus, symptoms should not be present in the first half of the menstrual cycle (that is, from the first day of the menstrual period to the time of ovulation). PMDD differs from PMS in that it is a psychiatric disorder; the diagnosis of PMDD is made only when the symptoms are associated with significant distress and impairment. For example, the mood changes should be so severe as to cause the woman to feel anxious or depressed, to miss work, or to cry excessively.

According to the *DSM-IV*,[1] the diagnosis of PMDD is made when a woman has five (or more) of the following symptoms (including one of the first four symptoms):

1. Markedly depressed mood
2. Marked anxiety, tension, and nervousness
3. Marked mood swings—feeling sad, tearful, irritable, or angry without good reason; moods shift without warning
4. Persistent and marked anger or irritability
5. Decreased interest in usual activities
6. Easily fatigued or decreased energy
7. Difficulty concentrating
8. Marked change in appetite or eating patterns
9. Feeling overwhelmed or out of control
10. Insomnia or hypersomnia (sleeping too much)
11. Other physical symptoms, such as breast tenderness or swelling, headaches, joint or muscle pain, bloating, or weight gain.

Why Do PMS and PMDD Occur?

At present, no one knows exactly why PMS and PMDD occur, and theories vary widely. Most scientist agree that they are not due to an abnormality of a specific hormone or brain chemical but rather to a shift in the relative balance or concentrations of these chemicals. The figure below shows the hormonal changes that occur during the menstrual cycle. As shown, ovulation induces a number of different chemical changes. Estrogen concentrations increase to their highest level shortly before ovulation and then fall dramatically after the egg is produced. Progesterone levels, on the other hand, are relatively low prior to ovulation and increase dramatically immediately after the egg is produced, to fall slowly in the week preceding menstruation. Thus, it may be the combination of falling estrogen and progesterone levels that causes PMS symptoms, or it may be sensitivity to progesterone concentrations or to the estrogen shift. The appropriate hormonal treatment depends on the individual woman's symptom pattern and its relationship to the hormone concentrations.

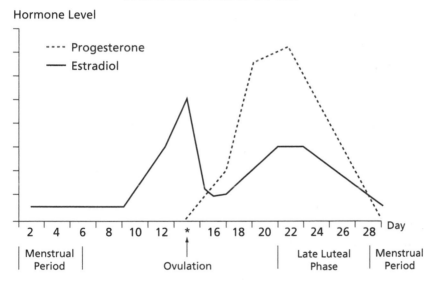

FEMALE HORMONE LEVELS
THE MENSTRUAL CYCLE

Treatment of PMS and Premenstrual Dysphoric Disorder

Because we don't yet know what causes PMS and PMDD, there isn't currently a cure for the disorders. However, a variety of treatments have been shown to be effective, either through medical studies or individual experiences. We present a partial list here. Noticeably absent are psychological therapies, such as psychotherapy or other forms of counseling; their omission is a reflection of the fact that none has been shown to be effective for the majority of women treated with them. For individual patients, however, psychotherapy or cognitive treatments may be helpful and should be considered with your therapist or doctor. Similarly, the nutritional, hormonal, and pharmaceutical treatments suggested here should be thoroughly discussed with your physician before treatment is begun; obviously, not every treatment is suited to every woman.

Nutritional Supplementation

A variety of anti-PMS diets have been published, and many women have reported at least some relief from these diets, which are rich in complex carbohydrates. The anti-PMS diets typically recommend several small meals per day to avoid dips in blood sugar concentrations. This is because studies have shown that PMS symptoms become worse when women get hungry or go for extended periods between meals.

Deficiencies of pyridoxine (or vitamin B_6), calcium, magnesium, and vitamin E are thought to contribute to PMS, and some physicians will recommend supplementation with these important vitamins and minerals.

Hormonal Therapy

Dr. Katharina Dalton (author of *Once a Month: The Original Premenstrual Syndrome Handbook*) and other experts believe strongly in the benefits of progesterone suppositories for the treatment of PMS.[2] However, a number of controlled trials have failed to show any benefits of such progesterone administration, so the therapy is not widely prescribed. For certain patients who have a clear association between decreased progesterone concentrations and PMS symptoms, progesterone supplementation may be helpful. If your symptoms seem to be closely tied to your menstrual cycle, then you might want to discuss this therapy with your doctor.

Oral contraceptives have been suggested as a treatment for PMS because they decrease the intensity of the hormone shifts. Many women have found oral contraceptives helpful in "smoothing out the edges" of their PMS, but controlled studies have not found them to be superior to placebos (inactive sugar pills). Other medications that suppress ovulation (such as Danazol) may be effective for PMS management because they also suppress the dramatic hormonal changes that occur following ovulation. But because of the potential negative side effects of the ovulation-suppressant medications, these drugs are usually reserved for women with PMDD and those with severe PMS who have not been helped by other treatments.

Medications

Several antianxiety and antidepressant medications have been shown to be helpful for PMS and PMDD. Among others, these include:

1. *Alprazolam (Xanax)* is an antianxiety medication that has been shown (in controlled studies) to decrease the anxiety and irritability of patients with PMS. Most of the studies used alprazolam during the premenstrual phase only. Alprazolam, like other benzodiazepines, can cause physical dependency or other negative side effects and should be prescribed only by a physician experienced in its use. The effectiveness of other benzodiazepines (such as Valium, Librium, Tranxene, and Ativan, among others) has not been established for PMS or PMDD. Because they work in a manner similar to alprazolam, they may also be helpful.

2. *Buspirone (Buspar)* is a nonsedating, nonaddicting, antianxiety medication that has been shown to be helpful for PMS and PMDD. Buspar takes a while to become effective and therefore should be started right after ovulation or continued throughout the menstrual cycle. Buspirone has some mild to moderate side effects, including nausea, headache, light-headedness, dry mouth, insomnia, and increased nervousness.

3. *D-fenfluramine* is a relatively new drug, and experience with it is limited. In controlled trials, it has been shown to reduce depressive symptoms associated with PMS and PMDD, as well as to suppress the carbohydrate craving and appetite increases that are problematic for some women. The most notable side effects of d-fenfluramine include nausea, anorexia, dry mouth, and headache.

4. *Fluoxetine (Prozac)* has shown the greatest benefit for treatment of both PMS and PMDD. A recent study in the *New England Journal of Medicine* (June 1995) reported that fluoxetine decreased all psychological symptoms to a greater extent than did a placebo.[3] In

another study, over half of the women taking fluoxetine had total remission of their symptoms, and all of the women participating in the study did significantly better while on the fluoxetine treatment. Fluoxetine is taken throughout the menstrual cycle because it takes several weeks to become effective.

The effectiveness of fluoxetine suggests that other serotonin reuptake blockers, such as sertraline (Zoloft) or paroxetine (Paxil), may also be useful. Because they work within a few days, these serotonin reuptake blockers may be helpful even if they are administered only during the luteal phase (last two weeks of the cycle). Studies are under way to determine whether or not such treatment regimens will be beneficial.

Baby Blues and Postpartum Depression

"My precious baby, my beautiful baby," murmured Sandy, as tears streamed down her face. She was lying quietly in her hospital bed, still recovering from the emergency C-section that had been done four days previously. Although she was feeling better physically, Sandy couldn't imagine having enough strength to go home. She had awakened this morning with a profound feeling of sadness and overwhelming fatigue. She couldn't understand why she was so depressed—her doctor assured her that she was recovering on schedule, her baby was gorgeous, and despite the frightening events leading up to the emergency cesarean section, Jeremy appeared to be fine. He had all his parts: ten precious fingers, ten tiny toes, and a beautiful little face that looked so much like her first son's when he was born that it brought tears to her eyes. Her new baby was not the only thing that could bring tears to her eyes; watching the sun rise over the treetops, or having her husband walk in the door with a bunch of flowers, or hearing a sappy TV commercial, or even having the nurse be fifteen minutes late with her pain shot—all of these made her weep.

Sandy had had the "baby blues" after her first son had been born, but it had started later and hadn't been as severe. Of course, Joshua's birth had been easier in every way—the labor and delivery were smooth and nearly painless, he nursed well, and they had gone home together after only twenty-four hours in the hospital. Joshua had thrived from the beginning, but even then, Sandy hadn't. For the first two weeks following his birth, she had been profoundly blue and had found herself crying for no reason several times a day. Her sister had reassured her that the baby blues were normal; she had had them after the birth of each of her three children, and they always cleared up in a week or two.

When the doctor came in later that morning, Sandy relayed her concerns to him, including the fact that these blues were so much worse than she had felt with her first son. Her doctor patted her arm and told that she was just suffering from the "baby number two blues" and that these too would pass. The doctor did not ask her to call him if the symptoms persisted or if she started worrying about the depth of her depression, so Sandy assumed that whatever happened would be within the normal range. But after she had been home for two weeks, it became clear that these blues were not normal; they were not going away as the others had with Joshua's birth.

Sandy sought professional help the day that she found herself contemplating suicide. She knew that she wouldn't do it, but as she sat in the rocker holding Jeremy, the thought came that it would just be easier to end it all. She felt so awful and there was no end in sight. Jeremy needed her constantly—he was colicky and nursed nearly nonstop during the daytime and every two to three hours at night. Joshua was equally difficult; he seemed to hate the new baby and was always trying to get between her and Jeremy. Even her husband seemed unusually demanding, nagging her about the state of the house, or her appearance, or what she was eating. In actuality, he was just worried about her and was nagging her to eat, to nap, and to take care of herself, for her own sake. But it didn't feel that way to Sandy; his concern felt like just one more demand on her—one more demand that she couldn't meet. And so she called her family doctor, Dr. Jones.

Dr. Jones saw Sandy that same afternoon. He took a careful history, performed a complete physical examination, and ordered some laboratory tests to make sure that she didn't have anemia or a thyroid problem. He told her that he thought she was suffering from postpartum depression and needed immediate help from a psychiatrist. Together, they made an appointment for her to see Dr. Schmidt, a psychiatrist who specialized in women's mental health disorders, including postpartum depression.

Dr. Schmidt had been briefed on Sandy's case by Dr. Jones. She asked Sandy some more questions, probed gently about the severity of Sandy's depressive symptoms, and made sure that Sandy wasn't still having thoughts of suicide. After confirming Dr. Jones's diagnosis, Dr. Schmidt explained that it was not at all unusual for a woman who has had postpartum blues with her first pregnancy to have a full-blown case of postpartum *depression in her second or third pregnancy. Dr. Schmidt gently informed Sandy that the depth of her depression (particularly the presence of thoughts about suicide) required immediate, aggressive treatment. Dr. Schmidt prescribed an antidepressant medication and suggested that Sandy begin psychotherapy; the frequent visits would prevent her symptoms from getting worse while the medication took effect.*

Sandy expressed concern about taking an antidepressant while nursing little Jeremy. Dr. Schmidt replied that she might need to stop nursing because the medication often enters the breast milk and can be passed on to the baby. Since very little is known about the effects of antidepressant drugs on newborn infants, she would usually advise against continued nursing if the drug was present in the breast milk. However, she would prescribe imipramine, one of the drugs with the lowest concentrations in the breast milk, and would check the drug levels in Sandy's breast milk at various times over the next few weeks while coordinating similar checks with Jeremy's pediatrician. Meanwhile, Sandy should take her medication immediately after nursing Jeremy for the last time in the evening and have her husband feed him a bottle of formula in the middle of the night. This would not only decrease the amount of drug that Jeremy might take in but would also allow Sandy to get six hours of uninterrupted sleep each night—which was the third part of her prescription.

Before Sandy left the psychiatrist's office, Dr. Schmidt reviewed the danger signals of worsening depression, and Sandy promised to call immediately if she noticed any of them, particularly the feelings of hopelessness and helplessness that had led her to contemplate suicide. Fortunately, Sandy didn't need to place the emergency call to Dr. Schmidt. Although the first few days were rough, she soon started feeling less hopeless and depressed and found that her energy level was increasing. Over the next few weeks, her depression lifted, and she eventually recovered completely. Now, when she murmurs to Jeremy, she does so with joy and happiness.

When we researched the material for this section of the book, we were disappointed to discover how little scientific research has been done on the subject of postpartum depressive disorders. This is particularly shocking given the estimates that 5 to 10 percent of new mothers have a postpartum depression. It is our fervent hope that the researchers currently looking at the question of postpartum depression will soon find the cause of the symptoms and be able to develop more effective treatments for this all-too-common problem.

Until very recently, there was almost nothing known about the cause or effective treatment of postpartum depression. The little research that had been done focused on the lack of social supports or the mother's negative feelings about her baby as the basis for the depressive symptoms. But these studies did not find any meaningful differences in rates of depression among women who were looking forward to the birth of their child and those for whom the pregnancy was problematic. This would suggest that such psychosocial factors cannot cause postpartum depression, although they might make the depression worse (as, for example, when the depressed mother has no one to provide relief or support and becomes more overwhelmed and depressed).

Recent research has shown that over half of all women suffer at least some degree of postpartum blues and that up to one in ten new mothers will have a full-blown postpartum depression. The symptoms frequently start about two to three weeks after the woman gives birth and peak at about three months. The frequency with which postpartum depression occurs and the consistency of the timing of the symptoms suggest that postpartum depressive disorders must have a biological basis. This seems inherently obvious, since the hormonal shifts that occur in the postpartum period are among the most dramatic at any time in a woman's life. If the monthly shifts in progesterone and estrogen concentration can cause PMS and PMDD, then it isn't surprising that the plummeting concentrations that follow labor and delivery can also cause depression and anxiety.

Biological Causes of Postpartum Depression

Both progesterone withdrawal and estrogen withdrawal have been hypothesized to cause postpartum blues. At present, the data are conflicting, and more controlled studies need to be done in order to determine whether the rapid fall in progesterone and/or estrogen levels contributes to postpartum depression. As with PMS, it is possible that women with postpartum blues have an unusual sensitivity to the levels of hormones and normal postpartum reactions are magnified by their hypersensitivity.

Other hormones have also been proposed as causes of postpartum depressive disorders. Chief among these is cortisol, a steroid hormone produced by the adrenal glands. Cortisol concentrations climb to high levels during late pregnancy, peak at the time of delivery, and then fall precipitously immediately after delivery. Levels continue to decline over the next few weeks to prepregnancy levels or below. Both an overproduction and the sudden withdrawal of cortisol have been postulated to cause post-partum blues. Support for this theory is provided by the many studies of the role of these hormones in other forms of depression. (See Chapter Nine for further discussion of the contributions of hormones to depression.) At present, however, there is no definitive proof that cortisol abnormalities cause postpartum depression.

Prolactin, another pregnancy-related hormone, has also been suggested to be involved in postpartum depression. Prolactin is secreted in large amounts at the end of the pregnancy in order to prepare the uterus for labor and delivery; prolactin is also the key control of milk production in breast-feeding women. Thus, prolactin concentrations would be a natural focus of attention. Studies that examine the relative rates of postpartum depression between breast-feeding and non-breast-feeding mothers may soon help answer this question.

Thyroid dysfunction is known to cause depression and also to cause symptom worsening in other forms of depressive disorders (see Chapters Five and Nine). It may also be a causative factor in postpartum depression, particularly when the blues start two weeks or more after delivery, the time when thyroid levels are changing most. The thyroid dysfunction is easily treated, and the depressive symptoms are rapidly relieved. Thus, any woman with postpartum depression should have a full evaluation of her thyroid gland, including a physical examination and blood tests of thyroid hormone function. It is important for the woman's doctor to test the thyroid-stimulating hormone (TSH) levels as well as the concentrations of active thyroid hormone (measured as T4) in order to determine whether or not the thyroid gland is functioning properly.

Factors Contributing to Postpartum Depression

A number of nonbiological factors have been proposed to contribute to the severity of postpartum blues. These include gynecological and obstetric factors, such as a history of previous postpartum depression, history of PMS or PMDD, obstetric complications including difficult labors and deliveries (such as C-sections), and stress surrounding the health of the baby. Negative life events—such as serious illness in a family member, unemployment, marital stress or strain, or financial difficulties—and lack of social supports, including single-parenthood, geographic separation from family members, and so on, have all been reported to contribute to the severity of postpartum depression. Of these, the marital relationship appears to be the most important, although a few investigators have suggested that a poor mother-daughter relationship is more frequent among women with postpartum depression then among those who do not suffer from the disorder. As already mentioned, it does not appear that these psychosocial factors can *cause* postpartum depression, but they can certainly worsen the severity of the illness and interfere with recovery.

Distinguishing Baby Blues from Postpartum Depression

The difference between baby blues and postpartum depression is a matter of severity—in other words, how distressing are the depressive symptoms, and how much do they interfere with the woman's ability to function? Are there physical changes, such as a change in appetite or sleeping habits? Does the inability to perform tasks or to think clearly interfere with the woman's ability to care for her child or for herself? If the answer to these questions is yes, then the woman is more likely to be suffering from a postpartum depression than from baby blues. If the symptoms are transient and short-lived or are only mildly distressing and cause no interference, then it is more likely that she has postpartum baby blues. In either case, if she is concerned about her mental well-being, she should seek help.

Severe postpartum depression can evolve into postpartum psychosis, a rare condition that occurs only one or two times in one thousand births. Postpartum psychosis can be the end result of a particularly severe postpartum depression, or it can sometimes appear without any preceding depressive symptoms. It almost always occurs within two weeks after delivery and is characterized by the presence of hallucinations or delusions of guilt, persecution, or worthlessness. Postpartum psychosis is so different from the other postpartum depressive disorders that it will not be discussed further in this chapter; rather, it is described in detail in Chapter Eleven.

Treatment of Postpartum Depression

The treatments for postpartum depression are similar to those for other depressive disorders and include medication, electroconvulsive therapy (shock therapy), and psychotherapies. These treatments are discussed in detail in Chapter Nine and will not be covered here. But there are several unique features of postpartum depression treatment that are worthy of note. The first is that postpartum depression is frequently the result of thyroid dysfunction or other hormonal imbalance. When this is the case, the depression is best treated by correcting the underlying hormone dysfunction. Again, a complete medical workup will help determine whether or not thyroid abnormalities are contributing to your postpartum depression.

As in Sandy's case, the question of whether or not it is safe to breast-feed during antidepressant therapy is one that is frequently asked but infrequently answered satisfactorily. There simply aren't facts available to allow physicians and patients to reach informed conclusions. There are a number of very good reasons why this question hasn't been answered: drug companies are unwilling to accept the liability of doing research with nursing mothers and their newborns, doctors are reluctant to prescribe medications that haven't been adequately tested, and mothers are afraid to be the ones to take a chance and have something go wrong with their precious babies. Each of these positions is entirely reasonable, but the net result is that the research hasn't been done—yet thousands of women have taken antidepressant medications while nursing. Based on these experiences, some guidelines have been established, as Dr. Schmidt outlined to Sandy.

If you require antidepressant treatment and wish to continue nursing, it is extremely important that you discuss all of your concerns with your doctor, rather than deciding to stop nursing (which can further aggravate the depression) or refusing to take the prescribed medication. Your physician can choose one of the antidepressants that is less likely to reach meaningful concentrations in the breast milk. He can monitor the levels in your breast milk, and your baby's pediatrician can follow drug levels in your baby's blood to ensure that both remain within acceptable levels. Sometimes it is necessary to pump and discard your milk at certain times of the day, but with careful monitoring of the drug levels, a woman is often able to nurse her baby successfully and receive effective treatment for her postpartum depression at the same time.

Because postpartum depression can be worsened by life stressors, supportive therapy (therapy designed to help the woman cope with excessive stress) can be quite useful. The support is directed at the area(s) causing stress to the new mother. Social supports include everything from a visiting nurse (who can provide instruction and assistance in the care of the baby) to marital counseling, parent education classes, and group support. Some Lamaze and other childbirth education classes continue for a few sessions after the birth of the babies to provide social support; this may be sufficient to keep postpartum blues from worsening into postpartum depression.

Menopause

The clock strikes 3:00 A.M., and Winifred finds herself once again lying in a pool of perspiration. She has been having hot flashes every few hours for the last several months—during church and business meetings and while she's eating dinner or visiting with friends. The hot flashes come so randomly that she never knows when they'll strike, but they always seem to come more often at night, and they feel so much worse at 3:00 in the morning. Tonight, she lies quietly for a few minutes, waiting for the burning, anxious feeling to subside, and in a few moments, it does, as suddenly and mysteriously as it began. Her friends tell her that the hot flashes are a sure sign that menopause is upon her. The process is not particularly distressing to Winifred, as she doesn't want more children and is looking forward to the time when she no longer has to worry about menstrual periods or the possibility of pregnancy. But even so, the hot flashes are a pain. She's pleased that for her, they're really the only unpleasant part of going through menopause.

When Winifred looks in the mirror, she sees a mature woman who is perhaps a little bit thicker in her waist than in previous years but is otherwise still quite attractive. As far as she can tell, menopause hasn't affected her life in any substantial way. She and her husband are physically close and have been so for a number of years. She is more fortunate than many women approaching menopause because her life has been relatively stable over the last few years: her children are successful in their careers and established in their homes and community, her husband is in good health, and they are financially secure. All is right with Winifred's world, and menopause is just another part of her life. Unfortunately, this is not the case for her friend Constance.

Constance started having hot flashes and night sweats at about the same time that Winifred did. Unlike her friend, however, Constance has been dreading the onset of menopause since she gave birth to her last child. She is certain that it will mark the end of her femininity and the beginning of old age. For Constance, the hot flash is the perfect symbol for menopause as a whole—it's uncontrollable, unpleasant, and omnipresent. Because this is such a negative life change for her, it is not a surprise that she has reacted to it with depression. Her mood is as negative and unpleasant as she perceives "the change" to be. Constance is snappish and irritable to others and critical and self-deprecating of herself. She is sad and miserable. When she went to her gynecologist to request hormone replacement therapy, her doctor recognized that she was having more emotional symptoms than expected and recommended a psychiatric evaluation.

The psychiatrist evaluating Constance also was concerned that her symptoms went beyond an exaggerated negative response to menopause. After taking a complete history, he determined that she was suffering from depression. At this point, it was impossible for the doctor to sort out whether her depression was secondary to the life changes associated with her menopause or whether it was an unrelated, biological depression, but the severity of her symptoms clearly warranted treatment. He prescribed both antidepressant medications and cognitive-behavior therapy. The purpose of the cognitive-behavior therapy was to change her mind-set about menopause — to help her see it more realistically, rather than as a completely negative experience. Although Constance initially balked at the idea of therapy, she agreed to attend a few sessions and was pleasantly surprised to discover that the therapist was helpful to her. The combination of medication and therapy allowed her to recover completely from her depression and also to come to terms with her menopausal changes.

Is Menopause a Psychiatric Disorder?

Menopause has been blamed for a variety of psychiatric symptoms, including depression, irritability, anxiety, tension, inability to concentrate, nervousness, and aggressiveness. But these associations are largely the result of folklore rather than scientific data — a few women's experiences have been reported as representing "the menopausal experience." There is no way to know whether or not these women's experiences are representative of all women going through menopause, of most women, of a few women, or only of those whose symptoms were reported. Taking a wide sampling of these anecdotal reports, we find that there is no one unique psychological pattern associated with menopause. Like Winifred, many women may sail through menopause without problems, while others suffer from anxiety or depression as Constance did.

Depressive disorders (see Chapter Nine) and anxiety disorders (see Chapter Twelve) may become evident for the first time during or after menopause, but the disorders do not appear to have any unique features when they occur during the menopausal years. A large survey, conducted by Dr. Myrna Weisman, of symptoms in 422 women with major depression found no difference in symptoms (or treatment response) between those who were premenopausal and those who were post-menopausal.[4] It appears that aging in and of itself is associated with an increased risk of depression. One-third of all depressions occur among persons age sixty or older, and it may be the aging process, rather than menopause, that contributes to the increased frequency of depressive symptoms among menopausal women. However, for women who have been suffering from menstrually related symptoms (such as severe PMS or PMDD), menopause may be another period of vulnerability.

Because so little is known about the effects of menopause, the Office on Women's Health of the National Institutes of Health (NIH) in Bethesda, Maryland, has recently launched a major investigation of the physical and psychological symptoms accompanying menopause. The targets of the study include osteoporosis, increased risk of heart disease, and depression. The depression associated with menopause is thought to result from decreasing estrogen concentrations. This would suggest that estrogen replacement may be helpful in treating the depressive symptoms. Hormone replacement therapy (usually a combination of estrogen and progesterone) is now widely used and appears to be effective. The NIH research will focus on whether or not the anecdotal claims can be substantiated by controlled trials.

Summary

Despite the popular belief that hormones make women "act crazy," there is little medical evidence to suggest that this assertion is true. For most women, female hormones cause only minor emotional and behavioral changes. For a few women, the hormonal shifts inherent to the menstrual cycle and/or the birthing process are problematic and result in PMS, PMDD, and postpartum depressive disorders. These disorders are clearly caused by hormonal changes and deserve prompt and effective treatment, but they do not occur in the majority of women and should not be thought of as inherent to womanhood. Similarly, although menopause has been blamed for a variety of psychiatric syndromes, there doesn't appear to be a unique pattern of symptoms associated with menopause. Much research remains to be done, however, on all of the hormone-related conditions, and we should demand (and support funding for) research for this important but neglected area.

Resources

Premenstrual Syndrome and Premenstrual Dysphoric Disorder

Dalton, Katharina. *Once a Month: The Original Premenstrual Syndrome Handbook*. Alameda, CA: Hunter House, 1994.

Gold, Judith M., and Sally K. Severino. *Premenstrual Dysphorias: Myths and Realities*. Washington, DC: American Psychiatric Press, 1994.

Martorano, Joseph, and Maureen Morgan. *Unmasking PMS: The Complete PMS Medical Treatment Plan*. New York: M. Evans & Co., 1993.

Postpartum Depression

Dunnewold, Ann, and Diane G. Sanford. *Postpartum Survival Guide*. Oakland, CA: New Harbinger Publications, 1994.

Kleiman, Karen R., and Valerie D. Raskin. *This Isn't What I Expected*. New York: Bantam Books, 1994.

Menopause

Cutler, Winnifred B., and Celso-Ramón García. *Menopause: A Guide for Women and Those Who Love Them*. New York: W. W. Norton, 1992.

Gillespie, Clark. *Hormones, Hot Flashes, and Mood Swings*. New York: HarperCollins, 1994.

Lark, Susan M. *The Estrogen Decision: A Self-Help Program*. Los Altos, CA: Westchester Publishing, 1994.

Sand, Gayle. *Is It Hot in Here or Is It Me?* New York: HarperCollins, 1993.

Sheehy, Gail. *The Silent Passage: Menopause*. New York: Pocket Books, 1995.

Notes

1. American Psychiatric Association, *Diagnostic and Statistical Manual of Mental Disorders*, 4th ed. (Washington, DC), 1994.

2. Katharina Dalton. *Once a Month: The Original Premenstrual Syndrome Handbook* (Alameda, CA: Hunter House), 1994.

3. M. Steiner, S. Steinberg, and colleagues. "Fluoxetine in the Treatment of Premenstrual Dysphoria," *New England Journal of Medicine* , no. 23 (1995), 1529–34.

4. Myrna Weisman, as cited in Lawrence M. Deemers, John L. McGuire, Audrey Phillips, and David R. Rubinell. *Premenstrual, Postpartum, and Menopausal Mood Disorders* (Baltimore: Irbin & Schwartzenberg Press, 1989).

CHAPTER 5

"My Doctor
Thinks I'm Crazy"

Barbara has just been admitted to the psychiatric ward of the local hospital with a diagnosis of "psychosis, not otherwise specified." This means
that the admitting physicians thought she was crazy when they checked
her out in the emergency room.

"Boy, see a few flashing lights and hear some strangers whispering
about you, and the next thing you know, you're in the loony bin," she complained to the nurse who escorted her to her room. "I had been feeling
kinda weird all day—sorta keyed up and high, you know? And then this
evening, these lights started flashing in the corner of my living room, but
my husband couldn't see them, and neither could my kids. They couldn't
hear the lady's voice either; she kept whispering that I was evil and that
God was going to punish me. It was really scary—it sounded like she was
standing right next to me. I guess maybe they're right—maybe I am crazy."

The psychiatrist on call for the hospital came in to evaluate Barbara
about an hour later. Dr. Saunders asked her what had brought her to the
hospital, and she answered, "A Ford Taurus," and then laughed. The doctor laughed too, and Barbara explained that actually her husband had
brought her because he was so concerned about her. He was worried because she was seeing things that he couldn't see and hearing voices that
he couldn't hear. Dr. Saunders asked her if she had ever had any similar
episodes in the past, and she answered, "No, not like this. I went a little
crazy after my baby daughter died, but that was more like I was hysterical

with grief; they had to give me a sedative to calm down. There weren't any lights or voices, though."

The psychiatrist asked Barbara question after question about her emotions and behavior. No, she'd never used street drugs; no, she didn't smoke pot or drink a lot of alcohol; no, she hadn't been depressed or excessively anxious before this happened; no, she wasn't under any particular stress at work; and no, she hadn't had any particular stress at home either.

Dr. Saunders then started asking Barbara questions about her general health. She told him that other than the birth of her four children, she'd never been hospitalized. She knew she wasn't pregnant because she had had her tubes tied after her fourth child was born seven years ago. Her last physical exam was less than six months ago and had been completely normal. The only medication that she was taking was something her doctor had prescribed last week for poison ivy.

"Is it prednisone?" asked Dr. Saunders.

"Yes, it is," replied Barbara.

"When exactly did you start taking it?"

"I started it a week ago Saturday, so I'm almost done — I just have one day's worth left," Barbara answered.

"Are you taking any other medications," the psychiatrist inquired, "any drugs that you can get without a prescription, like decongestants or antihistamines?"

"Both, actually," Barbara said. "I've had hay fever for the past few days, and I woke up feeling really stuffy, so I took a couple of sinus tablets and an allergy capsule this morning and again later this afternoon.

"Oh, I almost forgot," she added. "For the past month, I've been taking some of those diet pills that you can get without a prescription. I've lost ten pounds so far, but I still have another fifteen to go. The prednisone isn't helping that situation at all — it can make you gain weight, you know."

"Yes, it can," Dr. Saunders said. "Prednisone can also give you hallucinations like the flashing lights and strange voices that you experienced today. Antihistamines and decongestants can do the same thing, and so can diet pills. It's hard to know which one of the medications caused your problem or whether it was a combination of the steroids with the hay-fever medications and the diet pills. Sounds to me like you had a triple whammy. Unfortunately, it will take a few days for you to feel like yourself again. Meanwhile, we'll do everything that we can to make you feel safe and comfortable."

Barbara was relieved to hear that she would recover. But who would have believed that a prescription medication or a bunch of pills that she had bought in the grocery store could do this to her?

Over-the-counter drugs and prescription medications can cause a wide variety of behavioral and emotional changes. Physical illnesses, such as metabolic disorders, autoimmune diseases, infections, and neurological disorders, can also cause psychological symptoms. This chapter reviews the medical illnesses and medications that masquerade as psychiatric disorders. They are presented before the psychiatric disorders because we believe that medical conditions should always be considered first as the potential cause of a woman's complaints; once these conditions have been eliminated, then the examining physician can look at the possibility of a psychiatric disorder.

Medical Illnesses That Masquerade as Psychiatric Disorders

Anne hasn't felt well for a long time. She can't put her finger on when and how it all started, but it seems like months have passed since she had any fun or any energy. Things that she used to enjoy doing are just too much effort right now, so she's stopped going to the mall or to the movies or out to eat. She sleeps instead—up to eleven hours each night—but still feels tired and dragged out. Anne has also noticed a peculiar weight gain. She has been so tired and blue that she's had very little appetite and has eaten much less than usual. Despite this, she has gained ten pounds over the last three months. Admittedly, she hasn't been exercising as regularly as she used to, but she isn't eating either—it just doesn't add up.

Anne's friend Lisa noticed the changes in Anne's appearance and behavior and told her that she looked depressed. Lisa attributed it to the fact that Anne's long-term boyfriend had broken up with her several months ago, and she said, "Just snap out of it; there are other fish in the sea." But Anne doesn't agree that the end of her relationship could be the root of her problems. After all, her sluggishness and bad mood had started before she and her boyfriend broke up. In retrospect, she wonders if her lack of energy and interest hadn't actually contributed to the demise of the relationship.

Anne spends a lot of time contemplating these and other issues. It seems like all she does lately is worry and wonder. She wonders if she could have said or done something differently to prevent the breakup of the relationship. And as she lies awake at night, she worries that she's hurt someone's feelings that day or failed to do her best at work. The longer she lies awake at night, the worse she feels in the morning. And no wonder—she's exhausted.

Anne's exhaustion is compounded by her fuzzy thinking; it seems like she just can't concentrate. Soon this starts to affect her work. Although she tries to hide it and works extra hours to make up for her dysfunction, she can't get the job done. Finally, one afternoon, Anne's supervisor takes her aside to comment on her deteriorating performance ratings. She concludes by saying, "Anne, you just don't seem to be yourself anymore. Perhaps you should speak with someone in employee health." Anne knew that her supervisor was referring to the company's psychologist and decided that she would rather see her own physician, Dr. Lundquist.

As soon as Dr. Lundquist walked into the examining room, she could tell that Anne wasn't herself. At every other appointment, Anne had been so perky and excited about her life. This time, Anne sat slumped in the chair and said in a low voice, "I think there's something really wrong with me, Dr. Lundquist. I'm so wiped out and tired all the time."

Dr. Lundquist went through a careful history of what had gone on in the year since she had last seen Anne. She asked Anne dozens of questions about her physical symptoms and also asked whether or not she had taken any medicines prescribed by another doctor or any over-the-counter medicines. Dr. Lundquist continued the interview by asking Anne about her interests, her sleep, her energy level, and her appetite. She asked Anne what changes there had been in her personal life and in her job and probed about the impact these might be having on Anne's life. Then, Dr. Lundquist did a complete physical examination.

After Anne got dressed, the two of them had a long talk. Dr. Lundquist suggested that Anne's supervisor could be right and that Anne might be depressed. Each of her symptoms, including the lack of energy and the changes in her sleep and appetite, could be due to depression, and there certainly were some good reasons for Anne to be depressed.

"However," Dr. Lundquist continued, "it's important for us to make sure that you don't have a medical cause for your symptoms. Too many young women have been treated with antidepressants or psychotherapy while the true cause of their symptoms went undetected." Dr. Lundquist explained that there were at least fifty medical illnesses that could masquerade as depression and that she would order some simple laboratory tests to rule out as many as possible. The tests would include a complete *blood count, a vitamin B$_{12}$ level, general chemistry screenings, and tests of thyroid hormone function. After writing up the laboratory orders, Dr. Lundquist told Anne to call her in two days for the results of the tests. She concluded their session by reminding Anne to try to sleep on a regular schedule, to eat well, to refrain from drinking alcohol, and to exercise.*

Anne was lucky that she went to see Dr. Lundquist for her problems and that she had a complete diagnostic workup. Too often, women complaining of depressive symptoms are told, "It's all in your head," without receiving an evaluation that adequately determines whether or not a physical disorder is causing their complaints. For some reason (although there is ample evidence to the contrary), the myth persists that the mind is separate from the body. Psychological symptoms are still perceived as separate from physical ailments, and physical diseases are considered distinctly different from mental illnesses. The purpose of this chapter is to lay this myth to rest once and for all—to demonstrate that the mind and body are intimately interconnected and that what affects one, affects the other. We will review a variety of medical illnesses that have psychological, emotional, and behavioral manifestations, and we will also look at the medical causes of various psychiatric syndromes. The most common of these are vitamin deficiencies, hormonal disorders, infections, autoimmune disorders, neurological illnesses, and toxic reactions to medications or other substances.

Vitamin and Mineral Deficiencies and Excesses

Vitamin deficiencies and excesses can produce symptoms of depression, anxiety disorders, and psychotic disorders. The vitamins most commonly associated with psychological symptoms include thiamine, vitamin B$_{12}$, folic acid, niacin, and vitamin C. Although all are water-soluble vitamins and share features, each has a unique pattern of symptoms.

1. **Vitamin B$_{12}$.** Vitamin B$_{12}$ is crucial in the synthesis of several important brain chemicals. Because the vitamin is essential to so many different brain activities, there are several backup systems to ensure that its function is protected as long as possible, and vitamin B$_{12}$ deficiency can sometimes be tricky to diagnose. For example, although anemia is considered to be the hallmark symptom of vitamin B$_{12}$ deficiency, the blood count can be normal, even with severe deficiencies.

Vitamin B_{12} deficiency is usually caused by inadequate intake of this vitamin. A few women will have an inherited (autoimmune) inability to absorb B_{12} from the stomach, and others have had intestinal surgery that leaves them unable to absorb the vitamin. More commonly, however, it is a dietary restriction that causes vitamin B_{12} deficiency. Women who are severely limiting their caloric intake or those who are strict vegetarians are at greatest risk.

The onset of the symptoms is frequently slow and insidious, but once symptoms are present, the patient's condition can deteriorate rapidly and irreversible nerve damage can occur. The "textbook" diagnosis of vitamin B_{12} deficiency includes the following signs and symptoms: anemia, weakness, a sore tongue, and numbness and tingling of the extremities. However, this picture is frequently absent, and the core problem of vitamin B_{12} deficiency can be masked by other, more prominent symptoms, such as loss of appetite, diarrhea, constipation, weight loss, palpitations (pounding heart), chest pain, and fatigue. Although it would be unusual for depressive symptoms to be the only presenting symptoms of B_{12} deficiency, there are examples in the medical literature of people whose only complaints of this deficiency are apathy, depression, lethargy, and difficulty concentrating.

Vitamin B_{12} levels can be obtained from a blood sample. If the values are low normal or below, the physician may choose to do additional tests to determine whether or not the vitamin B_{12} stores are adequate.

2. **Folic acid (folate) and Vitamin B_6.** Deficiencies of folic acid and vitamin B_6 are also thought to cause neuropsychiatric symptoms, including permanent neurological damage in untreated cases. Folate deficiency can cause apathy, depression, withdrawal, memory lapses, and difficulty concentrating. Because the food sources for folate are nearly identical to those of vitamin B_{12}, the deficiencies frequently occur together. Thus, the risk factors for folic acid deficiency are the same as for vitamin B_{12} deficiency. In addition to those mentioned in the previous item, it is important to note that alcoholism is frequently associated with vitamin B_{12} and folic acid deficiencies, as well as thiamine and niacin deficiencies. Vitamin B_6 deficiencies have been reported to occur more frequently among women using oral contraceptives, and women taking

birth control pills may choose to supplement their diet with the B-complex vitamins (or with a standard multivitamin tablet, which is often much less expensive and equally effective).

3. **Vitamin C.** Vitamin C is another water-soluble vitamin that plays key roles in the synthesis and breakdown of a variety of brain chemicals. Many of its functions are related to those of the B-complex vitamins, and vitamin C deficiency can cause a similar picture of fatigue, weakness, decreased appetite, and depression.

   Vitamin C deficiency is relatively rare in the United States because of the wide availability of citrus fruits, green leafy vegetables, and other foods rich in vitamin C, such as enriched cereals and grains. Before vitamin C supplementation was so widespread, scurvy (severe vitamin C deficiency) was relatively commonplace. Vitamin C deficiency still sometimes occurs during pregnancy or lactation (because of increased demands) and in women following rigid diet plans. This emphasizes the need for providing your doctor with a detailed dietary history, because the signs and symptoms of vitamin deficiencies can be mistaken for those of more common illnesses.

4. **Fat-soluble vitamins.** Unlike the water-soluble vitamins just discussed, the problem with the fat-soluble vitamins (A, D, E, and K) isn't usually deficiency but excess. Because the fat-soluble vitamins can't be eliminated in the urine, they collect in your body and can build up to dangerous levels if taken in excess. Chronic excesses of vitamin A can cause numerous complaints, including nausea, vomiting, irritability, blurred vision, weakness, headache, fatigue, and sleep difficulties. These symptoms are indistinguishable from those caused by several other disorders. This once again demonstrates the importance of consulting with your physician before starting any therapy—even those available in health food stores.

Anne called Dr. Lundquist three days later to inquire about the results of her blood tests. Dr. Lundquist went over the tests in detail: Anne's blood count was normal, so she was not anemic and it was unlikely that she had a vitamin B_{12} or folic acid deficiency; her chemistries were normal, which meant that her liver and kidneys were functioning well; the normal sodium and calcium levels meant that she didn't have parathyroid illness; and her sedimentation rate was within normal limits, making it unlikely that she had an active infection or autoimmune disorder. Because Anne's illness had lasted so long, Dr. Lundquist had also ordered a test for anti-nuclear antibodies. It too came back negative, which offered additional evidence that she didn't have any autoimmune or connective tissue diseases. However, Anne's thyroid levels were low. Dr. Lundquist referred her to an endocrinologist, who completed the workup and determined that Anne had hypothyroidism (low thyroid levels). The endocrinologist prescribed thyroid replacement hormone, which soon began to help Anne's symptoms. She had more energy, began to lose weight, and found that her mood had improved. Anne still wasn't sleeping well, however, and she still got headaches frequently. The endocrinologist assured her that these symptoms would also eventually improve.

But over the next few months, Anne actually seemed to be getting worse. She was increasingly fatigued and noticed that she seemed to move more slowly and that her legs felt weak. When she began to have trouble with dizziness and keeping her balance, she scheduled another appointment with Dr. Lundquist. The doctor took another history and repeated the physical exam. This time, she noted some weakness and numbness over Anne's lower legs and distinct abnormalities of her balance. Dr. Lundquist was concerned about the change in Anne's condition and ordered some new laboratory tests, including a test for syphilis, AIDS, and Lyme disease, a prolactin level, serum lead level, and vitamin B_{12} and folate levels. She then called a consulting neurologist, Dr. Parker, and sent Anne right over to see her.

Dr. Parker confirmed that there were some abnormalities on the neurological exam and that the pattern was suggestive of nerve damage. She discussed the possibilities with Anne, including such things as multiple sclerosis, Lyme disease, lead or other toxic exposure, vitamin deficiencies, and a variety of rare metabolic disorders. Anne was terrified by the possibilities but agreed to complete the series of tests that Dr. Parker ordered; after all, it was better to know which one of the awful possibilities she faced than to worry about the whole group. Over the next several days, Anne completed the tests, and everything came back normal, except for the B_{12} test—it was slightly below normal. Subsequent tests confirmed that Anne had vitamin B_{12} deficiency.

The two doctors admitted that they were surprised by the findings. Anne had not had any anemia or other "classic" signs of the disorder, but a vitamin B_{12} deficiency would explain each of Anne's remaining symptoms. The doctors went over Anne's history one more time with her, and together they were able to surmise that the deficiency was due to Anne's strict vegetarian diet. Because she ate no animal protein and didn't take *supplemental vitamins, her vitamin B_{12} levels had fallen to an unsafe level. Anne began a regimen of vitamin B_{12} injections, and most of her symptoms disappeared. She still has occasional numbness and tingling around her ankles, but her balance and her energy level are back to normal, and her depression has disappeared.*

Anne's case shows how important it is to pay attention to a lack of response to treatment. If you don't have any benefit from a therapy, it may be the wrong treatment for you, or the dose may be inadequate to treat your symptoms. If you have initial improvement but then worsen, as Anne did, you may have more than one problem (just as Anne had both thyroid dysfunction and B_{12} deficiency). As doctors, we often fail to consider this possibility because we are trained to expect patients to have only one disease at a time.

Metabolic Disorders

Metabolic diseases that result from disorders of the endocrine system need to be considered in any woman with significant emotional symptoms. The endocrine organs that may be involved are the thyroid, parathyroid, pituitary, and adrenal glands. The disorders of the endocrine glands are of two types: those that cause excessive hormone production ("hyper-" or high hormone levels) and those that cause insufficient hormone production ("hypo-" or low hormone levels). Interestingly, the neuropsychiatric symptoms may be similar, whether the gland is hyperactive or hypofunctioning. Often the symptoms are quite nonspecific and include such things as fatigue, general malaise, restlessness, difficulty with concentration, depression, anxiety, apathy, and changes in mood and general functioning. The specific symptoms associated with each of the hormonal disorders are considered here.

Thyroid Disorders

The thyroid gland is located at the front and base of one's neck. It secretes thyroid hormone, which is very important in regulating metabolism and maintaining energy balance. Excess thyroid secretion results in hyperthyroidism and hypermetabolism, while decreased thyroid causes hypothyroidism and hypometabolism. Any thyroid dysfunction is serious and must be treated promptly. Thyroid dysfunction can be detected by a simple blood test, but more extensive testing may be required to pinpoint the specific thyroid problem.

Hyperthyroidism (overactivity of the thyroid gland) may have either a slow, insidious onset or an abrupt one. It is classically associated with nervousness, overactivity, heat sensitivity, sweating, weight loss, sleep difficulties, and fatigue. In addition, many women with hyperthyroidism notice that their hair gets thinner or that the individual hairs become fine and silky. Although neuropsychiatric symptoms are less common in hyperthyroidism than in hypothyroidism, excess thyroid hormone can cause moodiness and unexpected tearfulness. In addition, there are reports of hyperactivity, nervousness, anxiety, and jitteriness. In rare, extremely severe cases, thyroid overactivity can lead to psychosis and mental confusion.

Hypothyroidism (underactivity of the thyroid gland) usually has a slow, insidious onset. The physical symptoms of decreased thyroid function are fairly nonspecific and include such complaints as fatigue, cold intolerance, decreased appetite, weight gain, decreased energy, dry skin, muscle aches, and difficulty concentrating. Nearly every known psychiatric symptom has been reported to have been caused by decreased thyroid function, and there is a particularly strong association with depression. Although hypothyroidism isn't the most common cause of depression, it should be considered in each case. Further, hypothyroidism should be considered in patients who have trouble concentrating or have cognitive changes, such as a failing memory or increased forgetfulness. As with hyperthyroidism, hypothyroidism is easy to detect with a blood test. Treatment consists of hormone replacement. This is generally successful but depends on the diagnosis being made promptly. Sometimes the psychiatric symptoms require separate treatment while the thyroid hormone levels are regulated.

Parathyroid Disorders

The parathyroid gland is located in the same region of the neck as the thyroid gland. Parathyroid hormone is important for the regulation of calcium and phosphate in the body. Parathyroid disease is rare, but there are a variety of other medical illnesses that can produce changes in calcium levels. Hypoparathyroidism (too little parathyroid hormone) may be characterized by fatigue, weakness, and tingling sensations in the hands or lips. Hyperparathyroidism (too much parathyroid hormone) may be a "silent" disease and have no physical symptoms. Both hyperparathyroidism and hypoparathyroidism can produce psychiatric symptoms, including a depressive illness in which patients are overly calm and disinterested in life. The apathy is out of proportion to their low mood; some patients also have mental confusion or trouble concentrating.

Adrenal Disorders

The adrenal glands are located on the kidneys and produce a variety of hormones, including the stress hormone, adrenaline (discussed in greater detail in Chapter Three). The adrenal glands also produce steroid hormones, which help to control everything from growth and cellular repair to "energy balance" and glucose (sugar) consumption.

Steroid levels are very carefully controlled through an elaborate feedback system that senses when levels are too high (or too low) and decreases (or increases) production proportionately. However, when the system breaks down and adrenal steroid levels are too high, Cushing's disease results; when levels are too low, the woman will get Addison's disease. A variety of conditions can cause these adrenal disorders. Addison's disease can be caused by excess steroid ingestion, whether through a too-powerful prescription or use of illicit anabolic steroids (bodybuilding steroids).

In both Cushing's disease and Addison's disease, behavioral changes and neuropsychiatric symptoms are common. The symptoms, which can become quite incapacitating, include irritability, fatigue, excessive mood swings, depression, confusion, or psychosis. Patients with Addison's disease may also notice a sense of restlessness and increased acuity of their senses, particularly hearing and taste. Diagnosis of the adrenal disorders requires a careful history and complete physical examination (both disorders have telltale physical abnormalities), as well as laboratory tests.

Infectious Diseases

Infectious illnesses can cause psychiatric symptoms such as depression, anxiety, trouble concentrating, and memory difficulties. Some infections produce *only* neuropsychiatric symptoms; although this is rare, it does occur and is worthy of note. One such example is AIDS. Doctors now know that persons who are HIV-positive and have early AIDS may have only psychological symptoms. This disorder is called neuro-AIDS and is characterized by personality changes, excessive moodiness, irritability, and cognitive changes such as memory loss and confusion.

Neuro-AIDS has replaced neurosyphilis as the leading cause of infectious neuropsychiatric symptoms. In contrast to neuro-AIDS, which occurs early in the course of the illness, neurosyphilis is one of the last manifestations of syphilis; it occurs only after decades of infection. Fortunately, with improved detection, prevention, and treatment methods, this late complication of syphilis is becoming less common.

In both neuro-AIDS and neurosyphilis, the diagnosis is made by taking a careful history and evaluating the patient's risk factors, by finding neurological abnormalities on physical examination, and by laboratory tests that show evidence of infection with the AIDS virus or the syphilis bacteria.

Lyme disease has received a lot of attention recently as "the great mimicker." Before the illness was officially recognized (in the early 1980s), women were often labeled as "hysterics" because of the vagueness of their complaints. In addition to the characteristic rash, fever, fatigue, arthritis, and headache, Lyme disease can cause a wide variety of neurological and psychological symptoms, including facial nerve paralysis (causing one side of the face and/or mouth to droop), numbness and tingling of the hands or feet, irritability, and personality changes. Lyme disease is sometimes difficult to diagnose because the symptoms can begin long after the person has been infected, or the patient may not even know that she was bitten by a tick (deer ticks, which carry Lyme disease, are about the size of the head of a pin). Ticks in most parts of the United States are not infected with the Borrelia burgdorferi organism and therefore can't spread it to humans, but certain regions are heavily infested, particularly on the Northeast coast from Massachusetts to Maryland, the Midwest (especially in Minnesota and Wisconsin), and in California. Unfortunately, the blood test commonly used to detect the causative organism, Borrelia burgdorferi, is not very reliable. Therefore, antibiotic therapy is sometimes initiated solely on the basis of a suspicious history and physical examination.

Chronic Fatigue Syndrome (CFS)

Abby called in sick to work on Monday morning. It was the first time she had used a sick day in over four years of teaching. Abby was one of the favorite teachers at Barton Middle School because her vivacious energy made her algebra lectures come alive. The children seemed to spark to her enthusiasm, and they would excel even though the subject matter was new and difficult for most of them. There wasn't much question about her going to work that day, though; she didn't have the energy needed to get out of bed, much less teach her algebra classes. Over the weekend, Abby had felt like she might be coming down with something. She slept a little bit later than usual on Saturday morning and had not felt well on Saturday afternoon, but by evening, she had rallied somewhat and had gone out dancing with her boyfriend. Sunday had been a repeat of the day before, and she began to think that maybe she was pushing too hard.

Monday morning, Abby awoke to find that she had been run over by a Mack truck—or at least, that was how she felt. She didn't feel any better on Tuesday morning either, so she made an appointment with her doctor. By the time Abby was seen that afternoon, she had chills and a fever of 101 degrees, a sore throat, swollen glands, muscle aches and pains, and a headache. She felt as bad as she had in college when she had had infectious mononucleosis. The physician told her that she suspected Abby was suffering from influenza, although it was a little early in the year for such a diagnosis. She suggested that Abby go home to rest in bed, drink plenty of fluids, and take Tylenol for the discomfort. Abby did so and missed the rest of that week of school, feeling pretty crummy the whole time.

By the following Sunday afternoon, she felt a little bit better and thought maybe she could go to work on Monday. When Monday morning came, however, Abby was so exhausted by the effort of getting up to brush her teeth and take a shower that she called in sick again and went back to bed. By the end of the week, Abby was unable to cook for herself because she was so fatigued; even the effort of eating seemed too overwhelming, and she began to lose weight. On Wednesday, ten days after she had become ill, Abby returned to her doctor, who expressed surprise that she was still sick. The doctor examined her thoroughly and found that her lymph nodes were still a bit enlarged and that her throat was red and inflamed. She told Abby, "It's unusual for someone to get mono twice, but I've seen it before, so let's just do a blood test to make sure that you're not one of the unlucky ones." Dr. Larson also ordered tests for anemia and thyroid disease and sent Abby home with the same instructions as the week before (get plenty of rest and drink lots of liquids).

Dr. Larson called back two days later and told her that all of the blood tests were perfectly fine. She hadn't found anything to explain Abby's illness but thought that because of the severity of her symptoms, Abby should see her colleague, an internist specializing in infectious diseases.

The second doctor suggested that Abby might have chronic fatigue syndrome but said that they couldn't be sure until Abby had been sick for at least six months. He offered no treatment recommendations but did *suggest that Abby should arrange for a leave of absence from work. Abby did so and made arrangements to go home to her parents' house. There, it seemed that all she was able to do was sleep. She slept sixteen, eighteen, even twenty hours a day. The few hours that she was awake, she didn't have the energy to do anything except lie on the couch or sit in the recliner. Many days, she didn't have the energy to brush her teeth or comb her hair, much less shower and change clothes. Her mother soon had to care for her as she had when Abby was a baby.*

Abby ended up missing the entire school year and was still barely functioning by midsummer. Each of the doctors she consulted told her that she had chronic fatigue syndrome, but none could offer any explanation as to why it had occurred. Worse, they couldn't predict when she would start to get better. Abby just couldn't accept it. After all, she was the one who had been called "an overgrown cheerleader" because of her energy and vivaciousness. Now, she was a bedridden invalid. What had happened?

Chronic fatigue syndrome is commonly known as CFIDS or CFS. CFS is a relatively new disorder and was formally recognized less than a decade ago. Prior to that time, women who were suffering from CFS were frequently told that their fatigue was "all in their heads," and they were accused of dropping out of life or shirking their responsibilities for a variety of psychological reasons. Many physicians now recognize this disorder as a very real entity and respect it as a very debilitating illness—although there are a few who still persist in assuming CFS is not a real disorder.

The cause of CFS is not known, but there are several working theories. The most widely accepted holds a chronic viral infection responsible for the symptoms. This is because of the many similarities between CFS and infections with Epstein-Barr (EBV) viruses (such as infectious mononucleosis). In fact, many of the early CFS cases were positive for EBV, but as the disorder became more widespread, the association between CFS and EBV became less common. Other infectious agents can also cause symptoms of infectious mononucleosis (including toxoplasmosis and cytomegalovirus, among others), so it is possible to have a negative blood test for EBV and still have an infectious trigger.

Immune system suppression has also been suggested as a cause of CFS, as the symptoms suggest that the immune response is sluggish and underactive. The cause of the immune suppression is unknown, but chronic stress and depression are two excellent possibilities. Both chronic stress and depressive disorders are known to diminish immune reactivity so that the person is less able to fight off infections and less able to cope with various stressors. Immune system suppression may explain why the syndrome seems to last so long.

Recently, researchers at the Johns Hopkins Hospital in Baltimore reported that CFS is linked to a specific kind of low blood pressure known as "neurally mediated hypotension."[1] This condition is characterized by dizziness, light-headedness, and fatigue after standing for prolonged periods and is detected by tilt-table testing. The tilt-table test was abnormal in twenty-two of twenty-three CFS patients participating in the study, indicating that they might be suffering from neurally mediated hypotension. Nineteen of the patients elected to receive treatment with drugs commonly used to treat neurally mediated hypotension (such as fludrocortisone, disopyramide, or a beta-blocker). Sixteen of the nineteen had dramatic improvement in their CFS symptoms, and nine had nearly complete recovery. The authors of the study point out that neurally mediated hypotension is frequently caused by salt (sodium) restriction. All of the CFS patients had voluntarily restricted their salt intake in an effort to eat a healthy diet. Although these results are very preliminary and must be confirmed by further testing, they confirm other studies suggesting that salt restriction is not appropriate for anyone who doesn't have high blood pressure. Some physicians have gone so far as to encourage young women with low-normal blood pressures to increase their salt intake in order to reduce their risk of developing neurally mediated hypotension and possibly CFS. Obviously, this is not something that you should do without consulting your physician, as increased salt intake could be dangerous for someone with high blood pressure (hypertension).

Chronic fatigue syndrome is, as its name suggests, a chronic illness. On average, symptoms persist for nearly two years, with gradual improvement beginning about a year after onset. The course of improvement is often marked by periods of intermittent relapse and recovery, which has been described as taking two steps forward and one step back. The vast majority of patients are completely recovered, or at least functioning satisfactorily, by three to four years.

The diagnosis of CFS was codified in the late 1980s. In order to receive a diagnosis of chronic fatigue syndrome, the patient must have:

1. New onset of severe fatigue that persists for six months or more and causes at least a 50 percent reduction in activity
2. Exclusion of other illnesses causing similar symptoms.

In addition, the patient must have at least eight of the ten minor criteria designated by the Centers for Disease Control[2]:

1. Mild fever (less than 101.5 degrees)
2. Sore throat or throat infections without pus
3. Painful or swollen lymph nodes
4. Generalized muscle weakness
5. Muscle discomfort and/or joint pains
6. Prolonged fatigue worsened by exercise
7. Headaches that are described as different from any occurring before the illness
8. Irritability, depression, forgetfulness, confusion or difficulty thinking, and an inability to concentrate
9. Sleep disturbance
10. An acute onset of the symptoms.

There are also physical examination criteria. The patient should have at least two of the following:

1. Fever
2. Throat inflammation
3. Palpable or tender lymph nodes.

Treatment of CFS

At present, there is no cure for CFS, but several treatments have been found to be effective for some (but not all) patients. The most helpful of these include:

1. **Medications**
   a. **Antidepressants.** Depression is a frequent accompanying symptom of CFS, and antidepressants were first given to patients with CFS in an effort to relieve this symptom. The physicians found that the antidepressant medications were effective in treating the fatigue and physical symptoms, as well. Sometimes a patient receiving a prescription for antidepressants is concerned that this means her physician thinks once again that the CFS is "all in her head." This is not the case. The antidepressants are used because they work. No one yet knows why they are helpful, but it may be because of a nonspecific effect on the immune system. Improvement comes relatively soon after start-

ing the medications, which would add support to this theory, since depressive symptoms don't typically improve for three to four weeks after starting medication. Although no systematic studies have been done, the following antidepressants have been reported to be of use to at least a small number of patients: doxepin (Adapin, Sinequan), amitriptyline (Elavil, Endep), desipramine (Norpramin), nortriptyline (Aventyl, Pamelor), protriptyline (Vivactil), amoxapine (Asendin), and imipramine (Tofranil). Some of the serotonin reuptake blockers, such as clomipramine (Anafranil), fluoxetine (Prozac), fluvoxamine (Luvox), and sertraline (Zoloft), may also be useful.

b. **Antiviral agents.** Antiviral agents, such as Acyclovir, have been tried with some limited success. A few individual patients have benefited greatly, but in general, the antiviral medications have been disappointing in their effectiveness—perhaps because of the long delay between onset of symptoms and antiviral treatment or perhaps because the symptoms come after the virus has already left the body. The antiviral agents may therefore be more useful to patients with evidence of a recent viral infection.

c. **Benzodiazepines.** Benzodiazepines (tranquilizers such as Valium, Librium, Tranxene, Xanax, and others) are sometimes used to help improve the CFS patients' sleep patterns. Some researchers believe that CFS results from chronic sleep disturbance and that by inducing a more regular sleep pattern, the daytime fatigue and sleepiness will be relieved. Again, individual patients appear to have been helped, but there are no group data to demonstrate that the benzodiazepines are effective.

d. **Antihistamines.** Patients with a history of allergies may benefit from antihistamine treatment of their CFS. As already mentioned, dysfunction of the immune system has been proposed as a cause of CFS, and the antihistamines may be effective in restoring balance to the immune system. At present, however, there is not wide agreement that these medications are really useful for CFS.

e. **Blood pressure stabilizers.** Based on the recent research findings of investigators at Johns Hopkins University, some physicians are now using blood pressure stabilizing medications, such as fludrocortisone, disopyramide, and beta-blocking medications (like propranolol [Inderal] and others) to treat CFS. Additional studies are needed to determine whether or not such drug treatment is helpful.

2. **Nutrition**

   Many different diets have been proposed for chronic fatigue syndrome, perhaps as a reflection of the physical debility that accompanies CFS. At a minimum, it would appear prudent to ensure that the CFS patient is taking in enough calories, protein, vitamins, and minerals. Although there are no specific vitamin or mineral deficiencies known to be associated with CFS, a multivitamin supplement may be helpful, particularly during the periods where eating is difficult due to a sore throat or excessive fatigue.

3. **Rest and Exercise**

   a. **Aggressive rest therapy.** As in Abby's case, patients are frequently so fatigued and weak that all that they can do is rest. Some doctors have taken this symptom and turned it into a treatment called aggressive rest therapy or ART. Aggressive rest therapy means enforced bed rest—twenty-four hours per day, seven days a week for three months or longer. Even when the patient begins to feel better, she is required to stay in bed and rest. The theory behind ART is that the body needs time to undo the damage done by the triggering infection and to heal itself. This treatment may be found to be effective, in a manner similar to that of the rest cures used for tuberculosis and rheumatic fever in the early half of the century. Until a specific viral or bacterial trigger is identified for CFS, ART offers as much potential for relief as other treatments.

   b. **Exercise.** It seems contradictory to suggest exercise as an antidote for fatigue and weakness, but exercise has been shown to help speed recovery from CFS. There is some disagreement about the use of exercise for CFS, however, so exercise is usually prescribed only for patients who are beginning to recover from the illness or for patients in whom stress is thought to be a contributing factor leading to the fatigue. Exercise is an effective stress buster, so it might be useful if stress is contributing to the chronic fatigue syndrome.

4. **Psychotherapy**

   Individual psychotherapy is usually not possible during the acute phase of illness in CFS because the patients are too sick. It can sometimes be very useful for patients recovering from the illness, as they struggle to cope with their disability and their feelings of helplessness or rage. Supportive therapy (either from a clinician who helps the patient find easier ways to take care of herself or who teaches problem-solving and improved coping skills) might also be indicated, as the recovering CFS patient often needs some assistance in trying to get on with her life.

Autoimmune Disorders

Autoimmune disorders are those in which the immune system (our natural defense against infections and other pathogens) turns against itself or another part of the body. In so doing, it forms autoantibodies, which are infection-fighting cells that recognize cells in the joints, heart, kidney, brain, or other tissues as foreign intruders (even though they obviously are not), and sets up a cascade to destroy them. The autoantibodies can recognize a single type of cell (for example, antithyroid antibodies destroy only the thyroid gland) or can be more widespread, as in systemic lupus erythematosus (SLE, or lupus). Other autoimmune disorders include multiple sclerosis, temporal arteritis, rheumatoid arthritis, and Sjögren's syndrome.

Each of the autoimmune disorders has been associated with mood, behavioral, and cognitive changes. Depression is especially common and may be the result of inflammation of blood vessels within the brain. In lupus, depression is a common symptom and typically has a waxing and waning course (which corresponds to the fluctuating antibody concentrations). An episodic course of neuropsychiatric symptoms is also seen in mixed connective tissue disease (MCTD). In MCTD, infections and psychological stress can trigger exacerbations of both the physical symptoms (arthritis, fatigue, muscle pains, and weakness) and the psychological symptoms (depression, irritability, memory lapses, and difficulty concentrating).

Autoimmune disorders are usually diagnosed by considering the sum of the history, physical examination, and laboratory studies. Some disorders can be extremely difficult to detect because of the fleeting nature of the autoantibodies.

Neurological Disorders

Discussions of the previous disorders have considered the interconnection between the body and the brain. This section concerns the connections between the brain and the mind. As you might imagine, they are indivisible, and it is often impossible to tell where neurological symptoms stop and psychiatric symptoms start. Because of this, most of the disorders in this section are referred to as neuropsychiatric conditions — a combination of both neurological and psychiatric symptomatology. One of the most common neuropsychiatric disorders is headache, covered in Chapter Three.

Epilepsy and Seizure Disorders

Although we typically think of grand mal seizures (dramatic "fits") as typifying seizure disorders, there are many different kinds of seizures. Some are quite subtle and characterized only by staring spells (so-called absence seizures) or changes in language, cognition, sensation, memory, emotion, or behavior. All seizures represent an inappropriate electrical discharge within the brain; the symptoms that we see depend on which nerve cells are stimulated and how large an area is involved. When seizure activity spreads to the entire brain, a grand mal seizure results. Often, however, the seizure activity is limited to a small number of nerve cells, and the symptoms can be as subtle as an occasional slight stutter or a barely perceptible eyebrow twitch. These are called partial seizures or complex partial seizures.

The symptoms of complex partial seizures vary widely. Sometimes the individuals will have only a brief loss of consciousness, which may go unnoticed by themselves and those around them because they pass out for only a fraction of a second. Other times, there may be a constellation of symptoms, including such things as ritualized movements of the arms or legs, repetitive speech patterns, or altered sensations. Hallucinations may occur, and the woman will see or hear things that aren't really there. Aphasia, or the inability to talk, can also be a symptom of a complex partial seizure; so can memory and cognitive distortions such as *jamais vu* and *déjà vu*.

Jamais vu is the absence of an appropriate sense of familiarity (for example, feeling like a stranger in your own home), and *déjà vu* is the feeling of having had a particular experience before. Both are eerily discomforting and move beyond the sense of having walked down a street before or having had snippets of conversation previously.

Other thought disturbances that are reported to occur during seizures include dreamlike states, confusion, thought blocking (the inability to finish a thought or fully access a concept), not feeling real, not feeling like yourself, a sense of detachment, or a loss of contact. A common symptom associated with complex partial seizures is an abrupt change in emotion—becoming depressed in the wink of an eye or having an abrupt onset of overwhelming fear. If you have had a sudden onset of anxiety or depressive symptoms, and the mood changes seem to occur randomly and precipitously, you may have a seizure disorder; be sure to tell your doctor about these characteristic symptoms. An electroencephalogram (EEG) may help the doctor decide if a seizure disorder is present, but ultimately the diagnosis is made on the basis of clinical information.

Movement Disorders

Movement disorders are, as the name implies, neurological disorders characterized by the presence of abnormal movements. There are two main types of movement disorders: those with decreased motor activity, such as Parkinson's disease, and those with increased motor activity, such as tics, chorea, and dystonia.

Parkinson's disease is a neuropsychiatric disorder that is characterized by the presence of both abnormal movements and psychiatric symptoms. It affects mainly the elderly and causes decreased voluntary movements, muscle rigidity, tremor, and slowness. The psychiatric symptoms include irritability, depression, and anxiety. These symptoms are sometimes more troublesome than the movement disorder itself. Most studies have shown that over half of the patients suffering from Parkinson's disease also meet criteria for depression. The depression responds to typical antidepressant medications, but the dosage may require adjustment depending on what other medications the patient is receiving.

Tics are rapid, purposeless movements (or vocalizations) that occur repetitively. Eye blinks, facial grimaces, shoulder shrugs, and foot jerks are all examples of motor tics; vocal tics include grunts, coughs, sniffing, humming, and simple words (like *ha, oh,* or *no*). The tics can also be complex and involve more complicated movements and phrases. Sometimes, the patterns are so involved and look so peculiar that the woman is accused of "faking" her symptoms—of having a hysterical reaction. The correct diagnosis depends on taking a careful history and performing a complete evaluation of the movement disorder.

Careful evaluation is also necessary for sniffing and coughing tics. Often, these tics are mistakenly diagnosed as allergic disorders; the key to making the correct diagnosis would be noticing that the woman has year-round "allergies," that her sniffing and coughing tics are present not only during spring and fall hay-fever seasons but in the winter, as well.

Further, antihistamine treatment is usually not helpful, as it doesn't treat her underlying tic disorder.

The movements of *chorea* are more continuous and less repetitive than are tics. In mild cases, choreiform movements may only be visible during special neurological testing or may be seen simply as an increase in restlessness or clumsiness. In more severe cases, the movements can be quite debilitating and can interfere with voluntary movements, such as brushing one's teeth, writing, or walking.

Dystonia is characterized by slow, more sustained, involuntary movements. Frequently, dystonia affects the muscles of the torso and may cause to-and-fro movements. Dystonia can also affect specific muscle groups and interfere with writing or walking.

The movement disorders appear to be caused by dysfunction in the basal ganglia. This region of the brain is responsible for control of movement. Recently, scientists have found that the basal ganglia also play an important role in cognition (thinking and remembering), behavior, and control of emotions. Thus, when the basal ganglia are malfunctioning enough to cause movement disorders, there are almost always some accompanying psychological symptoms. The psychiatric symptoms common to the movement disorders include problems with attention and concentration, excessive mood swings, obsessive-compulsive disorder, depression, and anxiety disorders, including separation anxiety and panic disorder.

Tourette's syndrome is a specific type of tic disorder, characterized by the presence of both motor and vocal tics. Many people think of Tourette's syndrome as a bizarre illness in which the sufferers curse in public. This is not an accurate representation of the illness, as the majority of people with Tourette's syndrome do not even have this symptom. Instead, they have a variety of involuntary motor movements and vocalizations. Attention deficit disorder (ADD) appears to be more common among people with Tourette's syndrome, and there is an increased frequency of obsessive-compulsive disorder (OCD) as well (see Chapters Six and Thirteen for complete descriptions of ADD and OCD). There appears to be a very close link between OCD and Tourette's syndrome, so if a woman has chronic motor and vocal tics, she is likely to have obsessive-compulsive symptoms as well.

Head Trauma and Stroke

Head trauma, such as after a motor vehicle accident, may cause cognitive and behavioral changes. The psychological symptoms can occur even when the trauma appears relatively minor and no serious neurological signs or symptoms are present. This is because the cortex (the thinking and emotional part of the brain) is the most vulnerable to abrupt changes in motion. Stopping suddenly (as when you hit a car or fall off a horse) can jostle the brain; the back and forth movements can cause microscopic damage to the blood vessels and nerve cell fibers. Depending on which vessels or fibers are affected, the psychological symptoms might include a change in personality, increased impulsivity, irritability, attentional deficits, and memory lapses. Neuropsychological testing may be required to determine the nature and extent of the symptoms; psychological testing that looks at information processing can be particularly helpful. Sometimes, when the damage is detected early, rehabilitation is effective in decreasing the impairments.

Cerebrovascular accidents—or as they are more commonly known, strokes—can also cause a variety of neuropsychiatric symptoms. Depending on the nature and location of the stroke, the resulting symptoms may be quite mild, or they may be very severe. Strokes can cause neurological, cognitive, emotional, and behavioral symptoms. Each of the psychiatric symptoms described in the later chapters of this book has been reported to occur as a result of a stroke. An unusual example is provided by a woman who was stung by a bee and then had an abrupt onset of obsessive-compulsive disorder. The bee sting caused a stroke in the basal ganglia region of her brain; following it, the patient had an abrupt onset of excessive fears about dirt and germs, and she exhibited washing compulsions.

Toxins

Poisons and toxins, such as lead and mercury, can cause cognitive, emotional, and behavioral changes in adults, as well as in children. Although we typically think of lead poisoning as a disease of young children, it can occur in adult women as well. Lead concentrations can be increased by drinking water from lead-contaminated pipes or in the course of removing the lead paint from an older home. Some imported pottery contains lead, which can leak out through the glaze; if the dishes are used to serve food, toxic levels can be ingested. The symptoms of lead poisoning include headache, mood swings and tearfulness, fatigue, delirium, mania, and coma. Physical symptoms include abdominal cramps, paralysis, pins-and-needles sensations in the hands and feet, and anemia.

Other forms of poisoning are relatively rare among adult women and usually are the result of occupational exposure—for example, exterminators may have organic phosphates poisoning; printers may be exposed to toxic photochemicals.

Self-administered toxins, such as alcohol and street drugs, are the most common causes of poisoning among adults. Overdoses of both alcohol and narcotics can be fatal, but death is less common than chronic, long-term toxic effects (see Chapter Fifteen). Alcohol withdrawal is associated with a number of neuropsychiatric symptoms. The classic picture of alcohol withdrawal is known as "the shakes"—severe, whole-body tremors. The shakes usually appear within twelve hours after the last drink in people who are alcohol dependent. This withdrawal period is frequently accompanied by feelings of excessive guilt, panic, dread, or a generalized sense of doom. Delirium tremens or the "DTs" develop about three days after the last drink and are associated with continued tremors, as well as vivid auditory and visual hallucinations.

Several over-the-counter and prescription medications can give a withdrawal picture similar to that which occurs when alcohol is abruptly stopped. Sleeping pills are notorious for causing withdrawal symptoms. The drugs chronically suppress REM sleep, and when someone stops taking them, the REM cycle rebounds and can continue during periods of apparent wakefulness; this can cause true visual hallucinations. In addition, the person who stops "cold turkey" may feel jittery, anxious, and uncomfortable, just as the withdrawing alcoholic does in the first two to three days of abstinence.

Medications That Cause Psychiatric Symptoms

Doctors frequently tell patients taking a new drug to expect the unexpected. Sometimes, however, we forget to warn patients about the dramatic effects that can occur with over-the-counter medications or when different medications are combined, as in Barbara's case. Further, since each woman's body will metabolize the medications differently, it is impossible to predict what kind of reactions she will experience.

Most, but not all, of a drug's side effects can be predicted by knowing how the medication works. However, side effects can occur for which there is no reasonable explanation based on the drug's known properties. These side effects are known as idiosyncratic reactions. Fortunately, idiosyncratic reactions are rare, but when a drug is prescribed frequently, the chances of these reactions occurring increase. It's a little like playing the lottery—the more you play, the greater your chance of winning, even if the chance is only one in a million each time.

Some physicians and patients turn to the *Physicians' Desk Reference* (or *PDR*) for information about side effects.[2] The *PDR* is a reasonable reference text, although some critics maintain that listing so many side effects makes it difficult to read. Further, the side effects are reported in the manner required by the Food and Drug Administration, which is not very helpful to individual patients and practitioners. Every single side effect ever reported by a patient in a study is listed. There is no way to know how frequent the problem is or how severe the reported symptoms are. Sometimes the number of patients who experience the side effect with a placebo (a sugar pill) is also listed. In order to determine whether or not a symptom is meaningfully associated with the drug, we need to look at how much more frequent a side effect is with the active medication than with the placebo. Sometimes, the side effect is higher on the placebo than on the active medication (for example, excessive sleepiness, headache, or change in sex drive), which suggests that the complaint is one that is common in daily life and may not necessarily be attributed to the medication.

It is critical to remember that *all* over-the-counter medicines, prescription medications, and street drugs can cause side effects. In addition to physical symptoms, the side effects might include behavioral symptoms, mood changes, anxiety, depression, and cognitive difficulties, as discussed in the subsections that follow. Using combinations of drugs (for example, a cough syrup and an antihistamine) may produce side effects that would not be seen when either drug is taken alone. Further, certain combinations of medications can be deadly—for example, fluoxetine (Prozac) with the antihistamines terfenadine (Seldane) or astemizole (Hismanal). Thus, it is very important to consult with a physician or a pharmacist before combining medications, even if you can buy one or both of them without a prescription. In addition, you might wish to consult *The Pill Book* (see "Resources" at the end of this chapter). We have found it to be a helpful resource text as it provides side-effects information about most prescription drugs.

Depression

Depressive side effects are often seen with cardiac and antihypertensive (high blood pressure) medications, sleeping pills, tranquilizers, and hormone preparations, such as estrogen. Oral contraceptives are particularly likely to cause (or aggravate) depression, and the symptoms can be quite troublesome. Women who have had a previous depression should talk with their doctor about whether or not birth control pills are safe for them.

Drugs used to treat ulcers, such as cimetidine, can also cause symptoms of depression, as can over-the-counter appetite suppressants. Steroids, including body-building anabolic steroids, are well-known causes of mood swings; depression can result, and so can euphoria (feeling excessively "high" or happy), hypomania, mania, and psychosis (see Chapters Seven and Eleven).

Drugs used to treat neurological symptoms may be associated with depression and other behavioral disturbances. This is not surprising since so many have a direct effect on brain chemicals. Amantadine (Symmetrel), bromocriptine (Parlodel), levodopa (L-dopa, Dopar, Larodopa), and phenytoin (Dilantin) are all known to cause depression.

Anxiety

Anxiety symptoms are often precipitated by energizing and stimulating drugs, such as amphetamines. Over-the-counter stimulants, including decongestants and nonprescription appetite suppressants, can also cause jitteriness, nervousness, and anxiety. Stopping these medications abruptly can also cause anxiety. Both excess caffeine consumption and sudden caffeine withdrawal can create anxiety, which sometimes escalates to a full-blown panic reaction. In fact, caffeine injections are used to induce panic reactions in healthy volunteers participating in studies of anxiety. Surprisingly little caffeine is required to cause symptoms, so if you're experiencing nervousness, tension, or anxiety, try decreasing your caffeine intake — *slowly*, in order to avoid withdrawal anxiety.

Psychosis

At regularly prescribed doses, steroids (prednisone and others) are the most well-recognized cause of psychosis (hallucinations, delusions, and other distorted thinking patterns). Many drugs can cause psychotic symptoms if taken in excess or overdose. In addition, idiosyncratic (unpredictable) psychotic reactions can occur with any medication at regular dosages, whether it requires a prescription or is available over the counter; you might be the unlucky one-in-a-million who reacts badly to antibiotics or high blood pressure medications. Nighttime cold preparations have been reported to cause psychosis, perhaps because of the combination of antihistamine, decongestant, and high alcohol content. Drug overdoses can also cause psychosis. Amphetamine overdose causes a unique type of psychosis, characterized by unusual physical sensations, such as ants crawling over one's skin.

Cognitive and Behavioral Changes

In this category, the drugs that are most problematic are sleeping pills. These include the barbiturates, chloral hydrate, the benzodiazepines (Dalmane, Restoril, Halcion, and so on), and other prescription sedatives. These medications suppress normal sleep patterns so that the brain doesn't rest properly (see Chapter Seven). Chronic use (longer than five days) can lead not only to fatigue and tiredness but also to confusion, personality changes, memory loss, and concentration difficulties. Further, the drugs are rapidly addictive and can cause rebound and withdrawal syndromes that may make the user feel worse than before she started. In general, we recommend strongly against the use of sedatives or tranquilizers for sleep except on a very limited basis.

One must keep in mind that almost any medicine that can enter the central nervous system is a potential cause of emotional and behavioral changes. When the patient is taking more than one drug, it may be difficult to sort out which medication is causing the problem. A useful first step is to eliminate unnecessary or duplicative medications (for example, a cough syrup used at the same time as a cough-and-cold preparation) and then to reassess the symptomatology. In order for your doctor to decide whether or not your symptoms are related to medication side effects, it may be helpful for you to provide him with a list (or the actual bottles!) of all the medications that you have taken recently (including all nonprescription drugs). It often takes a bit of detective work to ferret out the culprit, but usually the elimination trials can pinpoint the source of the neuropsychiatric symptoms.

Summary

Beware of medical conditions that masquerade as psychological problems! Everything from vitamin deficiencies to side-effects of over-the-counter diet pills to viral infections can cause symptoms identical to the common psychiatric disorders. These medical mimics can be missed if you forget to mention that you are taking a new antihistamine or that you have been feeling unusually weak and tired. To ensure that you get optimum therapy, take extra care to report all your symptoms accurately to your doctor and to provide a complete history of prescription and over-the-counter medications that you are taking. Your doctor, in turn, should provide you with a complete medical evaluation—including a careful history, complete physical examination, and necessary laboratory tests. Each of you plays an equally important role: your doctor knows more about medicine than you do, but you know more about your own body than he or she does. The two of you should form an active partnership to ensure that you receive the best medical and psychiatric care possible.

Resources
Chronic Fatigue Syndrome (CFS)

CFIDS/CFS Society
P.O. Box 230108
Portland, Oregon 97223
503–684–5261

The CFIDS Association of America
P. O. Box 220398
Charlotte, North Carolina 28222
800–44–CFIDS (800–442–3437)

National CFS Association
3521 Broadway, Suite 222
Kansas City, Missouri 64111
816–931–4777

Further Reading

Bell, David S. *The Doctor's Guide to Chronic Fatigue Syndrome: Understanding, Treating, and Living with CFIDS*. Reading, MA: Addison-Wesley, 1995.
Feiden, Karyn. *Hope and Help for Chronic Fatigue Syndrome: The Official Book of the CFIDS/CFS Network*. New York: Simon & Schuster, 1992.
Lark, Susan M. *Chronic Fatigue and Tiredness*. The Women's Health Series. Los Altos, CA: Westchester Publishing, 1993.

References for Medications and Drug Side Effects

Gorman, Jack M. *The Essential Guide to Psychiatric Drugs*. New York: St. Martin's Press, 1990.

Physicians' Desk Reference. 50th ed. Montvale, NJ: Medical Economics Data Production Co., 1996.

Silverman, Harold M. *The Pill Book.* 7th ed. New York: Bantam Books, 1995.

Notes

1. Issam Bou-Holaigah, Peter C. Rowe, Jean Kan, and Hugh Calkins, "The Relationship Between Neurally Mediated Hypotension and the Chronic Fatigue Syndrome," *Journal of the American Medical Association.* 274 (1995): 961–67.
2. Dr. Gary Holmes and the Division of Viral Diseases, Center for Infectious Diseases, Centers for Disease Control, 1988. Atlanta, GA.
3. *Physician's Desk Reference,* 50th ed., 1996. Montvale, NJ: Medical Economics Data Production Company.

PART 3

THE MIND-BRAIN CONNECTION:

Psychiatric Disorders

CHAPTER 6

Disorders of Attention and Organization

Heloise raced into the meeting late with her briefcase half-open and her purse flying behind her. The meeting was an important one, and she had intended to arrive early enough to go over her materials, but here she was—late again! She had left the house late this morning because she hadn't been able to find her son's medical form; she had spent over twenty minutes looking for it before she remembered that she had put it on the dashboard of her car "so that I will know where it is." Then she had to make a detour to the grocery store; her daughter needed to provide the class with a snack that day and they didn't have any juice in the house. Heloise had known about both of these things for over a week, but she just couldn't seem to get it together ahead of time. Everything always got done at the last minute—or a little bit later.

As she made her way to the only seat left in the conference room, Heloise tripped over someone's feet and muttered, "Sorry." It seemed like she was always apologizing for something—missing a deadline, misplacing an important file, or neglecting to complete an assignment. Worse, she had been apologizing for things her entire life. Ever since she was a little girl, Heloise had been disorganized and "spacey." She was smart enough to get all A's, but she usually brought home B's and C's on her report cards because she had forgotten to turn in her homework, or she had missed the second half of an assignment, or she had failed an exam because she hadn't read the instructions carefully enough. Her teachers consistently complained that "Heloise isn't working up to her abilities." But she was. Heloise always tried really hard. In fact, it seemed like she put twice as much effort into everything as her friends did. It just wasn't enough.

In high school, Heloise earned the reputation of being a "space cadet"—sweet and well intentioned but not very dependable. She would sign up to bring cookies for the pep squad bake sale but then forget to bake them. She'd volunteer to write an extra-credit paper with two other girls but then put off doing her part until the others gave up and did her work for her. Or she would volunteer to help with the decorations for the homecoming dance but then get distracted by one of her friend's problems and spend the evening counseling her instead. She always felt terrible about letting people down, but it seemed like there was always someone who needed her more or something more important to be done than what she was supposed to be doing at that moment.

Heloise didn't outgrow these problems. If anything, they got worse as her responsibilities increased. Now, she had to try to balance her career responsibilities with those of being a wife and a mother. It was totally overwhelming; she'd spin around in circles trying to decide where to begin, and then when she'd finally decided, she'd get only halfway through one job before she'd remember another and go off to do that. Consequently, her house was a mess: laundry to be folded was sitting on the floor next to her bed (where she had moved it last night so that she could go to sleep), the dishwasher was loaded but she'd forgotten to turn it on so there was no room for the breakfast dishes, and bills and papers were stacked everywhere. Heloise knew that other people's homes didn't look like hers; other people's homes were nea; they were organized.

There was nothing organized about Heloise's life. Her purse was stuffed with everything from old receipts and dried-up mascara to unpaid bills and several books of stamps. (Heloise could never find a stamp when she needed one, so she just bought more.) Her date book was a jumble of little notes and scribbled bits of papers, and her briefcase wouldn't shut because she was still carrying around memos from six months ago. Her desk was equally a mess—unanswered phone messages were scattered about, yellow reminder notes were stuck everywhere, and unfinished assignments were piled high in both the "in" and the "out" boxes. Heloise felt like these things were a metaphor for her life—messy, undone, and out of control.

Heloise's life feels out of control because she is suffering from attention deficit disorder, or ADD. (In the past few years, the disorder has been renamed attention deficit hyperactivity disorder, or ADHD, but since hyperactivity is rare among adult women with the disorder, we will refer to it as ADD.) Heloise has trouble paying attention, setting priorities, and concentrating on a task from start to finish. She also is disorganized, and she frequently misplaces or forgets things. She is well intentioned, bright, and motivated, but she just can't seem to get things done, even though she works twice as hard as others do. Heloise has difficulty focusing on conversations or something that she's reading, because it seems her mind is always on the go, constantly searching for the next idea, the next thought, the next priority.

Attention Deficit Disorder

Attention deficit disorder (ADD) has received a lot of press during the past few years, but unfortunately much of it has been inaccurate. The disorder was blamed for the "impulsive" acts of the young man who spray-painted the cars in Singapore.[1] A Canadian professional hockey player successfully fought deportation from the United States for cocaine possession after his attorney argued that the drug abuse had stemmed from ADD. (Perhaps he did have ADD, but that would not excuse or explain his behaviors.) The lawyer cited studies that suggest that over half of the people hospitalized for alcoholism or drug abuse had ADD as children.[2]

In both cases, ADD was used inappropriately as an excuse for unacceptable behavior. This excuse is based on a summary of a few studies that found that 50 to 60 percent of prison inmates met criteria for ADD as children. Other studies, which found much lower rates, were not included in the defense arguments for these two men, nor were figures demonstrating how most children with ADD grow up to be responsible, law-abiding citizens. Further, these cases demonstrate how legal concepts of blame and responsibility are often confused with medical explanations, or attempts to understand the causes of behavior. The misuse of the ADD defense has put an extra burden on the millions of Americans who suffer from ADD, and it has also made it more difficult for people to seek legitimate help for their symptoms.

The *Wall Street Journal* had a more accurate account of ADD in January of 1993. The article asked, "Do you often procrastinate?

Daydream? Have difficulty completing tasks? Are you disorganized, forgetful, and restless in bed at night? Does your mind wander while reading this story? If so, you may suffer from Attention-Deficit Disorder, or ADD."[3] Adult ADD was considered newsworthy not because it had some sensationalistic value but because it is so common; estimates cite eight to fifteen million adults with ADD in the United States alone.

It has only been since the mid 1980s that researchers, led by Dr. Paul Wender of Utah, have recognized the continuation of ADD into adulthood.[4] Previously, children were thought to outgrow ADD because the hyperactivity associated with the disorder usually disappears by adolescence. Since the teens were no longer fidgety, overly disruptive, or talking excessively, they were presumed to have outgrown their ADD. However, long-term follow-up studies revealed that they remained inattentive, distractible, and impulsive and that they continued to have difficulties with concentration and organization.

Attention deficit disorder is thought to occur much less frequently in girls than in boys (only about 20 percent of diagnosed ADD cases are female), but the figures may underestimate its true frequency. ADD is much less likely to be recognized in girls because girls with this problem typically do not have motor hyperactivity. Girls with ADD work twice as hard as their classmates and keep their grades up, or if they can't, they are called underachievers and presumed to be poorly motivated. The chances of receiving the correct diagnosis decrease even further as these girls grow older because of the bias that ADD is seen only in children. Instead, women with ADD are often labeled as "spacey" or "disorganized" or "daydreamers," and like Heloise, they must struggle to find ways to compensate for their disabilities.

How to Know If You Have Attention Deficit Disorder

The hallmark of attention deficit disorder is inattention. *Inattention* is defined by the presence of at least six out of the following nine symptoms (adapted from the *DSM-IV*):

1. Often fails to pay close attention to details or makes careless mistakes
2. Often has difficulty sustaining attention
3. Does not seem to listen when spoken to directly
4. Does not follow through on instructions and frequently fails to finish duties in the workplace or at home

5. Often has difficulty organizing tasks and activities
6. Avoids or dislikes activities that require sustained mental activity
7. Often loses things that are necessary for tasks and activities
8. Is often easily distracted by outside stimulation
9. Is often forgetful.

As is apparent from the list, it may be difficult to determine whether or not an adult has difficulty with inattention. Therefore, symptoms present during childhood are considered when making the diagnosis of ADD in adults. The symptoms, such as inattention, distractibility, and difficulties with concentration, would still be present in the woman with ADD and should be of sufficient severity to cause interference in her daily activities and/or impairment of functioning. Again, this may be difficult to ascertain, as the woman has often learned to partially compensate for her disorder. Some women choose a career that doesn't require sustained attention—for example, being a waitress in a short-order diner or clerking in a busy convenience store. In both instances, the action is fast-paced, sensory input is high, and sustained attention is not required.

It is interesting to note that this combination of fast-paced action, high sensory input, and shifting attention patterns is characteristic of video games. We have been told so often, "My daughter *can't* have ADD, she can play Nintendo for hours!" This is actually characteristic of children with ADD. They can hyperfocus on intriguing, exciting, or engaging tasks. Children with ADD pay close attention to the video games or are mesmerized by television cartoons because they fulfill their need for *excessive sensory stimulation*. The child's focus is captured by the rapidly changing visual patterns, the music and audio feedback, and the motor activity of manipulating the controls. The child with ADD does well as long as she isn't required to inhibit a response— that is, as long as you don't ask her *not* to respond to a cue. She is quick with her responses and scores high on "go" tasks (such as capturing the fruit in Super Mario Brothers) but can't sift through the relevant information quickly enough to stop an inappropriate response (like sending the hero dashing into the dragon's cave without the protective charm), so she loses the game by getting caught in a trap. This inability to shut down inappropriate responses is known as impulsivity.

Impulsivity and *restlessness* may both result from a need for increased sensory input. This need for increased sensory input might cause people with ADD to drive fast, play hard, or take excessive risks.

While most women with ADD do not have motor restlessness, they may have mental restlessness, which means that they must be constantly challenged with new thoughts and novel stimuli.

Or the disorder might be much more subtle and manifest as *distractibility*. Distractibility is one of the major causes of dysfunction for adults with ADD because it prevents them from setting appropriate priorities, organizing their lives, and completing necessary tasks. Distractibility means that your attention is pulled away from the task at hand to whatever is more interesting or appealing. Consider the following example:

Heloise was in a meeting with her employee, Ms. Jones, when the phone rang. The caller was her boss, Mr. Smith, who asked if she could provide him with a copy of the minutes from yesterday's meeting "at your convenience." Worried that she might forget to deliver the papers to her boss, Heloise excused herself from the meeting to "run upstairs for a minute." As she waited for the elevator, she ran into her colleague Jane, and they discussed the latest proposal for increasing sales. That discussion caused Heloise to miss the elevator twice, so she decided to climb the stairs. There, she ran into her friend Betsy, and they exchanged pleasantries for a few minutes before she started on her way again. Heloise eventually delivered the papers to Mr. Smith, but as she made her way back downstairs to her office, she ran into Tom, who just wanted to ask her a "quick question." By this time, Heloise had completely forgotten about Ms. Jones, so she worked with Tom for over fifteen minutes before returning to her office. As soon as she saw her employee, she knew that she had really blown it this time: Ms. Jones was red-faced and sputtering with anger. She stayed only long enough to say, "I will not be treated this way. You are the rudest, most arrogant boss that I have ever had. I'm going straight to personnel to ask for a transfer. While I'm there, I think I'll file a complaint against you."

This time, Heloise's distractibility led to unforgivably rude behavior. At other times, it has created less crucial but equally embarrassing situations, such as asking her boss to repeat himself because she was distracted by a pigeon on the windowsill, or listening to the sound of a car's rough engine rather than the guest speaker, or daydreaming when she should have been paying attention to her child's story. Distractibility can cause problems in every area of a woman's life. It can make it impossible to finish a project in a timely fashion because the woman keeps getting sidetracked by unimportant details; she literally loses sight of the forest for the trees. She also can't organize her life, because to do so would require her to complete a series of tasks, and she always forgets what she's doing after the second or third step. She has *executive dysfunction*.

Executive Dysfunction

Dr. Martha Denckla, a world-renowned neurologist specializing in the treatment of ADD, has written that executive dysfunction is integral to the disorder. "Executive functioning" is the name given to the set of mental abilities required to organize, prioritize, and strategize tasks and responsibilities. It includes identifying what is important, developing a series of steps that lead to a completed goal, and sustaining attention and action in order to finish the task. In essence, executive function is the ability to formulate and carry out a plan, whether it be a proposal for work, a Sunday school lesson, or a dinner party. It is the ability to run a corporation or to get the family ready to go on vacation. Executive dysfunction can result from a glitch in any of the components: organizing, setting priorities, or strategizing.

The woman with ADD has difficulties in each of these areas. She cannot organize because she is distractible, so she cannot stay "on task" long enough to complete the planning sequence. Her impulsivity causes her to do things out of order and to ignore priorities. And her inattentiveness and restlessness cause her to become bored and to move on to something else long before she accomplishes her goal.

To determine whether or not you have executive dysfunction, imagine yourself giving a dinner party. (If you can't even imagine accomplishing such a task because it's too overwhelming to imagine planning and preparing such an event, the diagnosis is practically made: you may have executive dysfunction.) If you can imagine it, read on: How would you go about it? Would you plan it far enough in advance to send out formal invitations, or would you invite nearly everyone by phone a few days beforehand and then realize at the last moment that you forgot to invite the Smiths? How would you plan the menu—by looking through cookbooks and choosing a new recipe to try or by buying whatever strikes your fancy when you go to the market? When you shop for the groceries, do you use a preplanned list or just grab things off the shelf as you see them and hope that you don't have to make more than three trips back for forgotten items? How about setting the table? The executive sets a beautiful table that is perfect down to each detail; the woman with executive dysfunction runs out of time because she couldn't find a clean tablecloth and ends up having the spaghetti dinner "buffet style." Both parties may be equally enjoyable, but the woman with executive dysfunction is totally exhausted and frustrated by her disability.

Making the Diagnosis of ADD in Adults

To be diagnosed with ADD, as with all the disorders discussed in this book, you must be experiencing distress and impairment. If a woman has inattentiveness, distractibility, and impulsivity but these do not bother her in any way or cause significant interference in her ability to perform at home or at work, then the diagnosis of ADD would not apply. Even with distress and interference, the diagnosis can be difficult to confirm in adults.

Some have argued that psychological testing is necessary in order to diagnose ADD in adults. Psychological testing consists of testing that assesses specific mental skills, such as memory, attention, vocabulary, language, problem solving, and the ability to deal with abstract concepts. Women with ADD may show a specific pattern of difficulties with tasks requiring sustained attention and efficient processing. However, if they don't show this pattern, it doesn't mean that they don't have ADD. It may just mean that they are bright enough to have "topped out" on the test—that is, their score is near the maximum obtainable. Or the structured environment in which the test is administered may help the woman focus and perform well. Or it may mean that their ADD is "compensated" so that the measurable deficits are minimal and the ADD only becomes problematic in real-life situations. Consequently, we do not routinely utilize psychological testing to assist in making the diagnosis of ADD. It may be useful, however, when there are concerns about the woman's ability to comprehend certain types of information, as these can impact on educational or career goals.

Impulsivity is sometimes measured with a computerized game similar to the video game described earlier. The test has been carefully standardized so that clinicians can determine whether the woman is responding appropriately to the "go" situations and inhibiting her responses appropriately in the "no-go" situations. The test may add some valuable information but is not sufficient by itself to determine whether someone has ADD.

The diagnosis of ADD is best made by an experienced clinician based on a lifelong pattern of inattentiveness, mental restlessness, distractibility, and impulsivity. The profile of an adult with ADD has been well described by Drs. Hallowell and Ratey in their book, *Driven to Distraction*. They suggest that adults with ADD will characteristically have at least fifteen of the following symptoms:[5]

1. A sense of underachievement
2. Difficulty getting organized
3. Chronic procrastination
4. Trouble following through on projects
5. Tendency to say whatever comes to mind
6. A frequent search for novelty and stimulation
7. An intolerance of boredom
8. Easy distractibility and trouble focusing attention
9. Often creative, intuitive, highly intelligent
10. Trouble following proper procedures
11. Impatient and easily frustrated
12. Impulsive
13. Tendency to worry needlessly and endlessly
14. Sense of insecurity
15. Mood swings
16. Restlessness
17. Tendency toward addictive behavior
18. Poor self-esteem
19. Inaccurate self-observation
20. Family history of ADD or mood disorders, or substance abuse.

If you find that you have the majority of these symptoms, then you might have ADD and may benefit from evaluation and treatment. Your physician should be able to provide you with referrals to an experienced clinician. Don't be surprised if your doctor suggests that you see a child psychiatrist; they are the ones who are typically most experienced in the diagnosis and treatment of ADD. In fact, parents often first realize that they have a problem with ADD while they are completing the forms for their child's ADD evaluation.

What Might You Have If It's Not ADD?

Because ADD is a lifelong condition that begins in childhood, there aren't many disorders that mimic it completely. But there are several conditions that can masquerade as inattentiveness, impulsivity, and hyperactivity.

Side Effects of Medications. Almost all prescription medications and over-the-counter drugs have been reported to cause inattentiveness, impulsivity, and/or hyperactivity. These symptoms are particularly common with medications that stimulate the central nervous system, such as certain antihistamines and decongestants, over-the-counter and prescription diet pills, and many others. Bronchodilators (used to treat asthma) can make you feel "jazzed up" and agitated. Several psychiatric medicines, including the selective serotonin reuptake inhibitors, or SSRIs, can make you feel restless and "on the go." Steroids, prescribed for poison ivy, asthma, and arthritis, can cause similar symptoms. If your ADD-like symptoms started at about the same time that you began taking a new drug, check with your physician or pharmacist to see if the symptoms might be related to the medication.

Psychiatric Disorders. Sometimes, anxiety disorders or depression can mimic ADD. For example, patients who are anxious often appear restless, distractible, and inattentive. Women who are depressed also may be preoccupied and distractible so that they appear to be forgetful and inattentive. The key to the diagnosis is to examine the whole picture: in anxiety disorders, there are accompanying symptoms of tension and worry; in depression, there will be mood changes or accompanying physical symptoms. It's also possible for ADD to coexist with anxiety disorders or depression. In such instances, the secondary diagnosis can cause the ADD symptoms to worsen.

Medical Conditions. Medical conditions that can cause inattention, hyperactivity, and distractibility include thyroid dysfunction, other endocrine disorders, lead poisoning, and neurological problems. Chapter Five contains a complete description of the medical mimics of ADD and other psychiatric disorders.

Excessive caffeine intake can cause a picture similar to that of ADD. Again, it should be relatively easy to distinguish the chronic condition of ADD from a short-lived caffeine excess, but the distinction cannot be made if the questions aren't asked. Caffeinated coffee or cola drinks can cause a woman to feel "revved up" and distractible. This can be a particular problem for the woman who has ADD, and some clinicians recommend that their patients with ADD abstain from caffeinated beverages.

Chronic fatigue (see Chapter Five) and sleep disorders (see Chapter Seven) frequently cause inattention and, occasionally, feelings of motor restlessness.

Treatment of Attention Deficit Disorder

Attention deficit disorder is probably the only condition in medicine in which there is more experience with the treatment of children than there is with adults. It is almost always the other way around; treatments are usually well worked out in adults before they are tried in children. However, since ADD was considered to be exclusively a pediatric condition until the last decade, there is little adult literature. For the first time, clinicians find themselves extrapolating up the age range rather than down. Based on these extrapolations, two treatments appear to be effective: behavior therapy and medications. The two probably work best when used in combination.

Behavior Therapy

The behavior therapy of ADD differs from that of other disorders in that it is directed at dealing with the outcome of the deficits, rather than trying to correct the deficits themselves. In other psychiatric disorders, such as obsessive-compulsive disorder or the anxiety disorders, the goal of the behavior therapy is eradication of the symptom. In ADD, the symptoms (inattentiveness, disorganization, distractibility, and so on) cannot be completely eradicated because they are an inherent part of the woman's makeup. Thus, the goal of behavior therapy for ADD is to improve functioning. In a sense, it is similar to rehabilitation therapy following a stroke.

The keys to improved functioning with ADD are *structure* and *consistency*—building an external system by which the woman with ADD can orient, organize, and focus so that she no longer has to depend on her overworked internal framework. This external structure will vary somewhat among individuals, depending on their personal and professional requirements. In general, it involves establishing set routines, requiring the woman to stick with them, and practicing organization: making lists and physically checking off completed items, planning things ahead of time (perhaps using a computerized schedule), following through on what's been assigned, and breaking tasks down into manageable units. Some people with ADD have found that it helps to wear a watch with a built-in timer that goes off at certain times to remind them about meetings or to set their watches ahead by ten to twelve minutes to avoid being late. Others use a day planner or a "peripheral brain" in which they keep everything vital to their day's activities. Or they might hire closet-organizing companies to come in and provide structure to their bedroom and kitchen. There are many tricks that can be helpful, and a skilled behavior therapist will know how to individualize them so that they are optimally beneficial.

Decreasing external distractions can be quite helpful. Turning the phone off can help you avoid getting caught up in a series of distractions and time-wasters. Having a quiet work environment is crucial (but sometimes impossible to obtain, as we all know). At home, women with ADD should have a quiet corner where they can pay bills or catch up on correspondence. Not only should this center be free of distractions but it should be of sufficient size to ensure that it acts as the "nerve center" of the home—the one place where everything important is deposited. If Heloise had had such a nerve center, she wouldn't have had to spend twenty minutes looking for Sam's medical form.

Drs. Halloway and Ratey (*Driven to Distraction*) suggest a behavioral technique called "OHIO—Only Handle It Once."[6] It requires the woman with ADD to focus immediately and carefully on the issue at hand, to make a decision, and to act on it. By creating a "minicrisis," it allows her to have sufficient sensory input to accomplish the task. More important, it avoids the well-intentioned but disastrous strategy of "doing it perfectly—later." That strategy just creates huge piles of undone work, and these piles totally overwhelm the woman with ADD because she has no idea where to start.

Another important part of therapy for ADD is to gain knowledge about the extent of the woman's dysfunction. It is very helpful to have a full understanding of the disorder and its implications. We have provided a partial list of references at the end of this chapter; in addition, we recommend that you contact one of the ADD support organizations. These resources can help you to understand what you can change about yourself and what you can't. Having reasonable expectations helps to defuse the feeling of being overwhelmed and helpless, and it improves your self-esteem as you have repeated successes rather than a series of failures.

Medications

Stimulant medications are the mainstay of pharmacological treatment of ADD. In 1937, Dr. Charles Bradley noticed that Benzedrine, a stimulant that was being prescribed for another purpose, was quieting down hyperactive children. It seemed like such a contradiction then, and it still does. Stimulants are called stimulants because they stimulate the nervous system, yet in hyperactive children, they have the opposite effect. Scientists now know that the stimulant medications actually may help the inhibitory part of the hyperactive child's brain to function better; they make the brakes stronger. The medications appear to have a similar effect in adults with ADD; they help brake the impulsivity and increase the brain's ability to tune out extraneous information.

The stimulant medications that have been found to be most beneficial for the treatment of ADD are methylphenidate (Ritalin), dextroamphetamine (Dexedrine), and pemoline (Cylert). Although these drugs can be abused, women who have taken them for ADD do not typically become addicted to them. A number of studies have shown that patients with ADD do not become physically or psychologically dependent on the stimulant medications, and they do not abuse the medications by taking excessive doses. It is interesting that they don't; amphetamine abuse occurs somewhat frequently among persons who have used them when trying to lose weight or when cramming for final exams. (Women with a previous history of drug abuse or alcoholism may have different susceptibilities and should receive careful evaluation before beginning stimulant medications. Pemoline may be a better choice than methylphenidate or dextroamphetamine.) Most women who have ADD can feel confident that taking stimulant medications, as prescribed and monitored by an experienced physician, is safe.

Methylphenidate (Ritalin) is well tolerated and quite effective. Its effect is seen within about forty-five minutes, and it lasts from four to six hours. Ritalin is one of the most commonly prescribed drugs for ADD and is available in five-, ten-, and twenty-milligram tablets. Usually, the woman will know within a day or two if the medication is helpful to her. If it is, then the dosage schedule can be adjusted to maximize the beneficial effects and minimize side effects. The woman will need to remain on the medication indefinitely and may need to have her dosage adjusted periodically.

Ritalin is available in a slow-release formulation that was designed for convenience. With slow-release capsules, the person takes a pill once a day rather than every four hours. While it is quite effective for some patients, others don't find it helpful and have nicknamed it the "no-release" formula—as if none of the medication is entering their system. Some physicians have found that a single twenty milligram SR tablet is roughly equivalent to fifteen milligrams of regular Ritalin. Also, many patients can feel the difference between the brand name (Ritalin) and the generic compounds (methylphenidate). If so, the physician should indicate that generic substitutions are unacceptable.

Ritalin has some side effects, including appetite suppression, weight loss, agitation, headache, nervousness, and insomnia. Both heart rate and blood pressure should be checked periodically while the woman is taking the medication, and the drug should not be used if there are reasons for concern about increasing the heart rate or blood pressure.

Dextroamphetamine (Dexedrine) is another stimulant that is very effective in the treatment of ADD. It offers an advantage over Ritalin in that it remains effective for longer periods of time and avoids some of the ups and downs seen with the shorter-acting drug. The disadvantage of this drug is that it may cause insomnia. The dosage of dextroamphetamine is started at five or ten milligrams a day and slowly increased to the point where the person's attention is maximally improved with minimal side effects. Again, the woman's blood pressure and pulse should be normal before starting the medication and should be followed over time.

The side effects of Dexedrine are the same as for methylphenidate, including problems with sleep. Each of the stimulants interferes with sleep, and the medications usually should not be taken after 6:00 P.M.

Pemoline (Cylert) is a third kind of stimulant that is sometimes used for ADD. It is as effective as Ritalin and Dexedrine, although it may take longer to reach peak effectiveness. Pemoline has an advantage over the other two stimulants in that it is taken only once each day. The side effects seen with pemoline are similar to those of methylphenidate and dextroamphetamine. Periodic blood tests are required during pemoline treatment as the medication has been reported to cause problems with liver function in rare instances.

Stimulants are the most effective way to treat the core symptom of inattentiveness in both children and adults. But some clinicians are reluctant to use stimulants as a first-line therapy in adults and will begin therapy with other medications, such as antidepressants or clonidine.

Antidepressants—such as the tricyclic antidepressants, imipramine (Tofranil), desipramine (Norpramin), and nortriptyline (Pamelor)—are often prescribed for ADD. They are not as effective as the stimulants in improving attention, but for individuals who cannot or should not take stimulants, they can be helpful. Bupropion (Wellbutrin) has been somewhat successful in treating the inattentiveness and irritability associated with ADD. The drugs that block serotonin reuptake (fluoxetine [Prozac], sertraline [Zoloft], paroxetine [Paxil], and fluvoxamine [Luvox]) have been used recently as well. It has been our experience that these drugs may sometimes help with the behavioral manifestations of ADD—such as the mood swings and irritability—but they don't actually help with the primary symptom of inattention. (The SSRIs are also used occasionally in conjunction with the stimulants to obtain complete symptomatic relief. Although there are no scientific data to suggest that the combination is more effective than stimulants alone, individual reports suggest that this may be helpful for some women.)

Clonidine (Catapres), which works on a different biochemical system than do the stimulants, is often used in children with ADD to help control some of the behavioral symptoms. It is not as successful as the stimulants in treating inattention, so it is not usually a first choice for adults with ADD. It might be used in some individuals when stimulant therapy is not advisable (such as in a woman with a history of drug addiction).

In general, drug treatment of ADD is quite effective and can have a dramatic impact on the person's life. However, because of the nature of the stimulant medications, they should be prescribed only after the diagnosis of ADD has been confirmed, and they require ongoing monitoring.

Heloise left work early the afternoon of her ill-fated meeting with Ms. Jones—in part because she felt that she needed to recover a bit, but more important, she and her son Sam had another appointment with Dr. Silver, a child psychiatrist. They had been seeing Dr. Silver for a few weeks, ever since the school had referred Samuel for evaluation of his hyperactivity, inattention, and behavior problems. Today's appointment was the final one in a series of diagnostic appointments. Sam had talked with Dr. Silver and a psychologist, and then, while Heloise and her husband spoke privately with the doctors, Sam had completed several psychological tests and computer games. Today, they were going to discuss the results.

As expected, Dr. Silver told the family that Sam was suffering from Attention Deficit Hyperactivity Disorder (ADHD). He had problems in each of the key areas: motor overactivity, impulsivity, and inattentiveness. At school, these problems were obviously having a profound effect on his performance in the classroom; less obviously, it was also hurting his social development and his performance on the playground—none of the children would play with him because of his temper tantrums and impulsive behaviors. At home, Sam's life was equally miserable. He spent the majority of his time in time-outs—his punishment for sassing back, breaking rules, or lashing out. He struggled with his homework; he seemed really to try, although Heloise would always have to remind him to "get back at it" and to check his work. Even his sleep seemed to be affected; each morning, it looked like his bed had been hit by a tornado: covers were tossed everywhere, his pillow was on the floor near the window, and even the sheets were ripped from the bed. It was clear that Sam's ADHD was affecting his life twenty-four hours a day.

Dr. Silver recommended dual treatment for Sam: both behavior therapy and a stimulant medication. "Fortunately," he said, "Sam's school is used to working with behavior therapy programs. They are currently our partners in the treatment of several other children with ADHD, and those kids have made marvelous progress. The medication is primarily to help him focus and pay attention. It will help the impulsivity somewhat as well, but I really use medication for the inattentiveness. That is the thing that will stick with Sam—the hyperactivity is the major behavior problem right now, but the inattentiveness is what will keep him from succeeding in the long run."

Heloise said quietly, "I think that's what has held me back, Dr. Silver. As I read the materials you provided, I felt like it was talking about both Sam and me. Do you think that I could be treated for my ADD?"

Dr. Silver replied, "Why do you think that you should be, Ms. Fox?"

"I have all of the symptoms of inattention that you listed for Sam. Plus, I have struggled all my life to get organized and to plan ahead—I just can't do it. Everything is twice as hard for me as for anyone else, because I have to do it all twice. Today, I forgot about an employee sitting in my office, and now she's going to file a complaint against me"—and with that, Heloise started to cry.

Dr. Silver offered reassurances to her, including the fact that she certainly might benefit from treatment. "But," he said, "I'll refer you to my colleague, Dr. Black, for evaluation and treatment. I think that it's not a good idea for one therapist to treat both you and your child, as you might have conflicting needs."

Heloise scheduled an appointment with Dr. Black for the next week. She also scheduled a general physical examination with her family doctor and checked out fine physically. Her workup by Dr. Black was as comprehensive as Sam's had been, and after three sessions, the psychiatrist informed her that she did indeed have ADD. He suggested that she would benefit most from combination therapy: behavior therapy to help her organize her life and to learn some tricks for coping with her disability, and stimulant medication to improve her attention span. Heloise agreed to his recommendations and started treatment the next morning. Within twenty-four hours, she found that she was more focused and less distractible. She could concentrate better and pay attention for longer periods of time.

Over the next few weeks, Heloise worked with Dr. Black to get the dosage of her medication adjusted to the optimal level. She was no longer inattentive and restless and was also having fewer problems with side effects, such as headaches and trouble sleeping. Sam was doing well too; he was excelling in school, had several new friends, and hadn't had a time-out in over two weeks. To celebrate, the Fox family went out to dinner at a nice restaurant. Heloise thoroughly enjoyed herself; she was able to pay full attention to the dinnertime conversation, and Sam stayed seated throughout the entire meal.

Summary

Attention deficit disorder is much more common among adult women than had been realized previously. The disorder can cause life-long difficulties with attention, concentration, and organization. Behavior therapy and stimulant medications can correct these problems and allow the woman to reach her full potential—without expending twice as much effort as women without ADD.

Resources

Attention Deficit Disorder Association (ADDA)
P. O. Box 972
Mentor, Ohio 44061
800–487–2282

CHADD (Children and Adults with Attention Deficit Disorder)
(Local chapters in most communities)
499 NW 70th Avenue, Suite 308
Plantation, Florida 33317
305–587–3700

Further Reading

Barkley, Russell. *Attention Deficit Hyperactivity Disorder: A Handbook for Diagnosis and Treatment.* New York: Guilford Press, 1990

Hallowell, Edward, and John Ratey. *Driven to Distraction.* New York: Touchstone Books, Simon & Schuster, 1994.

Hechtman, Lilly, and Gabrielle Weiss. *Hyperactive Children Grown Up: ADHD in Children, Adolescents and Adults,* 2nd ed. New York: Guilford Press, 1993.

Kelly, Kate, and Peggy Ramundo. *You Mean I Am Not Lazy, Stupid, or Crazy?!* (1993) Tyrell and Jerem Press, Box 20089, Cincinnati, OH 45220.

Wender, Paul. *Attention Deficit Hyperactivity Disorder in Adults.* New York: Oxford University Press, 1995.

Notes

1. David Grogan and Karen Emmons, Luchina Fisher, and Tom Nugent. "Whippingboy." *People.* April 18, 1994, 41-43.
2. Krystal Miller. *Wall Street Journal.* January 11, 1993.
3. Miller. *Wall Street Journal.*
4. Paul Wender, *The Hyperactive Child, Adolescent, and Adult.* New York: Oxford University Press, 1987.
5. Edward Hallowell and John Ratey, *Driven to Distraction* (New York: Touchstone Books, Simon & Schuster, 1994), 73-76.
6. Hallowell and Ratey, *Driven to Distraction,* 99.

CHAPTER 7

Rhythms and Blues:
Sleep/Wake Disorders
and Bipolar Disorder

Jessica was feeling great. She was flying through her paperwork and knew that she would soon be able to finish the presentation that she had been trying to get done for the last couple of weeks. It seemed so easy tonight. She was productive, focused, and energetic. Why couldn't she always feel like this? Jessica glanced over at the clock—2:00 A.M. No wonder she felt so great—it was her time of the night. She was always at her best between 10:00 P.M. and 3:00 A.M. The house was quiet, her family was asleep, and there was nothing to distract her. If only she didn't have to go to work in the morning.

Jessica hated Monday mornings. Come to think of it, she hated the whole workweek. She always felt so awful—tired, irritable, and groggy. She sort of stumbled through her days, not really waking up until she was on her way home from work in the evening. The weekends were so much better. She could sleep in until 10:00 or 11:00 and have a second or third cup of coffee while she read the paper and ate brunch. Then she was ready to go—awake, alert, and full of energy. If only the weekdays could start at noon.

Jessica didn't know it, but that was exactly what her body needed: a day that started at noon. Jessica has a sleep/wake-cycle disorder known as night-owl (or delayed sleep-phase) syndrome. But before we can discuss the disturbances of the sleep/wake cycle and other cyclic disorders, we must understand the importance of biological rhythms to our physical and mental health.

Biological Clocks

Nearly every one of our body's systems has a natural biological rhythm, a built-in clock that regulates its function. Biological rhythms affect blood pressure, temperature, hormone levels, breathing rates, blood sugar levels, pulse rates, bowel functions, sleep and wakefulness, and the production of enzymes necessary for key chemical reactions. Each of these functions has a different rhythm, and each has a different cue to keep it on schedule; some use daybreak, others sunset, and others, temperature. Thus, the clocks can get out of sync from one another and cause problems with sugar regulation, or temperature control, or sleep and wakefulness.

Many of our internal clocks are on an approximately twenty-four-hour cycle and are known as "circadian rhythms" (from the Latin words *circa*, about, and *dies*, a day). Of all the body's circadian rhythms, the sleep/wake cycle is the most noticeable and impacts all aspects of our daily life. As its name implies, the sleep/wake clock tells your body when it's time to gear up for wakefulness and when it's time to shut down for sleep. Sunlight, particularly at dawn and dusk, is necessary to keep the sleep/wake cycle on a twenty-four-hour schedule. Numerous experiments have shown that without sunlight, the sleep/wake cycle gradually lengthens to twenty-four and a half to thirty-three hours. When Stefania Follini lived alone in a cave for 131 days, she found that her sleep/wake cycle extended to a thirty-three-hour "day" with twenty-three-hours awake and ten hours asleep. Even if we just spend all our time indoors under artificial lights, our sleep/wake cycle can get out of sync with the environment—and with our daily life. Without strong sunlight, our biological clocks no longer can tell us what time of day it is!

Occasionally, just one of our biological clocks (usually the sleep/wake cycle) will get out of sync. It becomes disconnected (desynchronized) from the cycles controlling body temperature, hormonal controls, and others. For example, it's midnight, your temperature has dropped in preparation for deep sleep, and the sleep-inducing hormones have been produced, but your sleep/wake clock says it's time to be awake, so you are. You lie there—cold, groggy, sluggish—but wide awake and miserable. Or perhaps the three systems (sleep/wake clock, hormone control, and temperature) stay connected to each other but become disconnected from the external world. Now your biological rhythms are "free-running," and you'll *really* feel miserable. Because instead of being cold and groggy and sluggish at midnight, you'll be cold, groggy, and sluggish at 8:00 A.M. or 6:00 P.M. or for the entire day.

The regularity of our circadian rhythms changes as we age, and sleep disorders are more common at some life stages than at others. Newborns begin to establish a circadian rhythm within the first few weeks of life, and this helps them eat at predictable times, wake at predictable times, and fall asleep at predictable times (thank heavens!). During childhood, the circadian rhythms remain fairly strong, so children tend to get up about the same time every day and go to sleep at about the same time every night. During adolescence, however, the sleep/wake cycle often becomes unreliable. The hormonal shifts of puberty wreak havoc on all of the body's circadian rhythms, including the sleep/wake cycle. In some teens, the sleep/wake cycle is prolonged, and in others, delayed; both have the same effect: the teenagers have trouble getting up in the morning, difficulty falling asleep at night, and they remain irritable and groggy throughout the day.

Fortunately, in our twenties and thirties, our sleep/wake clock usually returns to a predictable twenty-four-hour cycle. If it doesn't, sleep disorders can result (or persist). As we grow older, the sleep/wake cycle can become disrupted again. Many elderly persons have a cycle that is moved ahead or is shorter than twenty-four hours in length; this might explain their frequent catnaps during the daytime and insomnia at night; their bodies are out of sync with their environment.

Disorders of Circadian Rhythms

Jessica finally went to bed at about 3:00 A.M. and immediately fell into a restful sleep. However, morning came much too quickly, and when it did, she felt awful. She could hear her alarm going off and her husband getting dressed, but she just couldn't wake up yet. So she turned over to catch "just five more minutes" of sleep. Forty-five minutes later, she was roused by her husband yelling at her, "The kids are fed and I'm taking them to school. You're really late—get up. Do you hear me? GET UP!"

As her husband came up the stairs to make sure that she was finally up, Jessica tried to pull herself out of bed, but she just couldn't do it.

When he came into the room, she said, "I think I'm sick; please call work for me."

To which he replied, "You're not sick. You're having a Monday morning, just like every other Monday morning since I married you. You got enough sleep this weekend, so you can't be tired. You're just sleepy. Get up, take a shower, and drink some coffee. I've gotta go; you've made me late. I'll see you tonight." And with that he left, hoping that Jessica wouldn't fall back asleep as she had done so many times before.

Jessica struggled out of bed and made her way slowly down the stairs, yawning as she went. She downed two cups of strong coffee and headed back upstairs to shower. Only thirty minutes to get to work and she had a thirty-five-minute commute—guess she'd have to hurry. Later, maybe. Right now, she needed to rest.

Jessica finally managed to get herself dressed and into the office. She knew she looked terrible because she felt terrible. Her presentation was terrible too. As her kids would say, "It stunk—badly!" Too bad she couldn't have given it last night—then she felt like she was on top of the world; this morning she felt like she was lost in a fog. And the fog didn't clear until about 4:00 in the afternoon. Jessica had had three cups of coffee and two Diet Cokes by then, and she was finally awake. As she became alert, she made a decision: she wasn't going to live like this anymore.

Jessica scheduled an appointment with her internist. She told him how difficult it was for her to get out of bed in the morning and how hard it was to force herself to go to bed at night. "The only time I feel OK is on weekends when I can sleep in. Oh, and when I travel to California on business. The time change is great. They're three hours behind us, and that's just about how much time I'm behind myself." Jessica had just diagnosed her problem. She had delayed sleep-phase disorder. Fortunately, her internist was astute enough to recognize this and referred her to a physician who specialized in the treatment of sleep disorders.

The sleep expert explained to Jessica that the key to curing delayed sleep-phase disorder was a regular wake-up time. The doctor explained that Jessica couldn't force herself to go to sleep at night, so she had to reset her sleep/wake clock by forcing herself to wake up at a certain time in the morning. Even though her body was telling her to sleep late on the weekends, she had to get up. Sleeping in was the very worst thing that she could do, because it knocked her sleep/wake clock out of sync with her weekday schedule. In addition, the doctor recommended that Jessica use bright-light phototherapy early in the morning to ensure that her sleep/wake clock was getting a strong enough external signal.

It took a few weeks for Jessica to reset her sleep/wake clock, but when she finally did, she noticed a big improvement. She was awake and alert in the morning, productive throughout the day, and able to fall asleep at night. Jessica couldn't really believe that a bright light and an alarm clock (always set for the same time) could have made such a difference, but they did. She was back in sync and feeling on top of the world!

Night Owls (Delayed Sleep-Phase Disorder)

Night owls or "night people" consistently go to sleep late (typically, 2:00 to 3:00 A.M.), fall easily into a restful sleep, and then get up late in the morning. They feel their best and are their most productive in the late afternoon and evening hours. These night owls have delayed sleep-phase disorder. They essentially have jet lag without having traveled; their body tells them that it's not really as late as the clock on the wall says that it is.

Women may be able to adapt to delayed sleep-phase disorder if they work the evening (the 3:00 P.M. to 11:00 P.M.) shift or if they have a job where they don't have to show up at a certain time, such as a free-lance writer who can write at home and set her own hours. Sometimes, however, even these women will have difficulties. They may feel irritable, inattentive, or tired. This is due to the desynchronization of their different biological clocks: their sleep/wake cycle becomes disconnected from the other biological cycles, as described earlier.

The "Sunday night insomnia" and "Monday morning hangover" described in Jessica's story are characteristic of delayed sleep-phase disorder. The night owl sleeps late on Saturday morning because that is closest to her natural sleep/wake rhythm. But in so doing, she causes her clock to be pushed further off schedule, and by Sunday night, she is unable to fall asleep. When it is midnight, her body thinks it's 9:00 P.M., so she's wide awake and hours away from being ready for sleep. On Monday morning, her sleep/wake clock is still delayed, and she feels like it's the middle of the night (4:00 A.M.) when it's really time to get up (7:00 A.M.). The night owl will feel "hung over" because her sleep/wake clock is still set for sleep. Sometimes the Monday morning hangovers are so bad that others may wonder if she has a drinking problem.

You may have delayed sleep-phase disorder if you have a chronic, persistent pattern of:

1. Feeling that you are at your best late at night
2. Having difficulty falling asleep before 2:00 or 3:00 A.M.
3. Having difficulty getting up or waking up in the morning
4. Sunday night insomnia and/or Monday morning hangovers
5. Excessive daytime sleepiness, especially in the morning
6. Irritability, inattentiveness, or concentration difficulties in the morning.

Obviously, a physician familiar with sleep disorders should make the diagnosis of delayed sleep-phase disorder, because other sleep disorders, as well as other medical and psychiatric disorders, can have similar patterns.

Treatment of Delayed Sleep-Phase Disorder

The treatment for people with delayed sleep-phase disorder is regulation of their sleep/wake cycle. Two treatments—chronotherapy and phototherapy—are used to do this.

Chronotherapy is time therapy—an external means of keeping the sleep/wake cycle constant. The night owl must get up at the same time (early) each morning and go to bed at the same time each night. This external control is usually sufficient to keep the night owl's sleep/wake cycle in sync once it has been reset, but resetting the clock is the hard part. Some doctors suggest *advancing* the sleep schedule to reach the desired target bedtime. This often requires that the woman take time off from work in order go to bed two to three hours *later* each day until she has reached her chosen bedtime. For example, if she currently gets sleepy at 2:30 A.M., but she needs to go to bed at 11:00 P.M. in order to get eight hours of sleep per night (the amount that she usually sleeps on weekends), then she will go to bed the first night at 5:30 A.M., the second night at 8:30 A.M., the next at 11:30 A.M., then at 2:30 P.M., then at 5:30 P.M., then at 8:30 P.M., and finally at 11:00 P.M. As you might expect, this can be very disruptive, but that appears to be one reason why it works: the clocks are "shocked" back into synchrony.

The other approach is more gradual; it takes longer to be effective but is easier to accomplish. This method requires the woman to move her awakening time back ten to fifteen minutes (for example, from 8:30 to 8:15 A.M. and then to 8:00 A.M. and so forth) every two to three days (including weekends, of course). In a few weeks, her sleep/wake cycle should be in sync with job requirements and the traditional twenty-four-hour day. (This early-awakening technique can also be used by students at the end of summer vacation in order to be ready for the first days of school in September. Don't forget to set the alarm on weekend mornings too!)

Light therapy (or phototherapy) is also very effective for delayed sleep-phase disorder. It can be used alone or in conjunction with chronotherapy. It is helpful both in the short run to reset the clock and on an ongoing basis to keep the clock on schedule. The timing of the light therapy is crucial, in order to ensure that the sleep/wake clock is reset correctly. The bright lights are used for thirty minutes each morning for at least a month. Some women place their light box next to the bed and attach it to a timer so that they can receive their phototherapy "automatically" each morning. Many people who respond find that they have to keep using the bright-light box each morning, or they relapse within a few days. Phototherapy is a medical treatment and should be used only "by prescription" and with ongoing monitoring by an experienced physician. (See Chapter Eight for a complete description of phototherapy.)

Morning Larks (Advanced Sleep-Phase Disorder)

As the name implies, morning larks are the opposite of night owls. They have advanced sleep-phase disorder; their clocks are set ahead, and their sleep/wake cycle is on the short side. Advanced sleep-phase disorder is seen most often among the elderly, perhaps because of the natural shortening of the sleep/wake cycle that occurs as we age. Morning larks wake up very early in the morning (3:00 to 5:00 A.M.) and feel sleepy very early in the evening (7:00 to 9:00 P.M.). Thus, they make great surgeons but lousy concertgoers. Advanced sleep-phase disorder is less common than delayed sleep-phase disorder and typically causes fewer problems. In fact, it may go unnoticed unless the morning lark needs to stay awake and alert for several evenings in a row. Advanced sleep-phase disorder is also diagnosed only when the condition is chronic and persistent.

Treatment of Advanced Sleep-Phase Disorder

Treatment of advanced sleep-phase disorder is best done by a sleep disorder specialist. The doctor will prescribe a plan of sleep/wake schedules and light therapy to slow down the lark's fast clock. Thus, the morning lark will be encouraged to "sleep in" in the morning and required to stay up later each evening. Evening exercise or bright-light phototherapy may help provide the stimulation needed to help reset the sleep/wake clock. In addition, stimulant medications may be used to treat advanced sleep-phase disorder.

Disruptions of the Sleep/Wake Clock

Short-term disruptions of the sleep/wake clock are common; caring for a newborn baby, studying for final exams, and traveling can all cause the sleep/wake clock to be thrown out of sync. Treatment is rarely required for these temporary disturbances, as the sleep/wake cycle is quickly restored when the disruption is removed. In some cases, such as shift-worker fatigue and jet lag, specific interventions can be helpful.

Shift-Worker Fatigue. It has always amazed us that nurses, who must be alert and vigilant in their duties, are scheduled for rotating day and night shifts. One week they are assigned to the 7:00 A.M. to 3:00 P.M. shift, and the next to the 11:00 P.M. to 7:00 A.M. shift. Their bodies and their biological clocks can't keep up with the changes. Even women who are permanently assigned to the night shift may never really feel their best. They are trying to sleep in the morning, when their metabolic processes are revving up, and trying to stay awake at night, when their metabolism is slowed down. They may use alcohol (to help them sleep) and caffeine (to stay awake) to excess and may develop problems secondary to these drugs. They may also suffer from chronic fatigue, decreased alertness, and other symptoms.

It might be helpful to consult a sleep disorder expert about shift-work issues. The physician may find that the problem is being made worse by other sleep disorders or by unrelated medical problems. Once these are treated, the fatigue and physical symptoms may be alleviated. In the absence of complicating conditions, shift workers can be helped to reset their biological clocks in order to minimize the effects of the changing sleep/wake cycle. For example, a sleep schedule might be developed that would involve sleeping only in the afternoon, or taking a brief nap in the morning and getting five to six hours of sleep in the afternoon. Typically, sleeping pills are not used, as they can make the fatigue worse by interfering with restful sleep. Chronotherapy and bright-light therapy may be prescribed for the night worker in an effort to help regulate her cycles.

Jet Lag. Anyone who has flown from Hawaii to the mainland or from California to the East Coast has probably experienced "jet lag." Although you can get jet lag from flying in either the eastward or westward direction, for most of us, flying east is more disruptive. Jet lag is characterized by difficulty waking up in the morning, trouble falling asleep at night, and daytime sleepiness, irritability, and difficulty concentrating. It is the result of your circadian rhythms being out of sync with the external environment. Your body's clocks just can't adjust as fast as the jet can travel; you end up two, three, or eight hours behind the times.

You can help your body adjust to the time change and thus minimize the effects of jet lag by adjusting your light exposure or using melatonin, a naturally occurring hormone that appears to regulate sleep and wakefulness. Taking three to five milligrams of melatonin shortly before bedtime for two or three nights before you leave home, while you're away, and on your return home appears to help prevent jet lag. (Melatonin has been proclaimed recently to be a "miracle" compound, but it is highly unlikely that it is truly "nature's age-reversing, disease-fighting, sex-enhancing hormone."[1] Before starting melatonin therapy, you should check with your physician for specific recommendations about its use.)

Jet lag can also be treated by adjusting light exposure. Although we won't go into detail about these adjustments here, there are several resources that give specific plans for doing so. We particularly recommend the book, *How to Beat Jet Lag*, by Drs. Dan Oren, Walter Reich, Norm Rosenthal, and Tom Wehr (see "Resources" at the end of this chapter).

Sometimes the insomnia associated with jet lag is treated with a short course of sleeping pills. Although their use is controversial, some physicians believe that the sleeping pills speed up the process of resetting the sleep/wake clock by allowing the traveler to fall asleep on time for the first few nights in the new time zone. Alcohol is very disruptive to restful sleep and should be avoided during air travel and as a "treatment" for jet lag.

Sleep Disorders

Sleep is a very vital and active process. Rapid eye movement (REM) sleep (the stage of sleep in which we dream) plays a crucial role in revitalizing and restoring us in many ways. The amount of sleep you need is individually determined and appears to depend on the fraction of time that you spend in REM sleep. Some women get sufficient REM sleep with only five to six hours of sleep per night, while others need nine or ten hours of total sleep time. Further, many factors can interfere with REM sleep, and it is possible to spend a full night sleeping and yet be deprived of truly restful sleep. Not having had enough restful sleep for several nights in a row begins to affect one's mood, memory, attention, and energy. With long-term sleep deprivation (such as occurs in the sleep disorders), fatigue, irritability, depression, paranoia, disorientation, memory loss, inattention, and concentration difficulties are common.

Do You Have a Problem Related to Sleep?

It is estimated that 100 million Americans have occasional sleep problems and that nearly thirty million have some type of chronic sleep disorder. There are so many sleep-related disorders that we cannot begin to describe them in detail here. However, sleep is so vital to your mental health that a sleep disorder must be considered whenever you are having trouble with irritability, depression, anxiety, or inattentiveness. The following symptoms are also associated with sleep problems:

1. Tiredness and fatigue during the daytime
2. Sleepiness during the daytime
3. Waking up and not feeling rested
4. Needing several naps during the daytime
5. Feeling disoriented, confused, or "drunk" when waking up in the morning
6. Falling asleep taking more than twenty to thirty minutes
7. Waking up repeatedly during the night
8. Snoring loudly or excessively
9. Waking up during the night because of breathing difficulties
10. Having restless movements during sleep (such as legs kicking a lot)
11. Grinding and clenching one's teeth during sleep
12. Having trouble falling asleep again after awakening in the middle of the night
13. Falling asleep while driving
14. Waking up extra early in the morning and being unable to go back to sleep

15. Having terrible nightmares or night terrors
16. Wetting the bed as an adult
17. Sleepwalking as an adult
18. Trouble paying attention during the daytime
19. Problems with irritability, anxiety, or depression during the day-time.

Motherhood is perhaps the most common cause of sleep problems for women. Breast-feeding every two to three hours means that you aren't getting sufficient REM sleep, even if you're lucky enough to sleep for a total of eight hours each night. More often, new mothers are deprived of enough of either type of sleep; this can lead to both physical and mental exhaustion, with resulting fatigue, concentration difficulties, forgetful-ness, irritability, and depression. This condition doesn't require medical treatment, just increasing the number of hours of consecutive sleep. Until your newborn baby learns to sleep through the night, it is impor-tant to have occasional "nights off"; bank your milk and have the baby's father give the middle-of-the-night feedings once in a while.

Sleep can be disrupted by other external forces, including excessive stress, caffeine consumption, alcohol intake, over-the-counter and pre-scription medicines, and environmental irritants (like noise from a nearby airport). Sleep problems can also arise from medical illnesses, such as asthma or emphysema, which interfere with your breathing at nighttime, as well as stomach ulcers or hiatal hernias, which produce heartburn when you lie down. Most psychiatric disorders, including de-pression, anxiety disorders, panic, bipolar disorder, and psychosis, are associated with sleep problems.

Sleeping pills are a common but curious cause of sleep disorders. The sleeping pills are initially prescribed for short-term problems with insomnia, but over time, they induce such physical and psychological addiction that the woman can't fall asleep without them. Further, sleep-ing pills alter sleep patterns and decrease REM sleep so that the woman doesn't get enough REM sleep and may develop a secondary sleep dis-order. Physicians are becoming increasingly aware of the dangers of sleeping pills and now usually prescribe them for only a few nights at a time.

Insomnia and Hypersomnia. The most common sleep disorders fall into two general categories: insomnia (difficulty with falling asleep or staying asleep) and hypersomnia (excessive sleepiness during the day-time). Occasional difficulties with falling asleep aren't serious and don't require medical interventions, but nightly insomnia, particularly the kind that leaves you feeling exhausted the next day, should receive attention. People who are suffering from insomnia may feel sleepy the next day, and those who have hypersomnia may have slept so much during the daytime that they have difficulty falling asleep at night, so it can often be difficult to sort out which disorder is the primary problem. Therefore, if you think you might have a chronic sleep disorder, we recommend that you ask your physician for treatment or a referral to a sleep disorder specialist.

Parasomnias (Abnormal Events During Sleep). Parasomnias occur when the sleeping person becomes partially aroused. The most common parasomnias, sleepwalking and night terrors, affect about 1 percent of adults. These disorders are more common during childhood, but most people outgrow them. If you first begin to sleepwalk or have night terrors as an adult, you should see a doctor to make sure that you aren't having epileptic seizures and to receive treatment for this potentially dangerous condition. Safety measures (such as hiding the car keys, double-locking doors, and sleeping on the ground floor) may be sufficient for mild parasomnias.

Night terrors are different from nightmares. Nightmares usually occur late in sleep, can often be remembered, and may feel frightening, but they do not cause any physical symptoms. Night terrors occur early in sleep, are usually not remembered, and are accompanied by racing heart rate and sweating. The person appears to be wide awake, but she's actually still half-asleep. She may scream in terror, cry inconsolably, or appear confused. When the night terror is over, she will lie back down and immediately return to deep sleep. Night terrors require assessment by a physician to determine whether the parasomnia is due to a treatable medical or neurological condition. The physician would also want to be sure that the woman isn't suffering from flashbacks associated with post-traumatic stress disorder (see Chapter Ten) or from nighttime panic attacks (which occur during a different phase of sleep than do night terrors). The treatment for night terrors is fairly simple; it involves sleeping longer hours, which decreases delta sleep (the phase in which night terrors occur). On occasion, medications that decrease delta sleep are used, as well.

Bipolar Disorder and Other Cyclic Mood Disorders

Maureen was feeling great. No, she was feeling better than great—she was feeling fantastic! She worked the room, chatting with this VIP, flirting a little with that one. She knew that she was the most beautiful and most desirable woman at the party tonight. All of the men wanted her. And why not? Not only was she drop-dead gorgeous, she was clever and smart. She had really wowed them with her presentation today. It had been perfect—no, better than perfect, it was awesome. It had taken weeks and weeks of effort and then working around the clock for the past three days, but she'd done it. And almost single-handedly too. Her stupid assistant hadn't been much help at all, insisting that he had to go home at midnight to catch some z's. But who needed him? She had done it herself, and it was brilliant stuff. She was a superwoman. Time for superwoman to find a superman. She spied one across the room and pushed her way through the crowd to meet him. Oh, yes, he was yummy. And obviously important too.

"Hi, there, what's your name, stranger?" she asked.

"Uh, Toby, ma'am. Do you need something?"

"Yes, you, sugarplum. Do you think we could go somewhere together?"

"No, ma'am. I can't. I'm working. I'm the busboy. I mean, I have a girlfriend and . . . and I have to be home by eleven." Toby stammered as he backed away from her.

Maureen turned away, nonplussed by her misjudgment.

Oh, well, there were bigger fish in the sea. Maybe she'd go out and get some air. She didn't need food or sleep anymore. But she needed air—she liked air, especially the night air. It made her feel even more alive. Oh, look at the lights; they were so twinkly. And look at the stars. And the moon—it was shining just for her. Oh, it was going behind a cloud. Too bad. But, no, it was a lovely little cloud. Everything was so beautiful. She'd sit down and enjoy the beauty.

Maureen sat restlessly for several seconds before getting up again to pace. A few seconds later, she looked at her watch. Hmm, midnight, time to get out of here. Where can I go in this town for some action? I know, the all-night diner on the edge of town.

She sailed back through the reception room, blowing kisses to one and all. They were all so beautiful. She was beautiful. The night was beautiful.

Maureen drove quickly on the rain-slick roads. She had her window wide open, and the damp wind felt so good on her cheeks, especially when she got onto the interstate highway. It seemed like the faster she went, the better the wind felt, the better she felt—and soon she was doing ninety miles an hour. She saw the exit for the diner just as she was about to pass it. Swerving across three lanes of traffic, Maureen barely reached the ramp in time, and she hadn't slowed down at all when she hit the curve marked twenty miles an hour at the top of the ramp. The last thing Maureen can remember is a sense of flying—flying through the air as her car left the road and flew over the embankment.

Maureen "woke up" the next morning in a psychiatric ward. She had been very lucky. Her car had been totaled, but she had suffered only a dislocated shoulder and a few scrapes and bruises. It seems that she had begun talking gibberish after she regained consciousness in the emergency room, and the consulting psychiatrist, Dr. Barney, was called in to help determine whether or not she had a head injury. Dr. Barney had recognized Maureen from her last admission to his ward and arranged for her to be committed. It was his voice that had awakened her: "Hi, Maureen. I'm glad to see you're awake. Can you tell me what happened? Did you stop taking your lithium?"

"I guess so, doc. I don't remember. I was working really hard on this project, and everything just started speeding up. You know how it is right before you go over the top—it's so incredible. I could think, I could work, I could create. I was a superwoman. I figured I could hold it at that level. Use it, you know. But I lost it. It got out of control. I guess I screwed up," she said. "What happened to me, anyhow? I can't remember anything after my presentation Thursday morning."

The doctor explained what had happened to her and how it was related to a manic episode. He told her that she would need to stay in the hospital until they could re-regulate her medications and arrange for supportive therapy. After a week in the hospital, Maureen's lithium level was regulated once again, and she was discharged. This time, she was given a case manager to help her monitor her sleep/wake schedule and to ensure that she didn't overdo it or forget to take her medication. Maureen was determined to keep her illness under control this time. She knew that if she didn't, she could wind up with more than a sore shoulder.

The cycling of mood, energy, and creativity common to the cyclic mood disorders was first described by the Greeks. This rhythmicity appears to be linked to internal forces, such as our biological rhythms and menstrual cycles, and external forces, such as day length, the seasons, and even the cyclic orbiting of the moon. (The Latin word for moon, *luna*, is the origin of the term "lunacy," and it refers to the ancient observations that madness seemed to peak when the moon was full.) But the nature of the relationship between these forces and the cycling of moods is unclear, and in bipolar disorder, no discernible rhythmic pattern has been found.

Cyclothymic disorder is characterized by cycling moods: the woman alternates between feeling low and feeling high, between feeling bad and feeling good. The lows aren't quite as low as depression and the highs aren't as high as mania, but cyclothymic disorder is sometimes a precursor to bipolar disorder. Bipolar disorder is divided into two types: bipolar I, which has recurrent episodes of both depression and mania; and bipolar II, which is characterized by recurrent episodes of depression and at least one episode of hypomania (a milder form of mania). Bipolar II can be missed if the doctor isn't specifically thinking about it; the woman won't recognize her hypomania as a problem, and there are many people who have multiple episodes of depression. Hypomania and mania are described in the subsection that follows, and depression is considered in detail in Chapter Eight. The "switch" between mania or hypomania and depression is a dangerous time for the patient with bipolar disorder; she goes from feeling absolutely terrific to feeling absolutely terrible, and the contrast is even worse than having depression alone.

Anne Sexton, a Pulitzer Prize–winning poet, suffered from bipolar disorder and committed suicide during one of her periods of depression. In her poems, we see her struggles against both despair and her self-destructive urges. Despite the efforts of her family, friends, and therapist to save her from her illness, she was overcome by a combination of hopeless depression and self-destructive urges. And at the age of forty-five, she took off her rings, put on her mother's old fur coat, climbed into the driver's seat of her car, and turned on the ignition to poison herself with carbon monoxide.[2] Ms. Sexton's death is particularly tragic because it occurred shortly after lithium had been found to be useful for patients with bipolar disorder—but Ms. Sexton hadn't been given treatment with the drug. Even with modern therapies, suicide remains an ever-present danger of bipolar disorder. One in ten patients with bipolar disorder will take her own life.

The Diagnosis of Bipolar Disorder

Bipolar disorder is characterized by opposite mood states: depression and mania. *Mania*, or a manic episode, is a period in which the person has an abnormally happy mood (euphoria) and/or excessive irritability. *Hypomania* is also an episode defined by a euphoric or irritable mood, but it is less dramatic than mania—the woman never loses control. In both mania and hypomania, the woman seems to be energized, confident, and "up"; her creativity is increased, her energy is increased, and her mood is elevated. She moves fast, thinks fast, works fast. Often she is also excessively irritable or impatient. She doesn't wait for the answers to her questions and talks quickly and loudly. She eats little and sleeps little, seeming to have an endless energy source. As her mood and energy increase even further, she may cross over the line into mania; then her talking fast becomes talking nonsense, her working fast becomes working carelessly, and her increased socialization becomes an inappropriate interchange between her and a stranger.

Mania is characterized by grandiosity—the feeling of being larger than life, important, omnipotent, or invulnerable. Dr. Kay Redfield Jamison, in her book *Touched with Fire: Manic-Depressive Illness and the Artistic Temperament*, writes about the bipolar artist's "fine madness of the artistic temperament and intensity."[3] This creativity is frequently short-lived, however, as the manic episode gives way to depression and despair.

Manic episodes are also characterized by poor judgment and poor insight. Because the woman doesn't recognize her behavior as abnormal or dangerous, she can get into serious trouble. She may drive too fast or recklessly, putting herself and her passengers at risk. She might have a sexual liaison with a stranger, or run up huge credit card bills, or throw away large sums of money. Some patients who have had a manic episode "awaken" in the hospital to discover that they've invested their life savings in a ridiculous get-rich-quick scheme or that they've given all their worldly possessions to a stranger.

In true manic episodes, psychosis is common. (Psychosis, or being out of touch with reality, is described in Chapter Eleven.) The woman may hear special messages, or believe that she has important insights for the president of the United States, or worry that she is being followed by the CIA. The combination of grandiosity and psychotic delusions can be particularly dangerous. The woman might try to jump off a bridge because she thinks that she can fly, or she may deliberately take an overdose because she's stronger than death. If she has these kinds of delusions, she may need to be hospitalized in order to save her life.

Hypomania is less dramatic but much more common than mania. Usually a woman with hypomania will not recognize her "high" periods as problematic. How could she? She's "up," "alive," extraordinarily happy and productive. She doesn't need as much sleep, so she gets more done; she isn't hungry and loses those few extra pounds; she is very happy and truly feels great. So how could that be bad? It is bad because the presence of hypomania, in conjunction with recurrent periods of depression, means that the woman has bipolar II disorder. If it goes unrecognized and she is treated with certain antidepressants, she might be thrown into a manic episode, or the medications could increase the frequency and severity of her depressive episodes (see Chapter Nine). She might even develop rapid-cycling bipolar disease (a condition in which the person has at least four episodes of mania and/or depression per year); this is a disorder that is notoriously difficult to treat. So the missed diagnosis of hypomania can have some very real and potentially very serious consequences. Because the woman might not be able to recognize her own hypomanic episodes, it is important for her physician to consider the possibility of bipolar II illness and inquire about periods of euphoria (excessive happiness) or irritability.

Other Cyclic Mood Disorders

Cyclothymia is a cycling mood disorder that is similar to bipolar disorder; with cyclothymia, the patient alternates between hypomania and depressive periods. The highs aren't as high, and typically the lows aren't as low as in bipolar II disorder. Some patients with cyclothymia may settle into a chronic low-grade depression (dysthymia, described in Chapter Nine), while others will go on to develop bipolar disorder. Interestingly, if they do, the rhythmicity of the cycles remains fairly constant, even as their amplitude increases.

"Rapid cyclers" are patients with bipolar disorder who have frequent mood swings with at least four episodes of mood disturbance (either mania or depression) within the past year. "Ultrarapid cyclers" are women with bipolar disorder who switch frequently and quickly between depressive and manic symptoms, sometimes without a period of normal mood in between. Some ultrarapid cyclers swing back and forth between mania and depression on a daily basis. Rapid cycling is a very serious disorder and is associated with a poor outcome. It is these patients who are most helped by the mood-stabilizing effects of the anticonvulsant medications.

Premenstrual syndrome (Chapter Four) is defined as a cyclic mood disorder. So is seasonal affective disorder (Chapter Eight). These two disorders have recognizable triggers for the mood changes; when these triggers were identified, researchers were able to arrive at better clinical descriptions and more effective treatments. In bipolar disorder, the triggers for the mood changes are less clear but may include sleep deprivation, hormone shifts, or desynchronization of the body's rhythms. Clearly, more study is needed to understand the mechanisms by which the mood swings occur. It is already clear that external structure, such as strictly regimented patterns of sleeping, eating, and exercising, can help to prevent manic episodes.

Treatment of the Cyclic Mood Disorders

There is no cure for bipolar disorder, but mood-stabilizing drugs have dramatically improved the lives of patients suffering from the disorder. Recognition of the differences between bipolar disorder and schizophrenia led to the development of treatments that are effective for both the acute episode of mania and for the prevention of recurrences. Currently, the most effective treatment regimen involves a combination of medication, education, and psychotherapy.

Medications

The introduction of *lithium* was one of the most important breakthroughs in the treatment of bipolar disorder. Lithium has been used successfully to treat both the acute depressive and manic phases of the illness, as well as to prevent recurrences. Recent research suggests that the long-term use of lithium for prevention is important, as each recurrence seems to increase the chances of having yet another recurrence; this phenomenon is known as "kindling." It appears that the helpful effects of lithium may be lost by stopping the medication and restarting it during a manic episode, so patients should be encouraged to stay on their medication even when they are feeling well.

Lithium is the mainstay of treatment for bipolar disorder, but unfortunately, as many as one-third of patients either do not have a satisfactory response to lithium treatment or cannot take the medicine because of troublesome side effects. These side effects include increased thirst, increased appetite, weight gain, concentration and thinking problems, tremor, tiredness, diarrhea, and occasionally a low thyroid level (hypothyroidism). Hypothyroidism can cause both mania and depression. If the cause of these symptoms is not recognized as a side effect of the medication, the lithium dose might be increased to control the manic-depressive symptoms and cause further complications.

Lithium therapy requires ongoing care by a physician experienced in its use. During therapy, blood lithium levels need to be monitored, as too high a level may be dangerous and too low a level may not be effective. Although there tend to be more side effects at higher dosages, sometimes one can have troublesome side effects in the "normal" or therapeutic range. It is important for the patient to discuss these side effects with her physician so that alternative treatments can be found. Again, it is imperative that the woman continue treatment in some form, in order to prevent recurrent manic-depressive episodes.

Mood stabilizers are medications that decrease mood swings and prevent both mania and depression. The mood stabilizers include lithium (Lithobid, Lithonate, Lithane, Eskalith, and others), valproic acid (Depakene or Depakote), and carbamazepine (Tegretol). The latter two drugs can be used either alone or in combination with lithium. Valproic acid and carbamazepine are actually anticonvulsant (antiseizure) drugs. They have offered new options for patients who cannot benefit from lithium therapy. In particular, patients with rapid cycling of moods or mixed states (simultaneous symptoms of both mania and depression) may respond better to valproic acid or carbamazepine.

Each of the mood-stabilizing medications has its own set of possible side effects. Valproic acid may cause sedation, gastrointestinal problems, menstrual irregularities, and blood abnormalities (although this effect is rare). Carbamazepine is associated with tiredness, nausea, and dizziness. Because of an extremely rare side effect (one in 200,000 patients) called aplastic anemia, blood counts should be followed whenever the patient is on carbamazepine. In addition, women who are using oral contraceptives may need an adjustment of their medication dosage when they start carbamazepine therapy as the drug can decrease the effectiveness of the birth control pills.

The *antipsychotics* (or *neuroleptics*) are sometimes used during the acute stage of a manic episode, as they may work more quickly than a mood stabilizer started at the same time. Only in rare instances are antipsychotics prescribed in the maintenance phase of treatment, and then only if other agents are not effective. Any woman on an antipsychotic medication requires ongoing evaluation to determine whether any long-term side effects are present, such as abnormal motor movements (called tardive dyskinesias). (See Chapter Eleven for more information.)

Benzodiazepines, such as clonazepam (Klonopin), lorazepam (Ativan), and others, have several uses in patients with bipolar disorder. They are helpful in treating the agitation of an acute manic episode so that a lower dosage of the antipsychotic medications can be used. They may be used to provide treatment of symptoms such as anxiety, agitation, and insomnia. Long-term use of the benzodiazepines has not been well studied and should be done cautiously, as agitation and depression have been reported as side effects of these drugs.

Antidepressants are often prescribed for the bipolar patient who is suffering from depression. Although the mood-elevating effect of an antidepressant could theoretically "overshoot the mark" (improve the mood but cause someone to develop a manic episode), self-observation by the patient and careful monitoring by the physician can usually prevent this problem. In addition, certain antidepressants—impramine (Tofranil) and amitriptyline (Elavil)—may increase the frequency of mood swings and cause a woman with bipolar disorder to become a rapid cycler (see the description in the preceding section). During antidepressant therapy, physicians and patients must remain vigilant about side effects, including euphoria or feeling "too good."

Electroconvulsive Therapy

Electroconvulsive therapy (ECT) is a very effective treatment for both the depressive and manic phases of the bipolar disorder (see Chapter Nine). It offers an advantage in that its beneficial effects are seen much more quickly than those of medications. Despite this, it is rarely prescribed first, since most patients will respond to medications. It is usually reserved for patients who are so severely ill that they cannot wait for a medication response, or whose illness has not responded to other treatments, or for patients in whom medications should be avoided, such as pregnant women.

Education and Psychotherapy

Psychotherapy is often considered an important part of the treatment of women with bipolar disorder. Some studies have shown that patients do better when they receive both psychotherapy and medication. The goals of the psychotherapy are to improve medication compliance, reduce the risk of relapse, and improve social functioning. Supportive psychotherapy can be helpful in this regard, as can family therapy and psychoeducation (using psychotherapy sessions to teach the patient about her disease through role-playing and other techniques). Often, support groups can be very useful in keeping the woman informed of new treatment developments, as well as allowing her to develop a support system of people who are struggling with some of the same issues.

With bipolar disorder, it is particularly important that the patient, her family, and the psychiatrist work as a team. The efforts of each member of the team are needed to help identify the early warning signs of a manic episode, since the patient may be less willing or able to seek help when she is experiencing the pleasurable effects of hypomania (even though they inevitably lead to full-blown mania) or the poor judgment of a full-blown manic episode. It is equally important to identify the signals of an approaching depressive episode, since the patient is most vulnerable to despair during the "switch" between mania and depression. The team must also work together to ensure that the patient takes her medication exactly as prescribed, even during times when she feels well, in order to prevent recurrences. Bipolar disorder is clearly a chronic illness, and ongoing monitoring and assessment are essential.

Summary

Sleep disorders cause thousands of women to stumble through life half-awake and constantly tired. These disorders can be treated easily with light therapy and/or medications, but it's important to have the right combination for your particular problem, so an accurate diagnosis is essential. Be sure that the doctor you choose is experienced in the treatment of sleep disorders and that you follow his or her instructions carefully to get maximum benefit from the prescribed treatments.

Bipolar disorder is a chronic condition that causes serious psychiatric symptoms, such as mania and depression, and can result in suicide. Lithium and the other mood-stabilizing medications can prevent relapses (if taken on a daily basis) and allow the woman to lead a normal, productive life.

Resources

Sleep Disorders and Jet Lag

Further Reading

Becker, Barbara. *Relief from Sleep Disorders*. New York: Dell Publishing, 1993.

Dunkell, Samuel. *Good-bye Insomnia, Hello Sleep*. New York: Birch Lane Press, Carol Publishing Group, 1994.

Goldberg, Philip, and Daniel Kaufman. *Everybody's Guide to Natural Sleep*. Los Angeles: Jeremy Tarcher, 1990.

Hauri, Peter, and Shirley Linde. *No More Sleepless Nights*. New York: John Wiley, 1991.

Oren, Dan, Walter Reich, Norman Rosenthal, and Tom Wehr. *How to Beat Jet Lag*. New York: Henry Holt, 1993.

Regestein, Quentin, and David Ritchie. *Sleep: Problems and Solutions*. Mount Vernon, NY: Consumers Union, 1990.

Bipolar Disorder

National Alliance for the Mentally Ill
200 North Glebe Road, Suite 1015
Arlington, Virginia 22203
800–950–NAMI

National Depressive and Manic-Depressive Association
730 North Franklin, #501
Chicago, Illinois 60610
800–82N–DMDA

National Foundation for Depressive Illness
P. O. Box 2257
New York, New York 10116
800–248–4344

National Mental Health Association
1021 Prince Street
Alexandria, Virginia 22314–2971
800–969–NMHA

Further Reading

Duke, Patty, and Gloria Hochman. *A Brilliant Madness: Living with Manic-Depressive Illness*. New York: Bantam Books, 1992.

Goodwin, Fred, and Kay Redfield Jamison. *Manic-Depressive Illness*. New York: Oxford University Press, 1990.

Jamison, Kay Redfield. *An Unquiet Mind*. New York: Alfred A. Knopf, 1995.

Manning, Martha. *Undercurrents*. San Francisco: HarperSanFrancisco, 1994.

Notes

1. Walter Pierpaoli and William Regelson, *The Melatonin Miracle: Nature's Age-Reversing, Disease-Fighting, Sex-Enhancing Hormone*. New York: Simon & Schuster, 1995.

2. Diane Wood Middlebrook, *Anne Sexton: A Biography*. Boston, MA: A Peter Davison Book, Houghton Mifflin Company, 1991.

3. Kay Redfield Jamison, *Touched with Fire: Manic-Depressive Illness and the Artistic Temperment*. New York: Free Press, 1993.

CHAPTER 8

Seasonal Affective Disorder

It was mid January and Erica felt awful. She was listless, grumpy, and tired. She had gained fifteen pounds in the past three months, and that made her even more depressed. Things that previously had been enjoyable were now just too much effort, so she had stopped swimming at the club or going out to dinner with friends. Instead, she slept—up to fourteen hours a day. But sleeping just seemed to make it worse, and soon she was barely able to function. At work, her concentration was so poor and she had so little energy that even the simplest assignment seemed overwhelming. At home, it was even worse; her children were neglected, her husband distant, and the household routine had been abandoned as she struggled just to survive. The worst part was that Erica had had similar symptoms every January and February for the past five years.

Although Erica had always hated the dark, cold days of winter, it wasn't until her sophomore year of college that she had her first real symptoms. Perhaps it was because she was living away from home and there was no one to force her out of bed in the morning, or perhaps it was the heavy course load she was taking—whatever the reason, after Christmas break Erica began to fail, in every sense of the word. She couldn't get out of bed for some of her early morning classes; she completed only half her homework assignments and missed crucial deadlines. Even when she did manage to muster the energy needed to study, her concentration was so poor that she needn't have bothered.

By mid January, she felt so tired and hopeless that she went to the infirmary; there the health service physician diagnosed her as having infectious

mononucleosis, despite negative blood tests and a normal physical examination. The doctor told her to take it easy but didn't excuse her from any
of her classes since she had "such a mild case." And so it went, until
March when the days began to lengthen and Erica started to feel better.
In fact, it seemed that Erica's improvement was directly proportional to
the sun's increasing warmth. By early April, she was happy, energetic,
and able to concentrate, just in time to study effectively for final exams.

Over the next decade, Erica continued to have yearly wintertime
slumps. She joked that it was a good thing she was so productive for seven
months of the year, because the five months between November and
March were a "total loss." Erica finally sought help from her family
physician after reading a newspaper article about "winter blues." The
words had seemed to be describing her completely: recurrent wintertime
periods of depression, decreased energy, irritability, increased sleeping
and overeating (especially starchy foods and sweets). Her doctor confirmed that her diagnosis was seasonal affective disorder (SAD) and prescribed bright-light therapy. Erica was understandably skeptical that
sitting in front of a bright light source for forty-five minutes each morning
would help, but she complied with the doctor's recommendations. To her
surprise, three days later, she was feeling better, and within a week, she
had regained her energy and was no longer depressed or irritable. The oversleeping and overeating resolved over the next month.

Individual reports of SAD have appeared in the psychiatric literature
for decades, but it wasn't recognized as a separate disorder until the
1980s, when researchers at the National Institute of Mental Health noticed the seasonal pattern. Once recognized, SAD was found to be surprisingly common. The disorder is reported to affect 4 to 6 percent of
the population, and estimates suggest that one quarter of American
women may suffer from winter blues, a milder form of SAD.

The cause of SAD is unknown, but scientists suspect that it is related
to the shorter day length and decreased intensity of the sun in winter.
These seasonal changes affect not only the body's internal clock but
also the balance of particular messenger chemicals and hormones in
the brain. Because the hormones involved in SAD are so closely related
to the female hormones, women are more sensitive to SAD than are
men—particularly during women's childbearing years. The rates of
SAD among twenty- to forty-year-old women are so high that it caused
some to discount the syndrome; they attributed the symptoms to

women's increased stress associated with raising children or the struggles of balancing home and career. However, doctors now know that SAD is real; it causes measurable physical and psychological changes that are *not* all in the women's heads.

How to Know If You Have Seasonal Affective Disorder

You may have winter SAD if you have:

1. Extended periods of depression during the winter of several different years *and* no depressive episodes during the summer
2. Physical symptoms accompanying the depression—these symptoms include fatigue, increased sleeping, increased appetite, and decreased socialization.

Signs and Symptoms of Seasonal Affective Disorder (Table 8.1)

Seasonal Pattern:
Occurs every November through March
No symptoms in "opposite" months—that is, April through October

Impairment in Function:
Decreased capability at both home and work
Separates SAD from winter blues

Symptoms of Depression:
Feeling sad, blue, or depressed
Feeling overwhelmed and unable to cope
Feeling that life isn't worth living or that you'd be better off not waking up in the morning
Feeling isolated and alone
Feeling excess guilt or sense of responsibility
Low self-esteem
Decreased (absent) ability to find pleasure in activities
Frequent crying spells

Physical Changes:
Sleeping more and still feeling tired; having trouble getting out of bed in the morning
Lack of energy

Decreased sex drive
Changes in food preference—especially craving carbohydrates
Increasing appetite and/or binge eating; weight gain

Behavioral Changes:
Increased irritability
Decreased ability to think clearly and concentrate
Difficulty starting activities
Trouble getting things done
Failure at home, work, or school
Self-isolation and decreased socialization

Seasonal affective disorder is only diagnosed when the emotional and physical symptoms recur regularly during the winter months, cause distress and impairment, and do not occur in the summer. Of note, most patients with SAD will have some, if not all, of the *physical changes* listed in Table 8.1. It is these physical changes that distinguish SAD from the other types of wintertime blues.

The *mood changes* of SAD are similar to those of the other depressive disorders (Chapter Nine) and range from mild sadness to overwhelming despair. Often the depression that accompanies SAD is not as severe as other types of depression, and the woman may think that she just has the "blues." But if the low period lasts longer than two weeks and is associated with other SAD symptoms, it may represent a winter depression.

Anhedonia, or the inability to find pleasure in enjoyable activities, is common in SAD and may be the first sign of the disorder. This inability to enjoy life leads to social and emotional isolation—cocooning, in a sense. The SAD sufferer can't find pleasure in any of her usually enjoyable activities, so she pulls into herself and hibernates for the winter. Erica, for example, hibernated by not going swimming and by turning down dinner invitations from her friends. Other women find that they don't laugh in the winter; a joke that would be hysterically funny in July isn't even mildly amusing in January. Others might notice that their favorite TV show has become boring or that making love "just isn't worth the effort."

The SAD patient's *irritability* compounds her isolation. She feels so miserable that she just wants to be left alone, and her irritability ensures that everyone does so. Frequently, the onset of irritability is so insidious that it goes unnoticed or is blamed on others. Women with SAD tell us that everyone picks on them in winter, from their spouse to the grocery store clerk. But when this happens, it isn't the world that has become cranky—it is the SAD sufferer.

Increased sleep, fatigue, and lack of energy are frequent symptoms of SAD. They can severely undermine work and school performance, particularly when the woman is suffering from difficulties in focusing and concentrating—also common symptoms of SAD. Often, the energy required to do a simple task is more than the SAD sufferer can muster, but even when she is able to start a job, her inability to concentrate will prohibit her from finishing it, so checkbooks go unbalanced, letters unanswered, and work assignments undone. The impact of SAD on students and schoolteachers is particularly severe because of the overlap of the school calendar with the difficult winter months. (Some SAD researchers are so concerned about the impact of SAD on school performance that they have suggested that the school calendar should be reversed: classes in summer and vacation in winter.)

As in Erica's case, women with SAD may feel that they lose three to five months each year to sadness, fatigue, and concentration difficulties. While in summer they might sleep only seven to eight hours, in winter they sleep twelve to fourteen hours each night and still have trouble getting out of bed in the morning. In fact, it is a vicious cycle: the more they sleep, the less they are exposed to the beneficial effects of light and the worse the symptoms become, so that oversleeping on Saturday and Sunday results in missed work on Monday morning. (See also Chapter Seven's discussion of delayed sleep-phase disorder, a related condition.)

The *carbohydrate cravings* and *increased appetite* of winter SAD are sometimes the most troublesome physical symptoms. Women report that they switch from their summer "healthy" eating patterns to wintertime excess. It is not uncommon for women with SAD to gain ten to fifteen pounds each winter. If the weight isn't lost through summer restriction, obesity can result, with obvious effects on health and self-esteem.

Women with SAD often find themselves binge eating in response to food cravings, especially with chocolate, sweets, breads, potatoes, and other carbohydrates. Some researchers believe that the carbohydrate cravings are the body's way of trying to cure itself, since the carbohydrates are natural sources of chemical substances that may make the person feel less depressed. Others think that excessive carbohydrate consumption actually worsens the SAD by worsening the imbalance of brain chemicals.

If You Don't Have SAD, What Could It Be?

Other Types of Winter Blues (Table 8.2)

Winter Blues
Pattern is identical to SAD, but the winter blues don't last as long, are not as severe, and there is no significant interference with daily activities.

Holiday Blues or "Seasonally Affected Disorder"
Caused by holiday stress, including doing too much, stressful family relationships, and unrealistic holiday expectations.

Anniversary Grief Reactions
Related to a negative event or the loss of a loved one.

Other Depressive Disorders
Distinguished from SAD by the fact that the symptoms also occur in nonwinter months (see Chapter Nine).

Physical Illness
Illness: Viruses and low-grade bacterial infections can result in physical symptoms of SAD; usually would not recur with seasonal regularity.
Thyroid deficiency: Weight gain, excessive sleepiness, fatigue, sadness, and the "blues"—common but not seasonal.

Alcohol or Drug Abuse
Increased alcohol and drug use during winter months may result in physical symptoms and depression similar to SAD.

Vitamin B_6 or B_{12} Deficiency
These water-soluble vitamins are found in fresh fruits and vegetables; women may become deficient in them during the winter months because of decreased availability of fresh produce.

Winter Blues

Emily hated winter: getting up in the dark, coming home in the dark, and coping with five straight days of gray skies in between—what a downer! It was enough to give anyone the blues, and by mid January, Emily was feeling really blue. Oh, she could snap out of it if she had a crisis at work to attend to or if she went out for the evening with her friends, but she was in low spirits most of the time. Although she was sleeping and eating normally, she complained of being somewhat tired and listless. Emily felt like it had been winter for a year already. It was time for an escape. So she signed up for a Caribbean cruise and almost immediately felt better. Thinking about the warm sun and planning for the trip lifted Emily's spirits immensely, and she was soon back to her old self. She had a wonderful time on the vacation and returned to work rested, refreshed, and ready for spring.

The lack of physical symptoms accompanying Emily's depressed mood, the absence of impairment, and the rapidity of her recovery are all clues indicating that Emily had a bout of the winter blues rather than SAD. Severity is the key to distinguishing SAD from winter blues. The depression of SAD is deep and can lead to suicidal thoughts; the depression of the winter blues is milder and not associated with such despair. Similarly, while SAD causes significant interference with your performance on the job and ability to keep up at home, the winter blues results in only mild disturbances in functioning. Further, SAD sufferers typically have symptoms for several weeks to months at a time, while those with the winter blues feel blue for only a few days to a week at a time. Finally, SAD is associated with physical symptoms (described earlier), while winter blues are not.

Many patients with SAD report having had winter blues for several winters before the full spectrum of SAD symptoms was present. A physician experienced in the diagnosis of SAD can help sort out whether or not your symptoms are severe enough to be called SAD. Because the winter blues also respond to light therapy, people with recurrent episodes might wish to receive the benefits of this treatment.

Holiday Blues or "Seasonally Affected Disorder"

It was December 26 and Elizabeth was suffering from a bad case of the postholiday blues. Getting ready for Christmas had been so exhausting — baking dozens of cookies, decorating the house, buying and wrapping all the gifts (even her own!), and spending every spare minute since Thanksgiving in Christmas preparations. It was all just too much.

Elizabeth used to love getting ready for the holidays, but now she did it only because it was expected of her. And to make matters worse, no one seemed to appreciate her efforts. The children had greedily torn into their gifts and then gone off to play without even so much as a thank-you hug, her husband didn't notice the beautifully set table but did complain about having ham instead of turkey for Christmas dinner again this year, and her best friends had dashed off to attend someone else's party instead of lingering for a glass of eggnog and some home-baked cookies. She had expected Currier and Ives but had wound up with a Charlie Brown Christmas.

Like the winter blues, the holiday blues are neither as severe nor as persistent as SAD. Women with the holiday blues are typically overwhelmed by holiday preparations or dreading unpleasant family interactions. The best treatment is recognition and elimination of the unnecessary stress. To avoid "seasonally affected disorder," use your energy wisely and give of yourself only to the point where you still have something left. (We both know that this is easier said than done, but we'll say it anyway: put yourself first!) In the case of stressful family relationships or unrealistic holiday expectations, counseling or psychotherapy may be the best prescription.

In order to treat this version of the blues, you must fully understand and deal with the cause. Because decreased light exposure is not the cause of holiday blues, phototherapy is not the remedy. Before accepting a diagnosis of SAD or a prescription for light therapy, make sure that your clinician knows about any wintertime stressors in your life.

Anniversary Grief Reactions

Elaine, too, hates winter. Actually, she just hates the beginning of January; it depresses her. Elaine's mother died six years ago on January 5 of metastatic breast cancer. Elaine first found out about her mother's illness when they were watching the neighborhood Halloween parade, and her mother had complained of some fatigue and a nagging pain in the left side of her chest. The diagnosis was metastatic breast cancer. Despite the minor nature of her mother's initial complaints, the cancer had already spread too far to operate or to do much of anything except try to control the pain. The next two months were hell for Elaine and her mother. The two tried to spend as much time as possible together, but the pain was so severe that Mrs. Grant had to take increasingly large doses of morphine, and conversation was often impossible. Eventually, the pain became so excruciating that it was impossible to control, and Elaine secretly prayed that God would take her mother home. When she died in her sleep, Elaine was so relieved that she didn't think it was proper for her to grieve. And so she didn't that year.

But she did grieve the next year and in each of the following Januarys. The first year was by far the worst. Elaine had to miss several days of work because she just couldn't function. She spent hours thinking about her mother, wishing that she had been a better daughter, and longing for just one more chance to show her how much she loved her. Elaine felt miserable and had trouble concentrating, but she didn't exhibit any of the physical symptoms typically associated with SAD. If anything, she slept less and had a decreased appetite during this period. Further, rather than noticing an increase in the severity of her symptoms from year to year, her depressive periods lessened each subsequent year, until now she feels blue only for a few days around the anniversary of her mother's death.

Anniversary grief reactions are considered to be normal responses to the loss of a loved one or the death of a dream. They can occur not only in response to the death of a parent or friend but also after a miscarriage or abortion, a broken engagement, or being fired from a job. No matter what the trigger is, these grief reactions follow the pattern described in Elaine's case and usually can be distinguished easily from SAD.

When the annual depressive episodes don't seem to be lessening in intensity, the anniversary reactions may require treatment. Psychotherapy is usually the best treatment for problematic grief reactions, as it allows for resolution of the conflicts that help to perpetuate the grief.

Other Depressive Disorders

Seasonal affective disorder is one of several major depressive disorders. Other forms of depression should be considered before the diagnosis of SAD is assigned. In particular, bipolar disorder, with its episodic ups and downs, may resemble SAD, especially if the high (hypomanic) periods occur in summer and the depressive periods in winter. A careful history should be taken to identify any episodes of nonwinter depression, as well as symptoms of mania. For example, persons with SAD often feel particularly good in summer, but they do not have the euphoric highs or the negative symptoms of mania, such as irritability, recklessness, and excessive spending.

In some cases, it is impossible to separate SAD from bipolar disorder. Fortunately, there is evidence that phototherapy may help the depression of bipolar disorder as well as SAD, so such diagnostic ambiguity may not be too harmful. However, phototherapy can theoretically release symptoms of mania in a bipolar patient. An experienced health professional should always be involved in the diagnosis and treatment of SAD, and the patient should keep her follow-up appointments to ensure that the phototherapy is of optimum benefit.

Physical Illness, Substance Abuse, and Vitamin Deficiency

As listed in Table 8.2, medical illnesses and other disorders can mimic the seasonal depression of SAD (see also Chapter Five). For persons with alcohol and drug abuse problems, the holidays and the long cold winter nights are frequently associated with increased drinking and drug use. This increased use causes a variety of physical and psychological changes, including fatigue, irritability, and depression. If you use drugs or alcohol, be straight with your doctor about the amount and pattern of use so that this can be factored into your diagnosis.

Infections are more common in winter, so it is possible to have annual symptoms of decreased energy, malaise, and increased sleepiness. Although depressive symptoms can accompany such infections, they typically arise after a prolonged period of confinement and should not be confused with the depression of SAD. However, any person with her first bout of winter depression should have a thorough physical examination to rule out infectious mononucleosis and treatable illnesses. (Remember that SAD should *not* be diagnosed during the first winter of depression but only after a pattern of recurring winter depressions has been established.)

Thyroid hormone function should also be checked, as thyroid deficiencies can cause sadness, weight gain, and fatigue.

Vitamin B_6 and B_{12} deficiency should also be considered. Women are particularly prone to deficiencies of these water-soluble vitamins because of caloric restrictions, dietary patterns, and menstruation. Although a seasonal pattern should not be present, it might occur because of the lack of availability (or selection) of foods rich in these vitamins during the winter. B_6 and B_{12} vitamin deficiencies can cause symptoms of fatigue, decreased concentration, and sadness, which can be indistinguishable from the symptoms of SAD, or the deficiency could cause a woman's winter blues to worsen to full-blown SAD. Consequently, some clinicians prescribe B_6 and B_{12} supplements for all patients suffering from winter blues and SAD, although definitive proof of their effectiveness is still lacking. Health food stores and pharmacies sell B_6 and B_{12} supplements. There is no single right dosage, so ask your physician for a recommendation.

Treatments for Seasonal Affective Disorder

Once the diagnosis of SAD has been made, the treatment is surprisingly simple: light, light, and more light. Phototherapy and increased exposure to natural sunlight can decrease the physical and psychological symptoms of SAD for over 80 percent of patients. Exercise and careful attention to diet are useful additions to light therapy as they can reduce the physical symptoms of decreased energy and weight gain. Psychotherapy may play a role in helping the SAD victim learn how to cope with her disability, but psychotherapy alone has not been shown to be effective for the core symptoms of SAD. Medications, specifically tricyclic antidepressants and compounds that block serotonin reuptake, may be indicated for the treatment of severe SAD or when phototherapy alone is not sufficient.

Light Therapy

Phototherapy, or bright-light therapy, can be administered in a variety of ways, including light boxes, light visors, and dawn simulators. The amount of light required to treat SAD appears to depend on the method of delivery. Light boxes are designed to deliver between 2,500 and 10,000 lux, while light visors (which are similar to sun visors in appearance) have been found to be effective when delivering as little as 30 lux, perhaps because they shine the light more directly into the eyes. (Lux is a measure of the intensity of light. For comparison purposes, ordinary indoor lighting levels are about 300 to 500 lux, while light intensity outside on a bright summer day might exceed 20,000 lux.) Research studies have not yet established which light therapy is most effective, and this discussion will focus on the most widely available method: the light box.

Light boxes are available from a number of companies. If your physician cannot provide you with a referral, the National Organization for Seasonal Affective Disorder (NOSAD, listed in the "Resources" section) will send you a list of light-box manufacturers and distributors. Light boxes cost between $250 and $500 and are sometimes reimbursable through insurance carriers. Despite all the studies demonstrating their effectiveness, light boxes have not yet been approved by the Food and Drug Administration as medical devices, and insurance companies often refuse to pay for their purchase, even when prescribed by a physician. Nevertheless, it is worth a try to submit your receipt for insurance reimbursement, and the members of NOSAD have put together a packet to make that easier.

Fluorescent lamps have replaced full-spectrum bulbs in the majority of light boxes because of concerns about potentially harmful ultraviolet (UV) wavelengths. You should specifically inquire at the time of purchase what kind of light is contained in the box. Those boxes that use full-spectrum bulbs usually include a filter to screen out the UV wavelengths. If no such filter is provided, persons with sensitive skin or a family history of eye problems should ask that the full-spectrum bulbs be replaced by non-UV-emitting fluorescent bulbs (or they should buy a different model).

The time of day, dosage of light, and duration of treatment are individually determined. Some SAD patients are so sensitive to the effects of phototherapy that twenty minutes each morning of 2,500-lux light is sufficient to treat all their symptoms. Others use a 10,000-lux box (four times more powerful than the 2,500-lux box) and still must spend a total of ninety minutes in front of the light box to achieve maximum symptom relief. Usually, such therapy would be divided into two forty-five-minute periods, one done first thing in the morning and the other in the early afternoon. Most physicians recommend starting phototherapy administration in the morning to avoid the possibility of insomnia.

The benefits of phototherapy may be felt as early as the first session, although typically it takes about a week to feel better. Maximum benefit may not be evident for several weeks, so continued use is indicated if you have begun to see signs of improvement. The amount of phototherapy required to sustain a treatment response is frequently less than that required to obtain the initial response, so adjustments of the duration of light exposure may be necessary as therapy progresses.

Side Effects of Phototherapy. Side effects of phototherapy administration are mild and only rarely prohibit treatment. The most common complaints include headaches, eyestrain, irritability, overactivity, insomnia, fatigue, dryness of the eyes, nasal passages, or sinuses, and sunburn-type skin reactions (only problematic with the unshielded full-spectrum bulbs). Irritability and overactivity may indicate that the dosage of phototherapy is too high. Persons who feel irritable or "hyper" after finishing phototherapy treatments should check with their doctor to see if they should decrease the time they spend in front of the light box or shift positions to decrease direct exposure to the light. Eyestrain and headaches might indicate that the light box is too close to the face. Eighteen to twenty-four inches is the recommended distance for most light boxes. A humidifier used in the vicinity of the light box can decrease the drying effects of the treatment and prevent dryness of the eyes and mucous membranes. Persons who wear contact lenses should be particularly careful of the drying effects of the phototherapy boxes and may need to use artificial tears.

Despite the ease, safety, and effectiveness of phototherapy, it requires monitoring by a trained health professional. As already mentioned, phototherapy might precipitate mania in susceptible persons, and a physician would recognize this condition and prevent its progression. On the other hand, the phototherapy might not work, and a physician who is familiar with your case would be able to suggest alternative therapies.

Medications

The medications used to treat SAD are the same as those used to treat other forms of depression. (See Chapter Nine for a complete discussion of these medications.) Tricyclic antidepressants have been found to be effective, as have serotonin reuptake blocking compounds. Women suffering from SAD probably will only need to take the antidepressant medications during their symptomatic season. Symptom relief begins two to four weeks after starting the antidepressant medication but may not reach maximum benefit for several weeks more. If therapy is initiated late in the winter, it will be impossible to determine whether the medication was effective or whether the SAD symptoms resolved spontaneously as the days lengthened.

When SAD symptoms are severe and resistant to phototherapy, an antidepressant medication is probably necessary. In such cases, the side effects of the medication are clearly offset by the potential benefits. In other instances, although the SAD symptoms may be resistant to phototherapy, they are milder and less debilitating. The treating physician should explain the benefits and side effects of drug treatment and help the patient to make the decision. If you have to make such a choice, it may help to remember that antidepressant therapy, like phototherapy, is reversible, and if the side effects outweigh the benefits, the medication can be stopped. Again, a working partnership between the patient and her physician is essential.

Combination Therapy

A combination of phototherapy and drug treatment is becoming increasingly popular. Strict adherence to a phototherapy regimen is sometimes impossible—for example, when the SAD patient must travel for her job or when her hectic home life makes it impossible to find forty-five minutes each day to sit in front of the light box. So she may choose to use the light box for shorter periods and take antidepressant medications as well. The combination of phototherapy and medication appears to be more helpful than either treatment alone, so patients using both therapies may enjoy more rapid and complete recovery.

After a year or two of experimentation, Erica learned to begin using her light box in early November and to continue until late February to avoid her desperate winter plunge. She made sure that she exercised and watched her caloric intake to avoid winter weight gain. She kept a strict schedule of sleep and awake times to prevent oversleeping, and increased her light exposure by increasing indoor illumination, exercising outdoors during her lunch hours, and taking an annual winter vacation in the Caribbean. Although she has to make continued efforts each winter, Erica no longer suffers from SAD, and she hasn't lost the winter to the blues in a long time.

Summary

Seasonal affective disorder, or winter depression, causes seasonal sadness, irritability, and physical symptoms (overeating, oversleeping, and fatigue). Bright light phototherapy is usually sufficient to eradicate the winter blues. Antidepressant medications may be necessary in severe cases of SAD, and are also effective for women who cannot comply with a phototherapy regimen.

Resources

Patient Support Groups

The National Organization for Seasonal Affective Disorder (NOSAD) and the Society for Light Treatment and Biological Rhythms (SLTBR) offer support and information, including lists of knowledgeable physicians and sources of phototherapy equipment.

NOSAD
P. O. Box 451
Vienna, Virginia 22180

SLTBR
P. O. Box 478
Wilsonville, Oregon 97070

The patient organizations listed in Chapter Nine may also be helpful.

Further Reading

Rosenthal, Norman. *Winter Blues: Seasonal Affective Disorder: What It Is and How to Overcome It.* New York: Guilford Press, 1993. (For mail orders, call 1–800–FIX–BLUES.)

Smyth, Angela. *SAD: Who Gets it? What Causes It? How to Cure It.* London: Thorsons, 1990.

Thompson, C., and T. Silverstone, eds. *Seasonal Affective Disorder.* London: CNS Neuroscience Press, 1989.

CHAPTER 9

From **Sadness** to **Despair**

"Life is such a drag," said Anne's thirteen-year-old daughter, Meg.

Usually, Anne would correct her daughter, telling her that life was wonderful and that she should count her numerous blessings. But lately she just let Meg grumble. It was too much effort to argue. Besides, Anne's life was a drag right now; all the fun had gone out of her life, and where the pleasure used to be, there was just a kind of lonely, empty feeling. Little pleasures, like watching her favorite TV show or taking a walk at sunset, hadn't brought Anne enjoyment in over a month. Little problems, on the other hand, brought great distress. She would cry for hours after getting a parking ticket or having the dry cleaners lose her favorite blouse. In fact, it seemed like all Anne did was cry.

Crying had replaced eating, sleeping, and even making love. Long before Anne had begun to feel blue, her husband had started to complain that they never had sex anymore. Despite his complaints and her guilt, Anne couldn't muster either the energy or the interest to make love. It was like that part of her was shut off, trapped behind an impenetrable door along with all her other pleasures and passions. Food (even chocolate) didn't taste good, so she didn't eat. Aerobics didn't give her a "high" anymore, so she quit exercising. Sleep was elusive, so she didn't even try to go to bed until the late-late show was over. When Anne finally dozed off, she would toss and turn restlessly for a couple of hours, before awakening at 3:00 A.M. As she lay in bed and watched the clock read 3:30, 4:00, 4:30, and then 5:00, she would mull over the problems of the previous day and the possible problems of the day ahead. Usually, that would lead to more tears and more distress, and she would eventually get out of bed in disgust, angry with herself for being so weak and "such a baby!" All her life, Anne had been told that emotional problems such as hers were a sign of weakness and could be overcome by willpower. She just had to "tough it out."

During this time, Anne went to see her family physician, Dr. Smith, for an annual checkup. Fortunately, Dr. Smith was well versed in preventive care and administered the NIMH-D/ART questionnaire* to all her patients. Anne's responses indicated that she might be depressed, so Dr. Smith took a more detailed history about her mood, appetite, sleep, and energy. Although Anne's symptoms exactly fit the picture for a major depression, Dr. Smith knew that many other disorders can cause similar symptoms, so before making a diagnosis, she did a careful workup with a complete physical examination and several blood tests.

When Anne returned to see Dr. Smith, they talked about the physical disorders, such as thyroid disease, anemia, and other ailments, that had been ruled out. It was clear that the diagnosis was depression. Anne was still skeptical: How did she get depressed? She was usually a strong person who took good care of herself. What had she done wrong? Dr. Smith assured Anne that this depression was not the result of weak will or negative thinking but rather was a neuropsychiatric disorder that like other health problems, required specific treatment. Because Anne didn't want to see a mental health professional (after all, it was hard enough to admit that she was depressed, much less that she needed a psychiatrist), Dr. Smith recommended treatment with an antidepressant medication. Anne asked numerous questions about the medication, including what side effects she could expect and how long it would take before she started feeling better. She was relieved that the side effects were relatively minor but disappointed that it could take two, three, and sometimes even four weeks before her symptoms would begin to improve. Dr. Smith also told her that if the side effects were uncomfortable or if she started to feel more depressed, she should call her immediately.

The antidepressant medication did make Anne's mouth dry and her stools hard, but slowly, almost imperceptibly, her depression began to lift and she started to feel better. After the first month of treatment, she found that she was able to eat and sleep and even laugh occasionally. It took several more weeks for the depression to lift completely, but it eventually

---

*The NIMH-D/ART questionnaire is the National Institute of Mental Health Depression Awareness, Recognition and Treatment questionnaire.

did and Anne was able to get back to her normal activities—feeling well and happy.

Now, when Meg complains that "life is a drag," Anne replies, "No, Meg, depression is a drag. Life is pretty wonderful!"

How to Know If You Are Depressed

Everyone suffers from the blues once in a while, and in fact, the word *depression* is used to describe everything from disappointment, doldrums, and "the blues" to the kind of neuropsychiatric disorder described in Anne's case. In this chapter and throughout this book, however, we use depression to refer to "major depressive disorder," a neuropsychiatric condition characterized by persistent mood changes and specific physical symptoms. Even with that strict definition, depression is quite common. It is estimated that over six million American women suffer from major depression each year. For those women, the blues don't subside after a few days; they last for weeks at a time.

The National Institute of Mental Health has recently put forth a checklist that is being used by many doctors (like Dr. Smith) and in many clinics to help them recognize patients with depression. The checklist is as follows:[1]

1. Do you have a depressed mood most of the day, nearly every day, and has it been present for at least two weeks?
2. Have you had a markedly diminished interest in activities most of the day or nearly every day?
3. Have you had a significant change in your weight—either loss without dieting or a gain in weight?
4. Have you had insomnia or excessive sleepiness?
5. Have you felt sped up or slowed down?
6. Have you been fatigued or suffered a loss of energy?
7. Have you had feelings of guilt and worthlessness?
8. Have you had trouble making decisions and trouble concentrating?
9. Have you had recurrent thoughts of death or suicide?

Depression is likely when at least five of the nine questions are answered yes. It may seem incongruous that depression could cause both weight loss and weight gain, both insomnia and excessive sleepiness, and both acceleration and retardation (slowing down) of activities, but there are two kinds of depression. The first is melancholia or typical depression, which is characterized by weight loss, insomnia, and fatigue. Melancholic depression appears to be worse in the morning, and patients routinely complain of early morning insomnia, awakening at 3:00, 4:00, or 5:00 in the morning. The second type of depression, atypical depression, is characterized by the opposite symptoms of weight gain, excessive sleep (ten to fourteen hours a day), and feeling slowed down and fatigued.

Although these subtypes represent the most common presentations for depression, individual women may have symptoms of both typical and atypical depression. Further, some women with depression are also markedly tense, nervous, and anxious. They may be unnecessarily worried about things that normally would not disturb them or hypersensitive to stress or criticism. These women may have an anxious depression, which sometimes occurs in melancholic (typical) depression and other times indicates that two disorders are present—depression and an anxiety disorder.

Duration and Distress

Major depression is diagnosed when the symptoms have lasted for at least two weeks continuously and the mood changes are associated with emotional distress. It is not uncommon for someone to feel blue and even to have physical changes (such as decreased appetite or trouble sleeping) for a few days at a time, but this low mood would not be diagnosed as depression unless the symptoms are present for longer than two weeks. Bereavement, or the mourning of a deceased loved one, may cause a depressed mood lasting longer than two weeks; however, the grieving person usually isn't distressed by her depressed mood and considers her reaction to be "normal" (see "Grief Reactions" later in this chapter).

Distress is also characteristic of depression. The distress may be manifested as feelings of emptiness, profound sadness, hopelessness, and/or helplessness. In particular, feelings of hopelessness and helplessness have been found to be present in truly depressed individuals. When the woman becomes overwhelmed by her depression, she gives up hope of feeling better and feels helpless to improve her life. Normal blues, sadness over the loss of a loved one, and stress reactions are not associated with such distress; this is one of the ways they are differentiated from depression.

Suicide: A Special Risk of Depression

Jane drove home slowly from her job as a pediatric intensive care nurse. She drove slowly because it was hard to concentrate on her driving, and she was terrified that she might give in to the overwhelming need to end her pain and crash her car into a telephone pole. Her pain came from bearing the crushing burden of being so sad, so empty, and so overwhelmed. For her, all hope was gone. She knew she couldn't stand to live this way any longer, but somewhere, in the depths of her being, she knew that she didn't want to die either.

The sadness had started about two weeks earlier when Jane had lost three of her favorite patients in the same evening. Despite her training, her experience, and her efforts to steel herself against their inevitable deaths, she was overcome with grief. Her supervisor had suggested that she see one of the hospital's psychologists for some grief counseling, but Jane didn't think that was necessary. After all, this was part of her job; the children were patients, not family. There was no reason for her to go into a deep depression, as she had after her mother had died.

Jane took a clinical approach to her grief—observing it, measuring it, analyzing it—certain that she could keep it under control. And at first she did. Initially, there was only a gentle sadness that made her heart ache and her eyes fill with tears as she stood beside the empty cribs in the ICU; she missed her little patients so much. But gradually she began to feel a deep guilt that she had failed to save the children's lives: "Abby loved to watch the sunlight dancing on her mobile, but she'll never see it again"; "If only I had been more alert, maybe Julia and Sammy would be alive to see this sunset tonight"; and "Why did God spare me and take them?"

Jane's guilty ruminations overpowered her clinical detachment, and she sank into a deepening depression. Her self-loathing increased, and she felt that she didn't deserve to be alive. With that knowledge came a sense of incredible loneliness; she felt unworthy of her family's love and unable to stay connected to them. There was no longer any hope of rescue. It was impossible to go on. And so she drove slowly.

Some studies suggest that as many as one in ten women with severe depression will kill themselves. The number who attempt suicide is much, much higher—nearly eight times as many. Risk factors for suicide and for suicide attempts have been summarized in four categories: genetic (close relative that committed suicide), psychiatric (history of depression, schizophrenia, or other serious psychiatric disorder), psychological (recent loss or failure, decreased coping mechanisms, and many others), and biological (for example, low levels of the brain messenger chemical, serotonin). But the risk factors are only statistical and are calculated for large populations. They are meaningless for an individual woman.

If the risk factors listed here are not responsible for a woman's suicide, what is? Frequently, it is despair—despair about her inability to save herself, despair about the improbability of rescue by others, and despair about the impossibility of going on without being rescued. If you or someone you care about is depressed, it is important to ask the following questions:

1. Have you been thinking a lot about death?
2. Have you been wishing that you were dead or that you wouldn't wake up in the morning?
3. Have you had thoughts about hurting yourself? Killing yourself?
4. Have you made a plan to hurt yourself?

If the answer to any of these questions is yes, you need to get help immediately.*

What Might You Have If You Don't Have Depression?

Stress Responses and Variations of Normal

Being overworked, underpaid, and underappreciated can cause anyone to become down or "blue." Many American women who are trying to balance home, family, and career fall into this category. They are chronically stressed and consequently may feel overwhelmed and unhappy. However, they're not necessarily depressed. These "stressed-out women" have only a few bad days in a row, and even then, they eat and sleep normally and can still feel pleasure. The only "prescription" needed is to reduce stress. Counseling or short-term therapy may help

---

*Asking questions about suicide does *not* put ideas into someone's head—it does *not* cause the person to commit suicide. Therefore, if someone you care about is depressed, you can ask her the questions listed above without worry that you will plant the idea in her head. If she answers yes to any of them, get help immediately.

the woman identify and eliminate some sources of stress and learn more effective means of coping with others.

If you're not sure whether or not you're depressed, ask yourself the following questions: Can someone or something make me happy? Do I hear myself laughing occasionally? Do I enjoy good food, good friends, good sex? Am I sleeping and eating normally? If not, then you may be depressed. But if so, then the most likely "diagnosis" is the stressed-out blues. Even women suffering from stress-related mood changes may benefit from therapy (see Chapter Three). Often, counseling or self-help groups are the best relief for stress-related symptoms.

Grief Reactions and Adjustment Disorder

Everyone experiences grief when a loved one dies, and several days to weeks of sadness (sometimes accompanied by physical symptoms) are common and even expected. But we are less prepared for the grief that comes from the breakup of a marriage, the loss of a job, or a child's failure. Each of these circumstances represents the loss of a dream or ambition, and each stirs up feelings of anger as well as grief. There is an element of anger in all grief reactions, and some have said that anger turned inward *is* depression. Psychotherapy can be helpful in identifying and resolving the cause of the anger, as well as in dealing with the consequences of the loss.

June's husband, Bill, had recently lost his job and wasn't ready to start looking for a new one yet. In order to make ends meet, June was working a lot of overtime, and Bill had promised to take over for her at home, but he hadn't. In fact, he wasn't even doing his regular share. Instead, he slept till noon and then lounged around in his bathrobe the rest of the day. So June was forced to work twelve hours a day at the shop and then come home to a dirty house, unwashed dishes, and children sleeping in the clothes that they had worn to school that morning. She couldn't cope. She wanted to be angry at her husband, but how could she be? He was obviously depressed over losing his job and needed her love and support right now.

Although she couldn't admit it, June was deeply angry. Because she had no outlet for it, the anger turned against herself so that she began to feel depressed and anxious. Because the symptoms had such a clearly defined trigger, they most likely represent an adjustment disorder (a psychologically triggered psychiatric disorder—it too has biological underpinnings, even though it's caused by an external stress). However, the symptoms could easily persist or worsen to the point where they met the criteria for depression. (In neuropsychiatric terms, the adjustment disorder sets the stage for a biological depression to follow.)

For adjustment disorders, treatment is generally directed at removing the source of stress, using psychotherapy or marriage therapy to work through the crisis situation. In this particular case, the ideal solution would be for June's husband to get therapy for his depression and then to find another job. Meanwhile, the couple should be encouraged to recognize June's needs and to relieve some of her burdens and stress.

Dysthymia

Dysthymia is chronic low-grade depression. Patients with dysthymia feel low or unhappy and have numerous physical symptoms, including fatigue, feelings of tiredness, poor or excessive appetite, and sleep difficulties. Dysthymia is separated from major depression by its duration—with dysthymia, the symptoms last much longer. Dysthymia is diagnosed when patients feel depressed for most of the day, more days than not, for at least *two years*. If you think about feeling low or blue for over two years, you will quickly realize that the consequences of dysthymia are low self-esteem, feelings of failure, and a sense of hopelessness and helplessness.

The symptoms and consequences of dysthymia completely overlap those of depression; indeed, the distinction between dysthymia and chronic major depression is so difficult to make that it can be made only by a trained therapist. However, since both disorders benefit from similar therapies, the specific diagnosis may be less important then recognizing the presence of a depressive disorder.

Medical Illnesses That Masquerade as Depression

Depression is by far the most common psychiatric symptom to be caused by physical ailments (see also Chapter Five). The physical disorders that can cause depression include:

- Endocrine problems such as diabetes or pituitary, adrenal, or thyroid disorders
- Cancer (even before the diagnosis is made)
- Infections, especially with viruses like the Epstein-Barr virus

- Neurological disorders, such as Parkinson's disease, Alzheimer's disease, and strokes
- Collagen vascular diseases, like systemic lupus
- Heart disease (including heart attacks) and open-heart surgery
- Vitamin and mineral deficiencies and/or states of excess
- Alcoholism and substance abuse.

In addition, depression can co-occur with many medical illnesses and with any of the psychiatric disorders, including the anxiety disorders, eating disorders, obsessive-compulsive disorder, and personality disorders. It is because so many medical conditions masquerade as depression and so many other disorders may complicate the treatment of depression that we believe an experienced physician should examine any patient with depressive symptoms who is considering treatment with a nonphysician therapist. The consultation could be limited to the diagnostic evaluation but must include a complete history, physical examination, and laboratory studies sufficient to rule out hormonal problems, anemia, and other treatable conditions. Unfortunately, it isn't enough to see just any physician; rather, you need to see one who is conscious of the physical and psychological manifestations of each of the masquerading conditions. Some of these conditions are detailed here.

Thyroid Disease

Thyroid disorders—including Grave's disease, Hashimoto's thyroiditis, hyperthyroidism (excess thyroid hormone), and hypothyroidism (thyroid hormone deficiency)—are some of the most common medical causes of depression in women. (Notice that both hyperthyroidism and hypothyroidism can cause depression, even though they are direct opposites.) Any of the thyroid diseases can cause mood changes, weight gain or weight loss, insomnia or excessive sleeping, feelings of being revved up or slowed down, fatigue, and troubles with concentration or indecisiveness. When the mood changes are severe, they can be accompanied by anhedonia (loss of interest or pleasure in usually enjoyable activities). Thus, seven of the nine criteria for major depressive disorder can be met merely on the basis of thyroid disease alone.

To diagnose thyroid disease, your doctor should take a complete history, perform a physical examination, including carefully palpating (feeling) the thyroid gland (located in the front lower third of your neck) to detect masses or enlargement, and order several blood tests. If the blood tests show that there is a deficiency of thyroid hormone (hypothyroidism), thyroid hormone replacement is required. In other instances, the thyroid levels in the blood may be too high; in this case, your doctor will need to determine whether the thyroid gland is hyperactive (as with Grave's disease and hyperthyroidism) or whether an autoimmune disorder is interfering with the function of the thyroid hormone (such as Hashimoto's thyroiditis). The therapy for Grave's disease and Hashimoto's thyroiditis is more complicated than that for simple hypothyroidism, and care by an endocrine specialist may be necessary.

Collagen Vascular Diseases

The collagen vascular diseases are a widely varied group of disorders that have in common the production of antibodies (infection-fighting cells and their components) that mistakenly attack the cells within the body. When this happens, the antibodies are called autoantibodies (self-fighting antibodies). In systemic lupus erythematosus (commonly known as lupus), the autoantibodies attack the joints, the brain, the heart, and other tissues within the body. The particular complex of symptoms depends on which autoantibodies are being produced; a woman with autoantibodies that attack only the brain cells might have psychiatric symptoms as her only manifestation of lupus. Again, a careful history, complete physical examination, and selected blood tests should be sufficient to rule out a collagen vascular disease.

Vitamin and Mineral Deficiencies

Although the scientific evidence is sparse that vitamin and mineral deficiencies can cause depressive symptoms, most physicians have had a few patients in which depression and physical signs of fatigue, loss of energy, lack of interest in sex, and changes in weight and sleep were related to iron-deficiency anemia, zinc deficiency, or failure to take in enough of the B vitamins. Because of the blood lost during menstruation, many woman are chronically deficient in both iron and zinc. Further, use of oral contraceptives and chronic dieting (or even just decreasing calorie intake to a level necessary to maintain a reasonable weight in the face of a sedentary lifestyle) can lead to deficiencies, not only in iron and zinc and the other trace minerals but also in the B-complex vitamins.

The physical symptoms accompanying the vitamin deficiencies are quite similar to those seen in major depressive disorders; they include mood changes, fatigue, weakness, loss of energy, difficulty sleeping, weight loss or weight gain, and even trouble concentrating. The diagnosis of vitamin deficiency is usually made after detecting anemia (anemia results because the blood cells require iron, zinc, and the B-complex vitamins in order to be formed properly). A simple blood test can diagnose anemia, but because there are no inexpensive tests for vitamin levels, many physicians suggest that women supplement their diet with iron, zinc, and the water-soluble vitamins (B complex, C, and thiamine).*

Infectious Mononucleosis

Infectious mononucleosis or "mono" is commonly thought to affect only college students, but it can occur at any age, including childhood and middle age. Although people with a classic case of infectious mononucleosis have a sore throat, swollen glands, large spleen, fatigue, and low-grade fever, the disorder has many faces. Mono can look just like depression: feelings of sadness, loss of interest or pleasure in activities, weight changes, and loss of energy. Again, a simple blood test is usually sufficient to point the physician in the direction of infectious mononucleosis, although to confirm the diagnosis it is necessary to check specifically for the Epstein-Barr virus.

Chronic Mono and Chronic Fatigue Syndrome

Chronic fatigue syndrome, or CFS, is discussed in detail in Chapter Five. It is closely related to chronic mononucleosis (which is thought to result from a reactivation of an Epstein-Barr virus infection). In both CFS and chronic mono, the essential diagnostic feature is persistent: excessive fatigue. The fatigue is accompanied by other, more transient symptoms of aching muscles and joints, headache, sore throat, painful lymph nodes, muscle weakness, sleep troubles, trouble concentrating, and sadness. Some patients experience more sadness and mood swings than they do physical symptoms, and in those instances, even experienced physicians find it difficult to determine whether the patient has depression or CFS.

---

*Excessive supplementation of the water-soluble vitamins is probably not harmful because they are excreted in the urine; however, taking excessive quantities of any vitamin is not helpful, and excesses of vitamins A, D, E, and K must be avoided because they are harmful in high doses.

Depression is known to affect up to one-third of patients with severe medical conditions such as stroke, heart disease, diabetes, cancer, and Parkinson's disease. In the case of Parkinson's disease, the depression may be the direct result of the same biochemical abnormality that causes the motor symptoms of tremor, inability to move, and weakness. In the other conditions, it may be difficult to tell whether the depression is a direct result of the underlying physical ailment or is the secondary result of poor health and fears about one's mortality.

Jody had been diagnosed with breast cancer in her right breast in 1986. At that time, she sailed through a mastectomy and recovered in record time. She considered herself fortunate to have had no evidence of cancer in the lymph nodes and eagerly counted off the months until her five-year checkup. When the examination revealed that she was cancer free, she rejoiced and at last allowed herself to be considered a cancer survivor.

Six months later, she went to her family physician with complaints of insomnia, fatigue, weight loss, and feeling sad. The doctor found a lump in her left breast that was subsequently diagnosed as a new cancer — unrelated to her first. Devastated by the news, Jody underwent a second mastectomy, but this time she didn't bounce back. Instead, she took to her bed for a month, refusing to participate in the prescribed physical therapy and snapping at anyone who dared to disturb her. She cried easily and often and continued to have a poor appetite and difficulty sleeping. When she saw her doctor for her one-month checkup, he told her that she was suffering from a major depression and prescribed an antidepressant.

Jody refused to take the medication and hoarded the pills until she had enough to overdose. Fortunately, the overdose didn't do any serious harm, and it brought her to the attention of a psychiatrist experienced in treating breast cancer victims. The psychiatrist was able to help Jody work through her anger at being afflicted a second time, her loss of control, and her fear that the second cancer would be fatal. As she came to terms with these issues, she began to feel better, but it was clear that she still had significant depressive symptoms remaining and that she would benefit from further treatment of her biological depression. This time she took the antidepressant medication exactly as prescribed, and she soon noticed that her symptoms were improving.

As Jody's story unfolded, it became clear that her initial depressive symptoms weren't the result of a simple abnormality of brain messenger chemical levels but rather the interplay of a number of biological and psychological factors. In such cases, drug therapy alone will not be sufficient to relieve the depression.

Depression as a Side Effect of Medications

The psychological side effects of common medications are detailed in Chapter Five and will not be repeated here, except to remind you that many medications have been reported to cause depressive symptoms. Anytime depressive symptoms appear shortly after a medication is started or the dosage of a medication has been increased, it is sensible to consider that the depression is a side effect of the medication. Discuss this possibility with your doctor, and ask if the medication should be stopped or changed in order to determine if it is causing the symptoms. Remember that over-the-counter medications, such as cough and cold preparations, allergy pills, and diet pills, can also cause depressive symptoms.

The most common medications associated with depression include:

1. Drugs used to treat high blood pressure, such as Reserpine, the beta-blockers, and alpha-methyldopa
2. Hormones, including birth control pills, prednisone, and anabolic steroids
3. Histamine blockers used to treat ulcer symptoms, such as cimetidine and ranitidine (particularly in patients who have other illnesses)
4. Anticonvulsants or medications used to treat seizure disorders (particularly phenobarbital and carbamazepine)*
5. Levodopa, the drug used to treat Parkinson's disease
6. Antibiotics, including dapsone, isoniazid, amphotericin, and others.

Treatment of Depression

If you think that you might be suffering from depression, when, how, and from whom should you seek treatment? A good rule of thumb is that you should seek help whenever you are concerned about your ability to function or if your symptoms have persisted for more than two weeks. You *must* seek help immediately if you are having thoughts about suicide.

---

*These drugs can cause depression, but more frequently they cause nonspecific slowing and sedation.

As mentioned earlier, one of the first places to turn is to your family physician. Be open and candid about the impact of your symptoms on your daily life. Question your doctor about the possibility of a diagnosis of depression, remembering that many physical disorders can cause depressive symptoms as well. You can expect your family doctor to do a careful history (including an assessment of psychiatric and medical problems in your family members), a complete physical examination, and some blood tests, such as tests for anemia and thyroid hormone abnormalities. Once it has been determined that major depression is the most likely diagnosis, your physician may choose to treat you herself, or she may refer you to a mental health professional. There are two main categories of treatment for depression: psychological and pharmacological.

Psychological Treatments for Depression

Psychological treatments include a variety of methods ranging from traditional "talk" therapy to cognitive-behavior therapy. These therapies are used alone to treat mild to moderate depression and in combination with medications for severe depression. In addition to reducing depressive symptoms in the short term, psychological therapies have proved useful in improving the long-term outcome by reducing stressful situations that might prolong the depressive episode or provoke relapses.

Cognitive-behavior therapy of depression is based on the theory that changing your behaviors and your patterns of thinking will lead to changes in your emotional state. Because women with depression feel sad and hopeless, they tend to have negative thoughts. These negative thoughts lead to poor self-esteem, pessimism, hopelessness, and helplessness, and these in turn lead to more negative thoughts. Replacing the negative thoughts with positive ones breaks the cycle and leads to self-confidence, optimism, and hopefulness. The cognitive-behavior therapist works with the patient to reframe "automatic" negative thoughts as realistic, positive ones. For example, the automatic thought might be "I'm depressed so I can't enjoy myself at the concert"; this might be reframed as "I've been depressed and deserve a treat, so I will enjoy myself at the concert tonight."

Behavior therapy differs from cognitive-behavior therapy in that it focuses only on observable, measurable behaviors. It is even more goal-oriented than cognitive-behavior therapy. The patient is given homework assignments—specific tasks that she must accomplish by the next therapy session—and the therapist monitors her progress, encouraging her to move forward and preventing backsliding. The goal of behavior therapy is to replace negative, maladaptive "habits" with positive behaviors. As in cognitive-behavior therapy, the assumption is that this positive outlook will influence the emotional state and reduce the depression. In addition to specific homework assignments, the patient is encouraged to resume her social life and participate in pleasurable activities. Since these activities will bring enjoyment (probably only slight at first), they may also help to lift the depression. Even if they don't, the activities help to break the negative cycle of depression-causing fatigue and lassitude, which causes more depression, which causes more fatigue and lassitude, and so forth.

Cognitive-behavior therapy and behavior therapy have been found useful for one-third to one-half of the patients able to participate in treatment. However, it is important to note that these therapies require the patient to participate actively in treatment; for this reason, moderately to severely depressed women may not be able to benefit.

Interpersonal psychotherapy is used quite frequently to treat mild to moderately severe depression. There are two main types of interpersonal psychotherapy: supportive and dynamic. Both techniques appear to be helpful in depression. In *supportive psychotherapy*, the therapist provides support and "shoring up" for the patient. The patient's family may also be enlisted in the support of the patient. The goal of supportive therapy is not merely to reduce the severity of the depression but also to help the patient cope with the physical and emotional symptoms until they go away on their own. Most depressive episodes will resolve spontaneously within a year or two. Other treatments (such as medications, cognitive-behavior therapy, and dynamic psychotherapy) can help speed recovery as well as prevent some of the more serious consequences of depression, including suicide.

Dynamic psychotherapy or "talk therapy" is based on the premise that current difficulties are often the result of unresolved past conflicts. By bringing these conflicts into present awareness, the patient can understand and deal with them in a more appropriate manner. In dynamic psychotherapy, the patient is encouraged to talk about past relationships and to try to understand how these relationships are impacting her present experiences. The therapist acts as a guide helping to identify patterns of behavior and thereby building greater self-awareness and understanding. This allows the patient to gain control over her life—to make more positive choices, to form more satisfying interpersonal relationships, and to develop a healthier lifestyle. As with the other psychological treatments, these changes eventually lead to an improved emotional state: the woman feels better about herself and her life, and the depression lifts.

An abbreviated form of interpersonal psychotherapy (brief dynamic psychotherapy) is also used for depression. In *brief dynamic psychotherapy*, the woman takes on only those issues that are directly related to the depressive symptoms. This treatment has a slightly lower rate of effectiveness than other types of psychotherapy, but this may be offset by the fact that the short course of therapy is substantially cheaper than traditional psychotherapy. An example of the utility of psychotherapy follows:

Joan had lost her mother the previous year to uterine cancer and was still feeling quite depressed. (Any prolonged grief reaction or one in which the symptoms cause the woman distress may represent a major depressive episode.) Joan went into individual psychotherapy with a psychologist in order to explore the reasons for her continued symptoms. In weekly sessions, she learned that her grief was actually a manifestation of the deep-seated anger that she still held for her mother's withdrawn, distant parenting style. Joan had grown up feeling neither loved nor wanted. Joan was never able to confront her mother about these feelings, so when her mother was suffering the ravages of uterine cancer, it was Joan's turn to be emotionally distant.

When her mother died, Joan had tremendous guilt over her failure as a daughter—she too had failed to provide needed love and support—but she also had profound feelings of anger toward her mother for those still-unfulfilled childhood needs. In therapy, Joan was able to work through these feelings and eventually to let go of the anger. When she did so, her depression lifted, and she was able to get on with her life.

Selection of the ideal psychotherapy is often difficult for a depressed patient; that is why it is important to seek initial consultation with a psychiatrist or mental health professional experienced in a variety of treatments. Before starting therapy, you should know if the treatment has been shown to be effective for your kind of depression, know what the goals are (that is, is it time-limited and focused only on the current problems or more far-reaching?), and if the therapist is experienced in the use of this particular therapy for patients with major depressive disorder. A therapist who has demonstrated success in the use of behavior therapy for anxiety disorders may or may not be successful in applying these techniques to the treatment of your depression; you may be better off with a therapist experienced in treating depression. How progress will be measured should also be made clear from the beginning of the therapy. If there has not been any significant improvement in six weeks or nearly complete recovery in twelve weeks, then the therapy might need to be changed.

Pharmacological Treatments for Depression

The antidepressant medications have helped literally millions of women to recover from major depressive illnesses. But they are powerful medicines and should be taken only when prescribed by a physician and in the manner recommended. The depressions that respond best are those in which the mood changes are moderate to severe and are accompanied by physical symptoms. The patients who respond best are those who want drug treatment, rather than a nonpharmacological therapy, since compliance (taking the medication exactly as prescribed) strongly influences outcome.

There are five major classes of medications used to treat depression. These include:

1. The tricyclic antidepressants such as amitriptyline (Elavil), desipramine (Norpramin), doxepin (Sinequan), imipramine (Tofranil), nortriptyline (Aventyl, Pamelor), protriptyline (Vivactil), and trimipramine (Surmontil)
2. The heterocyclic antidepressants such as amoxapine (Asendin), bupropion (Wellbutrin), maprotiline (Ludiomil), and trazodone (Desyrel)
3. The selective serotonin reuptake inhibitors (or SSRIs) such as fluoxetine (Prozac), fluvoxamine (Luvox), venlafaxine (Effexor), paroxetine (Paxil), and sertraline (Zoloft)
4. The monoamine oxidase inhibitors (or MAOIs), such as isocarboxazid (Marplan), phenelzine (Nardil), and tranylcypromine (Parnate)
5. Anxiolytics, such as alprazolam (Xanax), diazepam (Valium), and buspirone (Buspar).

The anxiolytic medications should be reserved for use in melancholic depressions in which there are significant anxiety symptoms. The other antidepressants can be used for both typical (melancholic) and atypical depressions.

Tricyclic antidepressants frequently cause dry mouth, constipation, and difficulty with urination. The tricyclics can also cause weight gain, drowsiness, changes in blood pressure (particularly low blood pressure when first standing up) that could lead to fainting, and disturbances of the heart rhythms, which could be particularly problematic for women already suffering from some kind of heart disease, including mitral valve prolapse. The parent compounds, such as imipramine, tend to have more side effects than the second-generation compounds, such as desipramine. So if side effects are a concern, it may be worth it to pay the extra money to get the second-generation compounds.

The *selective serotonin reuptake inhibitors* (SSRIs) have enjoyed wide popularity because they are just as effective as the tricyclic antidepressants but have fewer side effects. Because these medications block serotonin reuptake, they can be associated with severe headaches, particularly in patients who have previously suffered from migraines or among women using oral contraceptives. They can also cause nausea, vomiting, diarrhea, or constipation. Side effects are a particular concern with fluoxetine because the drug stays in the body such a long time. Even one dose can take up to fourteen days to disappear, so if a woman has difficulty with fluoxetine side effects, she can be bothered for up to two weeks before the medicine is finally cleared from her body.

The *monoamine oxidase inhibitors* (MAOIs) are not usually first-line treatments for depression because they have severe dietary restrictions and can have very toxic (even lethal) interactions with other medications. If a patient has been unable to tolerate or has failed to respond to the tricyclic antidepressants and/or the SSRIs, then MAOI treatment may be indicated. The MAOIs appear to relieve depression by increasing the amounts of key brain chemicals. The drugs have a stimulating effect (unlike the sedating effects of the tricyclics) and can cause insomnia, restlessness or agitation, dizziness, and weight gain.

Frequently, patients ask us, "How long should I continue to take my antidepressant medication?" There is no one right answer, and this topic should be discussed regularly between the individual patient and her physician. However, as a general rule, once a patient has been symptom free for at least six to twelve months, the medication dose might be tapered, with careful watch for the recurrence of symptoms. If the symptoms don't recur after the medicine has been discontinued, then the patient is considered to be in remission and may even have been "cured" of her depression. On the other hand, long-term therapy is needed by many patients, particularly those who have had a previous depressive episode (the chances of having another depression increase dramatically when a woman has had two separate depressive episodes) and those who have other family members with a history of recurrent depressions or bipolar disorder (episodes of mania and depression as described in Chapter Seven). In these instances, antidepressant medications are continued indefinitely in order to prevent future depressions.

Electroconvulsive Therapy or Shock Therapy

The most effective treatment for severe depression is electroconvulsive therapy or ECT. Formerly known as shock therapy, ECT involves giving a series of treatments in which a small, controlled jolt of electric current is sent to the brain to induce a seizure. With modern anesthesia the ECT treatments bear little resemblance to the shock therapy used to torture patients in *One Flew over the Cuckoo's Nest*. However, ECT is still used only as a last resort in most instances, perhaps because of the memory loss and confusion that can result.

We highly recommend a recently published book, *Undercurrents* by Dr. Martha Manning,[2] to anyone considering ECT. The book details one woman's struggle with an overwhelming melancholic depression and her recovery from that depression following a series of six ECT treatments.

Summary

Any depressed mood that lasts longer than two weeks or is accompanied by physical symptoms (such as fatigue, lethargy, appetite changes, sleep problems, or difficulties with concentration) is defined as a major depression. Depression not only robs a woman of the ability to lead a normal, productive life, it also causes great emotional distress and can even progress to the point where the depressed woman feels so hopeless and helpless that suicide seems to be the only way out. Antidepressant medications and psychotherapy are both effective treatments for depression and offer real help to the millions of women who are affected each year.

Resources

National Alliance for the Mentally Ill
200 North Glebe Road, Suite 1015
Arlington, Virginia 22203
800–950–NAMI

National Depressive and Manic-Depressive Association
730 North Franklin, #501
Chicago, Illinois 60610
800–82N–DMDA

National Foundation for Depressive Illness
P. O. Box 2257
New York, New York 10116
800–248–4344

National Mental Health Association
1021 Prince Street
Alexandria, Virginia 22314-2971
800–969–NMHA

Further Reading

Emery, Gary. *Getting Un-Depressed: How a Woman Can Change Her Life Through Cognitive Therapy.* New York: Touchstone Books (Simon & Schuster), 1988.

Greist, John H., and James W. Jefferson. *Depression and Its Treatment.* Rev. ed. New York: Warner Books, 1992.

Hirschfeld, Robert M. *When the Blues Won't Go Away: New Approaches to Dysthymic Disorder and Other Forms of Chronic Low-Grade Depression.* New York: Macmillan, 1991.

Further information is also available from:
Office of Scientific Information
National Institute of Mental Health
5600 Fishers Lane, Room 7C-02
Rockville, Maryland 20857
301–443–4513

Notes

1. For more information, contact the Office of Scientific Information and the Depression Awareness, Recognition, and Treatment (D/ART) Program; National Institute of Mental Health, Room 10–85, 5600 Fishers Lane, Rockville, MD 20857.
2. Martha Manning, *Undercurrents* (San Francisco: HarperSanFrancisco, 1994).

CHAPTER 10

"On the Outside Looking In"

From her chair, Dr. Stone watched Jane curl up in the corner of the black leather couch and begin to cry. As she sobbed, Jane seemed to get smaller and younger, retreating from the painful memories that came as quickly as her tears. She cried for a very long time as Dr. Stone sat silently beside her. The therapist knew that this was a time of acceptance rather than reassurance, of empathy and not words, so she sat quietly. And then after a while, Jane straightened, her crying slowed, and she began to speak, to remember, to feel.

It had taken months of therapy to reach this point. Initially, Dr. Stone had focused the sessions on helping Jane to feel safe—safe from her battering husband, safe from her abusive family, and safe enough in therapy to confront the lifetime of memories that had been buried beneath layers of denial. Jane's denial served to protect her from the bad memories and the unpleasant feelings, but it also blocked out all of the good things. It took everything—all of her memories and all of her emotions. Jane had huge holes in her memory; she couldn't remember anything at all before the age of sixteen, and she had trouble remembering long periods of time even after she had left home. She still had frequent gaps, blank minutes or hours where it was as if she hadn't even been there—as if she had been locked outside herself.

Jane's emotions were locked up equally tightly. She could feel nothing, absolutely nothing. Over the years, this numbness had become unbearably frightening. Jane would do anything to get beyond it and prove that she was still alive—cutting herself, burning herself, or provoking her husband beyond the limits of his control. Sometimes, only his beatings could cut through the numbness. But these solutions didn't last, they didn't help, and the last time, they had nearly killed her. So Jane had started therapy; it was the only way to end the numbness once and for all.

Jane's story is that of every woman who has been abused or traumatized. She is the stranger who was beaten and verbally abused as a child. She is your colleague who was sexually molested by her teacher or her uncle or her stepfather. She is your friend who was raped by her date last night. She is your sister who was the unlucky one singled out for your father's sexual abuse. She is you. You might be the one who wants to huddle in the corner of the couch. You might be the one who struggles to find the words, to understand the feelings. You might be the one who needs to know that there is acceptance, there is help, there is hope.

The Aftermath of Trauma

Any woman who has suffered physical or psychological abuse may continue to suffer its reverberating repercussions throughout her life. Disturbances in consciousness, memory, perception, or identity can all occur in the aftermath of trauma. These repercussions are different for each woman. There is no single pattern of symptoms, but there are some common themes. If the trauma was particularly violent, post-traumatic stress disorder (PTSD) might occur. If the abuse occurred during early childhood, it will have left deep emotional scars impacting on self-esteem and personality development. If the abuse was perpetrated over a long period of time or by a close family member, the scars will be even deeper and result in depression, an anxiety disorder, or a dissociative disorder. Dissociation means to be cut off or distanced from yourself, and dissociative disorders, including amnesia (periods of total memory loss), depersonalization (feelings of being detached from or outside your own body and experiences), and multiple personality disorder (presence of multiple, distinctly separate personalities within one individual), are the hallmarks of severe, prolonged childhood abuse. Until the 1970s, these disorders were viewed as hysterical attempts to get attention and not as valid medical diagnoses. Now we know that these disorders exist, they are real, and they are treatable.

Children who are not valued are unable to develop a healthy self-esteem (self-concept). They are not taught that they are OK, that they deserve to be happy, and that they are worthwhile. Given the previous chapters in this book, you might expect us to tell you that these feelings are biologically based, and to an extent, they are. But they must also be learned. We must be shown over and over again that we are loved and therefore lovable, that we are valued and therefore valuable, and that we are respected and therefore worthwhile. Without such teaching, children grow up to be women with self-doubts, low self-esteem, and a lack of self-confidence. Some women tell us that they feel bound by unspoken rules that say that they cannot succeed, are unable to succeed, or should never try to succeed. They may feel undeserving of happiness or of having their basic needs met. Not uncommonly, these women have difficulty being assertive and asking for things that they need. They may feel that they don't deserve anything at all, so they deny many of their own basic feelings and needs.

Through childhood abuse and neglect, women are taught that they are worthless, that they deserve to be miserable, and that they do not have the right to feel safe. Often the abuse survivor feels (either consciously or unconsciously) that she must be bad, that there must be something wrong with her for such horrible things to have happened to her, that somehow she deserved it. She describes herself as worthless, unlovable, and despicable. She hates herself. She sees herself as worthy of punishment, so she punishes herself. She hurts herself, either directly through slashing at her wrists or making other suicide attempts or indirectly through choices that put her in danger or lead to continued abuse. These are often the women who stay in relationships with battering husbands or lovers. They don't leave the abusers, because they have come to believe that they deserve the abuse.

Abuse robs the woman of her basic right to feel safe. The abuse survivor is chronically anxious and fearful. She startles easily and feels that she must always keep her back to the wall. She is unable to trust her own senses. After all, those instincts didn't protect her from the childhood abuse. So she checks and double-checks, never quite sure that what she perceives as being there is what is really there. This can also cause her to put herself into a dangerous or abusive situation—not because she wants it or has deliberately chosen it but because she is unsure of how much she can expect in terms of safety. She lives with constant fear and doesn't recognize the difference between her own internal fears and those inflicted on her from the outside. This is one of the many reasons why women who have been abused as children put their own children at risk of abuse. They simply don't recognize the danger signs. It is only when they see the violence being perpetrated on their own daughters that they know that something is wrong.

Amnesia and Dissociation: Disturbances in Memory and Perceptions

Amnesia refers to the complete or partial loss of memory for a variable period of time. Amnesia, repressed memories, and subsequent recollection have been the subject of much attention and controversy recently. It is clear that amnesia about traumatic events is possible, as well as full or partial recollection of the event after a long period of time. This has been termed *dissociative amnesia*—a means of distancing oneself by forgetting all or part of the trauma. Dissociative amnesia has been well studied in combat veterans. Following World War II, for example, it became clear that soldiers could "repress" a particularly painful war event; later, it became clear that the memories could return in bits and pieces—the veteran would experience "flashbacks" to the repressed situation.

Children who have been molested also seem to develop amnesia for the events or the time period around the events as a means of coping with the terror. Some who experienced particularly horrific abuse may repress their entire childhood or long periods of time surrounding the abuse. Repressed memories explain why women who have been abused are able to recall only parts of a memory, or recall some facts incorrectly, or have no memory of the abuse until many years later when something triggers the release of the repressed memory. Arguments continue as to the validity of such recalled memories, particularly since there are examples of therapist-planted suggestions being recalled as "real" events (so-called false memory syndrome).

We are now beginning to understand how a memory could be forgotten and then recalled at a distant point in time or recalled only in bits and pieces. Studies of people who have had strokes have shown that the left half of the brain (the "left brain") stores the words or the verbal content of a memory (in general), and the right brain stores the perceptual and emotional parts of the memory. For a memory to be completely recalled, both halves of the brain must be activated simultaneously. Therefore, in very young children, where the connections between the two halves are immature and memories tend to be more emotional and perceptual, only the right brain may store the memory. Thus, attempts during adulthood to access it through language are difficult, if not impossible, but emotional and sensory triggers may inexplicably release the memory.[1] For example, try to conjure up a memory of some special meal that you ate as a child. If you're like most of us, you can't come up with very many. Now, go to the kitchen and get some cinnamon. Take a deep whiff and see if some vivid memories come rushing back. The cinnamon acts as a trigger to the right brain and releases the forgotten memories. The same thing can happen for a victim of abuse, only she doesn't know what emotional or physical stimulus will release her repressed memories. It would seem that such a memory would not be credible because of the intensity of the recollection and the pieces in which it recurs, yet this is actually a hallmark of dissociative amnesia.[2]

Dissociation

Although the term *dissociation* has been variously defined over the years, it is a neurological term and refers to disconnecting from a past memory or the current situation. Dissociation takes several different forms: depersonalization, derealization, and amnesia.

Depersonalization refers to the feeling of being detached from one's mind, body, or world. The woman who is experiencing depersonalization might say that she feels as if she were walking about in a dream or a trance.

Derealization is a state where the world looks somehow different than it did before or seems strangely distant. The woman may feel as if she is trapped in an alternate dimension, that she is "on the outside looking in." In both depersonalization and derealization, the woman usually recognizes that reality has not been altered but that she is the one who feels different or strange. This distinguishes the dissociative disorders from psychosis, where there is no recognition of the altered state.

The most extreme form of the dissociative disorders is that of multiple personality disorder (recently renamed "dissociative identity disorder"). Multiple personality disorder (MPD) represents an inability to integrate identity, memory, and consciousness. It is literally a condition in which a woman has two or more separate and distinct personalities. Each personality is referred to as an "alter," short for the "alternate" personalities that are present. Each alter operates independently from the others and has its own memory set; it is almost as if one alter is awake and the others are asleep at any single point in time. Therefore, the dominant alter may have large gaps in her memory. In one of the best-known descriptions of a woman with multiple personality disorder, *I'm Eve*, Chris Costner Sizemore describes her life with three separate personalities.[3] This is a courageous story of a woman who finally identifies that she suffers from MPD. For over forty years, she had three personalities, each of which was vastly different from the others. Ms. Sizemore's abuse occurred at such a young age that she spent most of her childhood with multiple personalities, and she describes being surprised when she realized that other children didn't have several selves. In her most recent book, *A Mind of My Own*,[4] Ms. Sizemore continues her true story and describes how she ultimately reintegrates (comes back together as a single personality).

Although there are increasing numbers of cases like Ms. Sizemore's, the diagnosis of multiple personality disorder remains controversial. There are two schools of thought—those who believe in the disorder as a real entity and those who do not. This question was recently debated by two leading psychiatrists in a well-respected journal of child psychiatry. On one side of the argument, Dr. Paul McHugh describes multiple personality disorder as "a socially created artifact for people who are looking for help." In contrast, Dr. Frank Putnam reports that multiple personality disorder is best understood as a complex form of posttraumatic stress disorder and that the dissociative disorder is almost always associated with a history of early severe trauma. Dr. Putnam argues that a person with multiple personality disorder does not seek a "sick role" in order to reduce life stress or access treatment but instead is attempting to cope with the aftermath of childhood trauma. Dr. McHugh disagrees and poses the following question: "Where is hysteria now that we need it?"—referring to the fact that these patients would have been diagnosed in the past as having hysteria.[5]

Post-Traumatic Stress Disorder

The diagnosis of post-traumatic stress disorder (PTSD) was first defined in 1980. Although the symptom profile has evolved somewhat since then, the diagnosis still reflects its origins in military medicine; the symptoms of PTSD most closely represent those seen in postcombat veterans. For the diagnosis of PTSD to be assigned, the trauma must have been quite serious, threatening your own or someone else's safety, and there must be long-lasting aftereffects. Examples of such a trauma include sexual abuse, rape, physical attack, physical abuse, severe accidents, and other life-threatening situations. Individuals who are victims of terrorist activities or natural disasters, such as floods or earthquakes, may develop post-traumatic stress disorder, and so may their loved ones who waited fearfully to learn if they were alive or dead.

The hallmark of PTSD is that the traumatic event is repeatedly reexperienced. There may be intrusive thoughts about the event during the daytime and nightmares when one is asleep. The intrusive thoughts interfere with reading or conversation, as they are so disturbing that they can't be ignored. Some women actually feel like they are reliving the event. This is described as a flashback. Any situation that reminds them of the event will invoke strong psychological and physiological responses (by triggering right-brain memories). This might cause the woman to avoid any person or place that reminds her of the event or to withdraw from her family and friends. It can also lead to a heightened sensory awareness and a feeling of always being "on guard" against danger. This hypervigilance and hyperarousal (part of the fight-or-flee reaction described in Chapter Twelve) may result in great difficulty in falling asleep or staying asleep at night.

"Psychic numbing" is typical for people with post-traumatic stress disorder and is characterized by decreased memory (especially for details of the event), decreased interest in activities, and feeling distanced or detached from others. This shutting down and blunting of feelings may be explained by "psychic avoidance"—the brain's attempts to avoid triggering the right-brain memories. Psychic avoidance is the mental equivalent of a person's avoidance of people or situations that remind her of the PTSD situation.

A similar syndrome, called *acute stress disorder*, describes a profound and pervasive anxiety that begins shortly after a trauma and lasts for up to a month. The diagnosis of acute stress disorder is made when a woman has experienced a severe trauma and develops profound anxiety symptoms, including dissociative symptoms, increased arousal, and recurrent reexperiencing of the event through nightmares or flashbacks. If it persists for longer than a month, it may be post-traumatic stress disorder.

Complex post-traumatic stress disorder is the term proposed by Dr. Judith Herman to describe the spectrum of symptoms that are found in people who have had repeated or prolonged trauma during childhood.[6] She emphasizes the *spectrum* of symptoms that can occur, including changes in personality, difficulties in intimacy with loved ones, self-destructive or self-mutilating behaviors, alcoholism, drug abuse, and patterns of repeated victimization. Dr. Herman details how psychiatry tends to disdain the syndromes that are common in abused women—somatization disorder, borderline personality disorder, and multiple personality disorder. The term *somatization* refers to women who have multiple medical symptoms that are presumed to be of psychic origin because they are so bizzare or at odds with medical knowledge. For example, a woman might complain of numbness in both of her hands in a glovelike pattern—this is completely inconsistent with the nerves supplying feeling to her hands, and so it is assumed that the symptoms are "just psychosomatic" or "all in her head." The diagnosis of borderline personality disorder is often used in an even more pejorative manner. Although it can be used legitimately to describe a constellation of symptoms common to women who have suffered from abuse, it is usually used as a means of writing the woman off, as in "she's just a borderline; ignore her complaints," or "everyone knows that borderlines don't respond to treatment." The women become their label—"borderlines"—and cease to be recognized as women with a problem.

Dr. Herman suggests that borderline personality disorder be replaced with the term "chronic post-traumatic stress disorder," and we agree. The term doesn't blame the woman for her illness but rather instructs us about its source and possible treatment.

If You Don't Have PTSD, What Could It Be?

Poor Memory. Absence of childhood memories is an important signal to indicate the possibility of childhood trauma and abuse, but it is not sufficient to make the diagnosis, and frequently this memory loss is caused by other factors. Just because you can't remember parts of your childhood, it doesn't mean that you have been abused or have experienced severe trauma. You simply may not remember well. Everyone has different memory capabilities—we all experience the world differently and store events and recall them with varying degrees of ease or difficulty. In addition, situations other than childhood abuse can lead to decreased childhood memories. For example, growing up in a home where one or both of the parents was alcoholic might have taught the woman to wall off her feelings, and this will make it harder for her to retrieve them as an adult.

Medical Conditions. There are many medical conditions that can cause alterations in perception and problems with memory (see Chapter Five).

The most common causes of perceptual disturbances are epilepsy and migraine headaches. (But it's important to note that these conditions are also overly common in women who have suffered childhood abuse.) Periodic memory losses are associated with epilepsy, migraines, concussions, and sleep disorders, such as narcolepsy (falling asleep unpredictably throughout the day). Drugs and alcohol abuse can cause absences of memory, particularly during alcoholic blackouts (see Chapter Fifteen). In addition, a variety of over-the-counter medicines, prescription medicines, and illicit drugs can interfere with memory, concentration, and perception.

One of the most important things to remember is that two disorders can coexist at the same time. If a woman has post-traumatic stress disorder, this does not exclude the possibility that she also has a medical problem. Too often, such women are dismissed with "Oh, that's just part of your PTSD," when in actual fact the symptoms are the result of an endocrine, metabolic, or neurological condition. Thus, it is extremely important for anybody with losses of time or distortions in memory or perception to have a complete medical evaluation by a physician who is familiar with the complexity of diagnoses that can mimic such distortions.

Treatment of PTSD

Crisis intervention is now being used to prevent the occurrence of traumatic stress responses and to lessen their severity. After disasters, such as floods, bombings, and fires, it is increasingly common for teams of therapists to be dispatched to the site. When a woman has been brutalized, she may receive similar crisis intervention therapy in the emergency room of the hospital. It is generally agreed that crisis intervention should be implemented as soon as possible in order to have maximum effect. Psychotherapy is commonly used in crisis intervention treatment to help the victim process the events of the trauma. The therapist-victim relationship provides an immediate source of support that can be sustained for as long as is necessary. Although crisis intervention is very useful, it is not curative, and some victims will still go on to develop PTSD.

Psychotherapy

Psychotherapy is the primary treatment for post-traumatic stress disorder and the dissociative disorders. The first stage of psychotherapy is establishing safety, the second is remembering and mourning, and the third is reconnecting.

Establishing safety both outside the office and within the psychotherapeutic relationship is very important. The woman's home and work environment must become safe and secure before therapy can progress to the next level.

The second stage is about remembering and understanding. The repressed memories are brought back to the surface and discussed in the context of the woman's feelings and experiences. This is not done to achieve a catharsis or to "clean house" of the bad memories but rather as a means of regaining control over the memories. Now, instead of acting out the partially repressed memories, the woman is able to examine them, to see them for what they are, and to gain control over them. She is empowered by the knowledge that they can't hurt her anymore.

The third stage of healing is reconnecting. This is the reason that the psychotherapeutic relationship is so important. It helps the woman to restore connections within herself and between herself and another person. The goal is to reconnect with the world at large and to be able to establish intimate relationships with her friends and family. This stage can be particularly long and difficult, because a woman who has suffered abuse is inherently mistrustful. She must be taught how to trust again, just as she must be taught that she is of value to herself and others.

Eye movement desensitization and reprocessing (EMDR) is a new form of psychotherapy. Although it is not yet widely known or accepted, EMDR is rapidly gaining popularity as a more rapid means of treating PTSD. Dr. Francine Shapiro first discovered the technique in 1987 and has used it to treat victims of rape, childhood sexual abuse, war, and natural disasters, such as the recent San Francisco earthquake. In EMDR, patients are instructed to focus their eyes on a rapidly shifting object or light and simultaneously to focus their attention on a single image from the traumatic event (for example, being held down by the rapist), the associated emotion and body sensations (terror, suffocation, and crushing weight), and the related thought (I'm going to die). This process appears to desensitize the patient rapidly to the traumatic event by breaking it down into these small units and allowing mastery of both the memory and emotions; it also helps the patient to reframe the automatic (negative) thoughts. The technique appears quite similar to cognitive-behavior therapy (see Chapter Twelve) but requires far fewer therapy sessions. EMDR has not yet been systematically evaluated, so it is impossible to say whether or not it will live up to its promises; if it does, it will offer new hope for the thousands of women suffering from PTSD.

Medications

Medications may play an important role as adjuncts to the psychotherapy. The drugs are chosen to provide relief of a specific symptom or set of symptoms. For example, antidepressants might be used for the woman who is depressed, while antianxiety medications might be right for the woman who is having difficulty sleeping or who is anxious and hypervigilant.

Medications that suppress the stress response are thought to be helpful to patients suffering from acute post-traumatic stress disorder and post-traumatic stress disorder. One such drug, propranolol, has been used to treat some of the intrusive thoughts and hypervigilance symptoms and appears to be somewhat effective. Clonidine, a similar medication, is also thought to be helpful, although there are no controlled studies demonstrating its effectiveness. Both medications block the anxiety response that can be triggered by right-brain memories. Similar to their effects in panic disorder, the drugs prevent the anxiety response from spiraling out of control, but they do not treat the underlying cause of the anxiety.

Antianxiety drugs (see Chapter Twelve), such as the benzodiazepines, have received some preliminary enthusiasm for their ability to decrease various PTSD symptoms. They are particularly useful in the short run for patients who can't sleep at night because of intrusive thoughts. They also have an antianxiety effect that may be helpful in decreasing daytime anxiousness and feelings of being "on edge." However, the benzodiazepines carry the risk of abuse, so these drugs are used sparingly and with caution.

Tricyclic antidepressants (see Chapter Nine), such as imipramine, desipramine, and amitriptyline, have been tested in controlled trials for PTSD and have been found to be helpful. The effectiveness of these drugs appears to be unrelated to their antidepressant properties. Instead, it may be related to their ability to decrease responsivity and hyperarousal.

Medications used to treat bipolar illness, including lithium and carbamazepine, have been reported to be helpful to a few individuals but have not yet been systematically studied.

The most promising drugs are those that work on the serotonergic system, such as fluoxetine (Prozac) and fluvoxamine (Luvox). In two separate studies, these selective serotonin reuptake inhibitors reduced PTSD symptoms in both men and women. The most potent effects were seen on the psychic numbing and hyperarousal symptoms, but the medications also helped the patient's associated symptoms of anxiety and depression. The studies' authors concluded that when people with PTSD feel less numb and more in tune with their surroundings, they are better equipped to deal with the flashbacks and intrusive thoughts.

Prevention

Prevention of post-traumatic responses is the only true "treatment" for these disorders. On a societal level, this means that we must work actively to address the desperate problem of violence against women. We must work together to stop rape, incest, and sexual abuse. We must support antistalking and victims' rights legislation. And, we must insist that the victims of these horrific crimes be protected. For example, AIDS testing should be made mandatory for accused rapists. Currently a woman who has been raped cannot force the rapist to undergo blood testing for AIDS, because this would violate his right to privacy. This is absolutely unacceptable, particularly in light of evidence that shows that immediate treatment with certain medications can decrease the victim's risk of contracting this deadly disease.

We should insist that our police officers become more sensitized to domestic violence and that they protect the victim from the potential repercussions of turning in her battering spouse. Recently, the state of Massachusetts implemented changes that allowed restraining orders to be initiated at the time that the police answer the complaint of domestic violence. Now, instead of giving the perpetrator time to talk his victim out of pressing charges, he can be removed from the home immediately, thereby ensuring the victim's safety, albeit temporarily. Resources for battered women must be increased, including access to medical and psychiatric care and legal assistance. Finally, medical professionals should be required to receive training in the signs of abuse so that they will recognize it and ensure that the woman gets help, even when she's too scared to ask for it.

Summary

It is especially important for women with post-traumatic stress disorders (such as PTSD and acute stress disorder) and dissociative disorders (such as chronic post-traumatic stress disorder and multiple personality disorder) to receive excellent psychiatric care. Too often, the aftermath of abuse is blamed on the victim, rather than being seen as the unfortunate consequences of an unconscionable act. As women, we must speak out against these acts of violence, demand further research into the biological underpinnings of the post-traumatic disorders, and actively defend our sisters' right to receive respectful medical care. Improved psychological and medical treatments offer new hope to many of the women suffering from PTSD and the dissociative disorders—it is important that they be able to receive this care from a knowledgeable mental health practitioner.

Resources

Nearly every community has an abuse hot line. In addition to providing advice and protection in an emergency, the hot-line volunteers are able to provide referrals for treatment.

Further Reading

Herman, Judith L. *Trauma and Recovery: The Aftermath of Violence from Domestic Abuse to Political Terror.* New York: Basic Books, 1992.

Kreisman, Jerold J., and Hal Straus. *I Hate You—Don't Leave Me: Understanding the Borderline Personality.* New York: Avon Books, 1989.

Putnam, Frank. *The Diagnosis and Treatment of Multiple Personality Disorder.* New York: Guilford Press, 1989.

Sizemore, Chris Costner. *A Mind of My Own.* New York: William Morrow, 1989.

Notes

1. Rhawn Joseph, *The Right Brain and the Unconscious: Discovering the Stranger Within* (New York: Plenum Press, 1992).
2. B. A. van der Kolk, *Psychological Traumas.* Washington, DC: American Psychiatric Press, 1987.

3. Chris Costner Sizemore, *I'm Eve* (Garden City, NY: Doubleday, 1977).

4. Ibid., *A Mind of My Own* (New York: William Morrow, 1989).

5. Paul McHugh and Frank Putnam, Debate Forum: "Resolved: Multiple Personality Disorder is an Individually and Socially Created Artifact," *Journal of the American Academy of Child and Adolescent Psychiatry* 34 (July 1995): 957–63.

6. Judith L. Herman, *Trauma and Recovery: The Aftermath of Violence from Domestic Abuse to Political Terror* (New York: Basic Books, 1992), 115-29.

CHAPTER 11

"She's Not in Her Right Mind"

Mary was anxiously awaiting the birth of her first child. She and her husband, Jerry, had tried for such a long time to conceive that when they found out that she was pregnant, both of them had cried with joy. The couple had attended childbirth classes, and parenting classes, and every other class that they could find in order to be prepared to bring their precious baby into the world. Mary was grateful that her pregnancy had gone smoothly. Oh, she had had a rough first four months (not three, as she had expected), what with the constant nausea and frequent vomiting, but that was over now. Now, the only thing that she noticed was that she had cravings for sleep and for certain foods, like citrus fruits. She was so huge that finding a comfortable position in which to sleep just wasn't possible, and Mary was beginning to feel extremely tired. So she was happy that her water broke a week before her due date. She was finally going to have this baby!

The labor and delivery weren't as difficult as she had expected, but it took nearly twenty-four hours before she gave birth at 2:48 A.M. on July 26 to a beautiful baby girl. As she stared at her precious baby, Mary was overcome by the enormity of the miracle of life. She wanted always to remember this moment. She memorized every tiny detail of her daughter's appearance—her long eyelashes, her semisquashed nose, her miniature rosebud lips, and her adorable little fingers and toes. Mary loved watching her daughter. She couldn't bear to let little Andrea out of her sight, even for the few minutes that it took for the nurses to check her out at the beginning of each shift.

Mary was able to take Andrea home after only one full night in the hospital. Her milk still hadn't come in, but the nurses reassured her that it could take a "day or two" since she was a first-time mom. When Mary's milk still hadn't come in by the third day after they got home, she became concerned and called her doctor. The doctor told her that this happened "all the time" and that she should just relax, drink extra fluids, and get some sleep. She wasn't sure that he was right. She still felt like she must be the only mother in the world who was such a failure that she couldn't even make milk for her daughter. But Mary agreed that she did need to get some sleep; she was totally exhausted. Little Andrea seemed to cry and whimper almost constantly, and Mary hadn't slept for more than an hour at a time since she was born—no, since the day before she was born.

Mary thought that her exhaustion was probably the cause of her increasingly low mood. She had been a little tearful in the hospital, but her childbirth classes had taught her that nearly every mother experiences the "baby blues," so she thought that this was normal. But now she was beginning to feel truly depressed. She found herself crying or snapping at Jerry for no apparent reason. Even little Andrea wasn't able to make her happy anymore. Mary's milk had finally come in and Andrea nursed hungrily, but even so, Mary felt awful. So tired. So depressed. So overwhelmed. And things only got worse. After another week had passed, Mary was feeling so low that she couldn't find the strength to get dressed in the morning, or to take her baby for a walk outside, or even to eat the food that her husband cooked for her. She just sat and rocked little Andrea. And as she did, Mary worried about her failures as a mother. "I don't deserve to have a little baby like you. I'm a terrible mother. A good mother would be bonded to you by now. I'm not bonded. I don't feel like your mother and you don't feel like you're my baby. You don't even look like my baby."

Jerry was so concerned by the deterioration in his wife that he called Mary's obstetrician and asked that she be seen. Dr. Fuentes was concerned when he saw how poorly Mary looked but could find nothing specifically wrong with her. He concluded that she wasn't getting enough sleep and recommended that Jerry "give her a night or two off. You can feed the baby a bottle in the middle of the night and make sure Mary gets at least six to eight hours of uninterrupted sleep." As the doctor had suggested, her husband took the night shift that evening, and Mary slept the entire night through—the first time in nearly three weeks that she had done so. She awoke feeling better than she had in weeks. She had some energy, and she even managed a smile as her husband joked, "Well, I'm not sure I'll come home tonight. You know how well I get along with your mom." That's right—her mother was coming. The cavalry had arrived.

As soon as Mary's mother walked in the door, Mary handed her the baby and announced, "I'm going upstairs to take a nap. Don't call me unless she needs to eat." Mrs. Lucas was a little taken aback by Mary's attitude, but agreed that her daughter needed a nap. Mary looked terrible to her—pale and drawn, with deep circles under her eyes. It must have been a long and difficult three weeks. She should have come down sooner to help, but Mary had wanted to settle into a routine by doing it herself for the first couple of weeks. She obviously hadn't been able to keep up; Mary looked exhausted, and the house was a mess. Well, she was here now and she'd just get busy and clean the house and make a nice dinner for the three of them. Mrs. Lucas checked on little Andrea every once in a while as she worked. Her granddaughter looked so beautiful as she slept. Mrs. Lucas hoped that Mary was sleeping too.

Actually, Mary wasn't sleeping. She was lying in bed, trying to nap, but she couldn't fall asleep. She was just too tired. Mary knew that it wouldn't do any good to try to force herself to sleep. So she just lay there and rested. And as she did, she thought about the past few weeks and about how many things had changed in such a short time. Everything had been so easy before she had come home from the hospital, and everything was so hard now. What was different? What had changed?

"I'm still the same as I was then, Jerry's still the same, my house is still the same, the baby's still the same . . ." Wait, the baby. That was it: the baby was different. The baby that she had given birth to in the hospital was beautiful, and quiet, and easy. This baby was ugly, and noisy, and difficult. She must have the wrong baby. Oh, my God, they switched my baby! They gave me someone else's baby. Where is my baby? What did they do with her? Maybe they hurt her or killed her or sold her to some strangers. That's what they must have done—they sold my beautiful little baby to some childless couple. Mary had heard about those shady adoption agencies; she'd seen a show in which an agency had kidnapped newborn babies and sold them to the unscrupulous rich. And I bet they made a lot of money off of her too, she thought. Andrea was so perfect, so wonderful.

"But wait, if they took our baby, why didn't Jerry say something? Surely he noticed, he had to have noticed. Of course he noticed. He just didn't say anything. Why? Why didn't he say anything? Maybe he's in on it. He must be in on it. That's it. That's why he didn't say anything. He planned *this all along. Jerry was the one who chose the fertility expert; they were in on this together. The two of them plotted to get me to have the perfect baby so that they could sell her for more money. Well, I'll fix them. I'm not going to take care of that brat downstairs as if she's my own. I'm going to find my baby. They're not going to get away with this. I'll fix them."*

And with that, Mary got up and slipped quietly out of the house. She used the back door so that her mother wouldn't hear her and try to stop her. Her mother might not believe her. Worse, her mother might be in on it too. After all, she didn't say anything when she saw that strange baby lying in the bassinet. She had seen her real granddaughter in the hospital, so she should have been able to tell the difference right away. Oh, no, her mother was in on it too. Well, that just meant she was on her own. She'd have to take care of this by herself. Mary drove quickly to the police station, went directly to the chief's office, and said, "I'd like to report a kidnapping. Someone has stolen my baby."

Mary was suffering from a postpartum psychosis. As you read her story, it becomes clear that she isn't thinking clearly or logically. Her thoughts are senseless and obviously irrational. Yet to her, they are very real. Mary's psychosis grew out of a postpartum depression (described in detail in Chapter Four). As she became more depressed and more sleep-deprived, she began to have unusual thoughts, including excessive guilt about her inability to nurse her baby and worries about her fitness as a mother, and then the "break" happened, during which she became convinced that her real baby had been kidnapped. When her thinking was no longer based in reality, she had a psychotic disorder or psychosis.

Psychosis is one of three disorders associated with irrational thinking; the others are delirium and dementia. When we say that someone is "acting crazy" or "is out of her head," she may be suffering from any one of these three. It is sometimes quite difficult to distinguish among them, particularly in the elderly.

Psychosis

Psychosis is a disorder of thought characterized by the presence of delusions, illusions, or hallucinations. In psychotic disorders, the woman's thinking patterns are unclear or disconnected from reality. These distorted thinking patterns can cause strange or bizarre behaviors, incomprehensible speech, and perceptual disturbances (such as delusions and hallucinations). Because psychosis is a *thought* disorder, the woman really believes her unrealistic ideas are the truth, and she cannot be dissuaded by proof to the contrary. For example, if all the doctors and nurses swore out affidavits that there had been no baby switch, or if they produced hospital footprints that matched the baby's at Mary's home, she still would not believe that the baby she had was little Andrea. In her psychotic state, she would become convinced that the doctors and nurses were lying to cover up their incompetence or that the footprints were fake. Nothing could shake her unrealistic beliefs.

Psychosis is characterized by a number of unique symptoms, each of which is the result of the distorted thought processes. Delusions are ideas or beliefs that have no basis in reality, such as paranoid delusions—in which the woman is convinced that someone is out to get her or is trying to hurt her (for example, aliens are sending her secret messages through her fillings and the FBI is trying to kill her in order to intercept the messages)—and delusions of grandeur, in which the woman is convinced that she is more important than she actually is (for example, the cleaning woman who believes that she is really in control of the company). Illusions are the misinterpretations of real experiences or feelings (such as seeing a window curtain moving in the night breeze and believing it is your long-dead aunt bringing you a message), and hallucinations are false sensory perceptions—seeing things that aren't there, hearing voices that speak to you alone, or smelling scents that no one else can smell.

A conversation with a woman suffering from psychosis can be frustrating, disconcerting, or downright eerie. It is frustrating because the psychotic thoughts may be disconnected from each other, so the woman's speech is disjointed and unclear. Her thoughts will meander, and she will appear to jump from one unconnected topic to another (this is called "flight of ideas"). It is disconcerting because the irrational nature of the conversation leaves you feeling that something is not quite right. The psychosis may be so subtle that you can't put your finger on the fact that her arguments weren't logical or the conversation just didn't make sense. And the conversation may feel eerie because the thoughts are often strange, bizarre, or frightening.

Obviously, if a woman is riding on the city bus wearing a huge aluminum foil hat on her head and a sign that says, "I'm protecting myself from the radio waves that are being bombarded at my head," you will think of psychosis. In other instances, the psychosis may be limited to a specific situation or setting, and it is much less obvious. Examples of such psychoses include erotomania (belief that a famous or important person is in love with you), delusions of jealousy (incontrovertible belief that your sexual partner is unfaithful to you), and somatic delusions (belief that you have a medical illness that cannot be diagnosed by others or is being "covered up" by the doctors).

Any time a woman is recognized as having delusions or other types of psychotic thoughts, she must receive medical attention immediately. The delusions and hallucinations can take on a sinister quality and cause the woman to try to hurt herself. For example, the "voices" of auditory hallucination might say, "You're bad, you don't deserve to live, just end it. Shoot yourself in the head. Do it now. Do it now." Or very rarely, the voices might tell her to hurt another person.

Psychosis Due to Medical Conditions and Medications

In Chapter Five, we described the many medical illnesses, medications, and substances (such as street drugs and alcohol) that can produce psychotic symptoms. These include:

- Hormonal shifts and endocrine disorders, such as thyroid disease, Cushing's disease, steroid administration, and the postpartum period
- Vitamin or mineral deficiencies or toxicities
- Infections, such as syphilis, AIDS, and Lyme disease
- Autoimmune illnesses, such as lupus and connective tissue disease
- Neurological illnesses, including migraine headaches, seizures, and movement disorders
- Sleep deprivation or chronic nonrestful sleep
- Fluid imbalances, such as those caused by dehydration or sunstroke
- Poisons and environmental toxins
- Medications, over-the-counter drugs, street drugs, and alcohol.

If the woman is young and she has had an abrupt change in thinking patterns, she is more likely to receive a comprehensive workup than if she is elderly, has significant life stressors, or already has another psychiatric disorder. But anyone with either gradual or sudden onset of perceptual disturbances deserves a thorough medical workup. Of note, the auras associated with migraine headaches are quite similar to some of the visual and auditory (hearing) hallucinations seen in psychosis, making it particularly important to have a complete neurological examination.

In addition to determining whether or not there is a medical condition underlying the psychosis, the examining physician should inquire about the use of over-the-counter drugs, street drugs or alcohol, and prescription medications. Sometimes, a woman may be able to tolerate a prescribed medication without problems until she combines it with an over-the-counter antihistamine, appetite suppressant, or cold medication; then she will have a toxic reaction. Psychosis is a surprisingly common symptom of such reactions.

Psychosis can be associated with starting a medication, prolonged use of the drug, or withdrawal from the medication. Prescription medications, such as sedative hypnotics (sleeping pills), can cause psychosis on rare occasions during use and, more frequently, when they are stopped abruptly. Amphetamines, cocaine, hallucinogens (LSD and PCP), heroin, and narcotic painkillers are all common causes of psychosis, during both the use of and the withdrawal from the drug. Even alcohol and marijuana have been associated with psychosis, particularly when the woman is taking certain medications. Thus, it is extremely important to ensure that the doctor examining a patient with psychosis is aware of all substances (both legal and illegal) that she may have taken.

Postpartum Psychosis and Other Psychoses Related to Mood Disorders

Postpartum psychosis affects one out of every one thousand women giving birth. It is frightening to both the new mother and those who care about her. In some tragic instances, the psychosis has gone unrecognized until the woman has murdered her child or has taken her own life. Postpartum psychosis frequently, but not always, arises from a postpartum depression (Chapter Four). The hormonal shifts accompanying labor, delivery, and the postpartum period appear to trigger the psychotic episode, although no one yet knows how or why this occurs. It is reassuring to know that most postpartum depressions do not lead to psychosis. However, both severe depression and mania are associated with psychosis, and in some cases, a postpartum psychosis is the first evidence of bipolar disorder (as discussed in Chapter Seven).

Depression is associated with feelings of guilt, inadequacy, and self-doubt. When these depressive thoughts lose their connection to reality, they have become symptoms of psychosis. Medications, electroconvulsive ("shock") therapy, and light therapy are all useful for the treatment of depression and bipolar disorder, but each has also been reported to trigger psychosis on very rare occasions.

Schizophrenia and Schizoaffective Disorder

The term *schizophrenia* is frequently mistaken for the word *schizoid* and is used incorrectly to indicate a split personality. Schizophrenia actually does indicate a split, but the schism is between perception and reality, not between opposite personality traits or contradictory behavior. Schizophrenia is a serious neuropsychiatric disorder that is believed to be caused by both structural and functional changes in the brain, particularly within the dopamine messenger system. In addition to the psychotic symptoms described earlier, schizophrenia is characterized by "negative symptoms"—a term used to describe a decrease or absence of normal, spontaneous feelings and behaviors. Negative symptoms include such things as disinterest in activities and people, social isolation, an inhibited or "flat" mood, and decreased speech and activities. It is as if the woman with schizophrenia is partially lacking the capacity to think, to react, and to respond. Thus, schizophrenia can have profound effects on her intellectual, emotional, social, and occupational functioning.

Schizophrenia is surprisingly common and is thought to affect 1 percent of all Americans. Typically, the symptoms start in early adulthood or later, with the first episode of psychosis (the psychotic "break") frequently occurring during a period of stress, such as leaving home or ending a relationship. The symptoms become apparent over the course of a few weeks to months, or less commonly, they may take several years to become obvious. The symptom course can be chronic and unremitting, or it can be episodic so that the woman appears to function well for prolonged periods before having another "break."

Schizophrenia is a chronic, lifelong disorder that is only diagnosed after symptoms have been continuously present for six months or longer. A schizophrenia-like picture that lasts less than six months is called schizophreniform disorder. A psychotic episode that lasts less than a month is called a brief reactive psychosis. Often, these brief reactive psychoses are not part of any ongoing psychotic disorder.

Schizoaffective disorder is also a serious psychiatric illness. It has features of both schizophrenia and of a mood disorder. A woman suffering from schizoaffective disorder has psychosis and depression simultaneously. She is in grave danger of hurting herself because the depression renders her hopeless and helpless and the psychosis interferes with her ability to think rationally enough to resist the urge to kill herself. Fortunately, the new antipsychotic and antidepressant medications offer these women hope for a longer, happier life.

Dramatic progress has been made in the treatment of both schizoaffective disorder and schizophrenia, but at present there is no cure for these debilitating illnesses.

The police chief listened to Mary for only a few minutes before he realized that her story didn't make sense. She was rambling and incoherent, referring to plots against her in one breath and the color of the wallpaper in the next. The chief excused himself from the room briefly and asked one of the female officers to come assist him with Mary's case. Another officer was instructed to try to find Mary's husband. Then the chief returned to his office to try to convince Mary to let him take her to the hospital. Eventually, Mary grudgingly consented—"but just to find out if they still have my baby there somewhere"—and they crossed the street to the emergency room. The staff had been alerted to expect her, and the attending physician examined Mary immediately. He took extra care to question her about any medications or pills that she might have taken, but avoided confronting her on the irrationality of her story, as he feared that she would become more upset or that she would flee.

By the time the doctor finished his evaluation, Jerry had reached the hospital. Concerned about his wife's welfare, he hurried into the emergency room and started for her cubicle. The doctor stopped him and told Jerry that because of her delusions, Mary might be very angry with him or very frightened of him. She was both. Jerry's presence sent her into a panic, and she began cursing and screaming at him, "How could you do it? How could you sell my beautiful baby? You're conspiring with the devil. I hate you! I hate you! You're evil. Don't hurt me. Don't hurt me."

The nurse was able to calm Mary down fairly soon after her much-shaken husband left the room. Mary agreed to sign herself into the hospital; she thought that she'd have a better chance of finding her baby that way. Once she had been admitted to the psychiatric ward, she asked for "something to help me sleep—I really need to sleep," and the doctors

prescribed Thorazine, an antipsychotic medication that also makes peo-
ple sleepy. Mary slept for nearly twelve hours, and when she awoke, the
head nurse oriented her to the unit and explained that she was there to
help her. "Oh, that's good," she said. "Maybe you can help me find my
baby."

   It took several days before Mary's psychosis began to improve. As it did
and Mary's thinking became more rational, the doctor was able to deter-
mine that her thought disorder had been the result of a deep postpartum
depression, rather than a symptom of bipolar disorder or schizophrenia.
He started her on an antidepressant medication, and she rapidly began to
recover. A few days later, the doctor asked Jerry to bring Andrea into the
hospital. The psychiatrist was sure that Mary was prepared, but Mary
was fearful that she wasn't ready, that she wasn't truly well. She tenta-
tively approached her husband and the baby that he held. As soon as
Mary saw her infant daughter's face, she knew that it would be OK. She
knew that the baby in her husband's arms was her own beloved Andrea.

Treatment

The key to the treatment of most psychotic episodes is determining the
cause of the symptoms. Often, the psychosis can be eliminated by treating the underlying cause (for example, correcting a thyroid hormone
dysfunction) or eliminating the psychosis-inducing substance (such as
steroid medications). If the medical and neurological evaluations fail to
reveal a treatable cause for the psychosis, then the woman is probably
suffering from a psychotic disorder, and antipsychotic treatment is indicated. Sometimes, antipsychotic medications are needed even when
the psychosis is the result of a medical condition. The drugs are used to
treat the delusions and keep the woman safe and more comfortable
until the underlying problem can be corrected.

Medications

Psychosis is usually treated with an "antipsychotic" medication (also
called major tranquilizers, dopamine-blocking agents, or neuroleptics).
The antipsychotic medications are divided into two groups designated
"typical" and "atypical." The typical antipsychotics all work in a similar
manner that differs from the newer atypical medications. Both groups
of antipsychotics are thought to work by blocking dopamine, which decreases the "overactivity" of the dopamine system; this overactivity is
the presumed cause of the delusions, hallucinations, and psychotic

thoughts. The negative symptoms of schizophrenia do not typically respond to the antipsychotic medications, and serious impairments can remain, even with effective control of the psychotic episodes.

Antipsychotics are appropriately prescribed for psychosis whether it is due to medical illnesses, major depression, bipolar disease, schizoaffective disorder, or schizophrenia. But they are *not* appropriate for the treatment of depression, anxiety, or insomnia, despite the fact that they are also known as major tranquilizers. When psychosis occurs in conjunction with a mood disorder, a combination of medications is often required, such as an antipsychotic plus an antidepressant and/or a mood-stabilizing drug. Antipsychotics should only be prescribed by clinicians who are experienced in their use, because the antipsychotic drugs carry a significant risk of side effects, and the patient should be maintained on the lowest dose possible.

The typical antipsychotics include haloperidol (Haldol), chlorpromazine (Thorazine), trifluoperazine (Stelazine), thioridazine (Mellaril), fluphenazine (Prolixin), thiothixene (Navane), and loxapine (Loxitane). The short-term and long-term side effects of these antipsychotics are the direct result of their therapeutic effects.

In the short term, one could develop an acute dystonic reaction, which is characterized by a painful spasm of the neck muscles, or Parkinsonian symptoms such as motor slowing, stiff gait, and hand tremors. These side effects can be prevented or treated by a variety of medications, but these drugs unfortunately have their own risks of side effects (such as sedation and dry mouth).

Tardive dyskinesia (TD) is the name given to the abnormal movements, such as lip smacking, facial grimacing, and abnormal gestures, that can result from long-term (or high-dose) treatment with an antipsychotic. The possibility of tardive dyskinesia must always be discussed with the patient prior to initiating therapy so that she can decide if she wants to accept this risk. For someone with schizophrenia, the benefit of having fewer (or no) psychotic episodes and the resulting improvement in the woman's ability to function will likely outweigh the risk of developing tardive dyskinesia. The risk does not outweigh the benefit for anxiety or sleep disorders, however, and that is why the antipsychotics (major tranquilizers) are not appropriate for these disorders.

The atypical antipsychotics include clozapine (Clozaril) and resperidone (Resperidol). They are the first of several new antipsychotics that are being developed in an effort to treat the negative symptoms of schizophrenia better and to reduce the risk of side effects. In addition, they appear to offer hope to patients who have failed to respond to the typical antipsychotics. The medications represent a major advance in the treatment of schizophrenia, but both carry a risk of serious side-effects. Several other drugs are under development, and it is hoped that one of these will offer advantages over the currently available antipsychotics, both in terms of safety and effectiveness.

Psychological Treatments

Antipsychotic medications are the mainstay of treatment for schizophrenia. As we have already said, though, they do not offer a cure for this devastating illness. Psychological therapies can play an important role in managing the illness and in improving the patient's ability to function. Group therapy, for example, offers support and practical guidance to improve social competency.

Flexible psychotherapy refers to the use of different psychological interventions at different times to treat the patient with schizophrenia. These psychotherapies include supportive, educational, and insight-oriented techniques. The treatments vary depending on the patient's particular needs and her symptoms at that point in time. Even though the therapies change, the therapist should remain constant, as the stability of the therapeutic relationship is important for improving outcome and encouraging the patient to remain in treatment. Unfortunately, this is frequently impossible, as patients with psychosis often have to get their care from low-fee clinics and public hospitals, both of which are notorious for their lack of staff stability and availability.

Recent studies have suggested that family involvement and family support can play an important role in the long-term outcome of patients with schizophrenia. Family involvement has become a major focus for the combined treatment of patients with schizophrenia; however, such involvement can be both physically and emotionally exhausting. Thus, family therapy must often serve to support both the family and the patient. Other sources of support available to families are listed in the "Resources" section at the end of this chapter.

Delirium

Agnes had been rushed to the hospital with severe pain in the left side of her chest. Fortunately, her heart attack had been diagnosed quickly enough to receive one of the new "clot-busting" drugs, and the doctors were able to prevent her heart muscle from being seriously damaged. She had been admitted to the coronary ICU for close monitoring, but the cardiologist had reassured her that it was merely a precaution and that she would be fully recovered and ready to go home in a few days. Over the next few hours, a nurse came in to check her pulse every fifteen minutes, and Agnes had difficulty settling down. She had an IV running fluids into her body, and they had given her several medications in the emergency room, so perhaps that was why she felt so restless and uncomfortable. Or maybe it was because she had almost died this morning—that was enough to make anyone feel a little anxious.

As the afternoon wore on, Agnes began to feel better. She was able to calm down and even to catch a few short naps between nursing checks. When her daughter called, Agnes told her to wait and catch the next day's flight instead of taking three separate planes to get there that evening: "I'm fine, honey. They think I'll go to the step-down unit in the morning."

The next day, her daughter didn't find Agnes in the step-down unit. Instead, she found her in the ICU lying partially uncovered and with both wrists tied down to her bed. Agnes didn't respond when her daughter called her name; she just mumbled some gibberish and thrashed about trying to pull her hands free from the restraints. Her daughter was terrified. The night before, Agnes had been clear and coherent. Now she was unresponsive. What had happened?

The nurse called it "ICU psychosis" and said that it was common after heart attacks. "We know it's upsetting to you, my dear. But try not to worry about it. We see it all the time—they always get better." Somehow, this was not reassuring, and Agnes's daughter demanded to speak with the physician. The doctor said basically the same thing: "Sometimes, in elderly people, the strange room is just too much for them. They get confused." Confused! Confused barely began to describe her mother. What on earth had happened?

Over the next few days, Agnes began to regain consciousness. As she did so, she seemed so anxious and uncomfortable that her daughter almost wished that she would pass out again. Agnes would claw at the sheets as if there were bugs crawling on them and mutter crossly to an invisible man in the corner of the room. This caused the I-know-it's-just-ICU-psychosis-nurse to ask her daughter if Agnes had a drinking problem: "She looks like she's having the DTs—you know, withdrawal symptoms. I took care of a lot of drunks at the VA hospital, and they all looked like that when they were drying out." Agnes didn't have a drinking problem, but her daughter did succeed in getting the nurse reassigned to a different unit.

Sometimes, Agnes would seem fairly alert and would recognize her daughter. At other times, she didn't know who she was or where she was. She would ask a question and then ask it again in a few minutes. Her speech was slurred, and she had trouble finding the right words. This made it hard for her daughter to understand her, and Agnes would get angry and irritated when she was asked to repeat herself. She also got angry when her daughter didn't follow her conversations, but it was impossible to follow Agnes's conversations—they made no sense. She was seeing things that no one else could see and hearing voices that no one else could hear. These bad periods seemed to come and go without warning. Gradually, though, they came less frequently and lasted for shorter periods of time. Finally, after about ten days in the hospital, Agnes's thinking had cleared enough for her to begin to wonder what had happened.

Agnes was suffering from delirium, which might have been caused by the medications she received following her heart attack or by fluid shifts within her brain induced by the rapid infusion of IV fluids. Delirium is defined as an acute deterioration of mental function and is characterized by confusion, delusions, hallucinations, memory impairment, and altered levels of consciousness. The disorder is quite common among hospitalized patients, and some have estimated that between one in ten and one in seven persons over the age of sixty will have a delirium during their hospital stay. Delirium usually starts abruptly and tends to fluctuate over the course of the day, so that the woman may appear clear and coherent in the morning but be quite confused and irrational by nightfall. In other instances, the patient shifts rapidly in and out of the delirium, and her symptoms might be missed if she is examined only during a lucid period.

Confusion is one of two hallmark symptoms of delirium. The confusion results from impaired thinking abilities. During a delirium, the woman can't reason well, is unable to organize her thoughts, and can't correctly process incoming information. If you ask her to "touch your right elbow with your right hand," she will try in vain to accomplish the task. Disorientation is another key symptom of delirium. Frequently, the woman will not know where she is, what day it is, or (rarely) even *who* she is. Cognitive misperceptions, including delusions and hallucinations, are also common in delirium. The symptoms look identical to those seen in psychosis and probably represent a similar brain malfunction. However, when delusions and hallucinations are part of a larger picture of confusion and shifting levels of consciousness, they are delirium, not psychosis.

"Shifting levels of consciousness" is the other hallmark symptom of delirium. This means that the woman randomly moves from being awake to being asleep, from being conscious to being unconscious. At the more subtle levels, this may mean that she is sleepy and "out of it" one moment, then alert and awake the next. These abnormalities are associated with particular electroencephalographic (EEG) changes, and the EEG can be quite helpful in making the diagnosis of delirium.

Delirium is often caused by a medical illness or by drug intoxication. The most common form of delirium in young women is delirium tremens, or DTs. DTs occur when a woman who has drunk excessive amounts of alcohol over a long period of time suddenly stops drinking. The DTs are a serious complication of alcohol withdrawal and have been reported to be fatal in rare instances (see Chapter Five for further discussion of DTs and other symptoms of alcohol withdrawal). Other causes of delirium include:

- Infections, such as encephalitis, meningitis, and syphilis
- Severe burns and heatstroke
- Fever (more common in children)
- Metabolic problems, such as fluid shifts, potassium or sodium deficiencies, liver failure, and kidney failure
- Toxins and poisons, such as carbon monoxide, lead, or mercury poisoning
- Vitamin deficiencies, including B_{12}, niacin, and thiamine deficiencies
- Anemia
- Endocrine disorders, such as Cushing's disease, and diabetes or hypoglycemia
- Neurological disorders, including strokes, seizures, and brain tumors
- Medications, including street drugs and over-the-counter preparations.

In almost every case of delirium, the underlying cause can be found if the evaluation is thorough enough. This may require laboratory studies, spinal taps, an EEG, MRI (magnetic resonance imaging), or CT (computerized tomography) scan, and other tests. However, in elderly patients, most deliriums are written off as an "ICU psychosis" or other meaningless term for an unknown cause, because they tend to resolve on their own.

Treatment of delirium is primarily aimed at correcting or eliminating the medical condition causing the delirium. In some instances, specific treatment of the delirium is required, particularly if the patient is extremely agitated and anxious or is suffering from hallucinations or delusions. In such cases, haloperidol (a typical antipsychotic drug) might be used with caution. Benzodiazepines (antianxiety drugs) are also used, although they have the disadvantage of inducing sedation, which makes it more difficult to assess the patient's mental state.

Dementia

It was 8:00 P.M. and Margaret was finally settled into her hospital room. She had sent her children and grandchildren home because she was exhausted. Besides, there was no reason for them to sit vigil with her. "Plenty of women have their gallbladder removed," she had told them. "It's not like I'm having open-heart surgery or anything." Just as she was about to relax, a medical student came in and told her that she needed to do a physical examination. Margaret grumbled that she had already had a physical—by a real doctor, her own doctor—but she agreed to let the student perform her exam. After all, they had to learn sometime. She hoped it wouldn't take too long, though. She had to get to sleep. She knew that the surgery would go much better the next day if she could just get a good night's sleep.

But Margaret wasn't going to get a good night's sleep that night. In fact, she didn't get much sleep at all. There were too many strange noises out in the hallway, and the light from the street lamp fell right across her bed. They had instructed her to leave all her medications at home, so she didn't even have her usual sleeping pill to help her relax and fall asleep. Finally, at midnight, she called the nurse and asked if she could have a sleeping pill. The nurse said that her doctor hadn't written a prescription for one, but she'd call the resident physician and ask. Margaret never heard back from her; at around 3:00 she finally fell asleep from sheer exhaustion.

She was awakened at 6:00 A.M. by the nurse taking her blood pressure. The nurse reminded her not to eat or drink anything, as Margaret was to have surgery that morning. Margaret snapped back at her, "Yeah, I know, that's why I'm here." Finally, it was time to go to the operating room. Sometime later, she woke up in the recovery room and felt very sick and sore. The next time she awoke, she was lying in bed in a darkened room, and a woman was standing next to her and putting something into her IV. Before Margaret could ask her what she was doing, she fell asleep again.

The next morning, Margaret woke up early. She wanted her breakfast. She rang her call bell and waited for the nurse to appear. When none did, she became increasingly annoyed and snapped at the candy striper who had arrived with a bouquet of flowers, "Where the hell is my nurse? With all the money I'm paying to be in this joint, you'd think I'd have round-the-clock attention." The young girl put the bouquet down and hurried out to find Margaret's nurse.

A few hours later, Margaret's family visited, and she complained bitterly about the "lousy" attention she was getting. "The nurses are ignoring me. I haven't seen one all day. My doctor hasn't been in all day, either. And they didn't give me any lunch." Her daughter, a surgical nurse, explained that she wouldn't get food until the next day but promised to talk to the charge nurse about her mother's complaints. While she was gone, Margaret's husband straightened his wife's bedsheets and brought her a fresh glass of water. He was used to taking care of his wife at home; it seemed like a natural thing to do in the hospital, as well. Just then, the attending surgeon came in to examine Margaret. After he was finished, Mr. Lowe followed him into the hallway and explained that his wife was concerned about the lack of nursing care that she had been receiving. The doctor said they were short-staffed but that he would see what he could do.

Meanwhile, Margaret's daughter Patty was speaking with Ms. Parks, the head nurse on the unit, and getting a very different accounting of the past twenty-four hours. It seemed that her mother was actually receiving excellent care. The nursing charts showed that Margaret had been checked at least every two hours, the last time by Ms. Parks herself. Each time, the nurses had been chastised for being late or neglectful. They had thought that Margaret's irritability was due to pain and that their visits to her seemed far apart because she was having such discomfort from her incision, so Ms. Parks had just asked her surgeon to prescribe a stronger pain medication. "But," the nurse said, "it doesn't seem to be helping. She's still so irritated that we're neglecting her. It's almost like she forgets that we've been in to see her," the nurse said. "Has your mother ever had problems with her memory before?"

When Patty went back into the hospital room, her mother greeted her with a scowl, "Where have you been all day? I thought you were going to come at 2:00. It's 3:00 now." Margaret didn't seem to remember that she had already seen Patty that afternoon, just a few short minutes ago. Patty knew in that instant that the nurse was right; her mother was having memory problems. Suddenly, it all became clear—the missed appointments, the wrong turns as they drove to a familiar restaurant, the many times her mother had apologized for being "a touch forgetful," the extra attention that her father gave to making sure that her mother was OK. But it had never been like this. Margaret had never had trouble remembering what she'd done a few minutes previously. And she'd never been so crabby and irritable.

After the consulting psychiatrist finished his examination, he sat down with the family and explained that Margaret was suffering from dementia. She had significant memory loss, irritability, slight disorientation, and by report, a change in her personality. These things had clearly been interfering with her functioning even before she was hospitalized. The condition seemed to have been made abruptly worse by the combination of the stress of surgery, the unfamiliar surroundings of the hospital, and the withdrawal of her sleeping pill. "I expect that you'll do a little better once you get back home and get some rest, Mrs. Lowe," he said, "but this isn't going to go away. It will never go completely away—the damage is permanent."

Dementia is the third cause of cognitive dysfunction. Alzheimer's disease is one of the most familiar forms of this neuropsychiatric disorder. In the end stages of dementia, the woman may have psychotic symptoms and/or delirium, but typically dementia refers to memory impairment and disturbances of language, motor activities, or executive functioning (such as planning, organizing, and abstract reasoning). The memory impairment makes it difficult for the woman with dementia to learn new information or to recall previously learned information. Often, the memory impairments may affect her short-term memory more than her long-term memory, so that she can tell you the birth dates of her eleven grandchildren but not what she had for breakfast. The language disturbance is characterized by difficulties with retrieving specific words, so that she will stumble over the name for a common household item, or she may have difficulty remembering the names of her friends and coworkers. The motor and sensory deficits are such that she may have difficulty writing, speaking, walking, or keeping her balance.

By definition, the dementia causes impairments in the woman's personal and professional life. She may be unable to balance her checkbook, keep house, prepare a recipe, or do crossword puzzles. She may forget simple instructions or mix up north and south on the map, so she is in danger of getting lost and of not being able to find her way home. Eventually, she may be unable to remember the way to get to the kitchen from the living room. The progressive nature of these symptoms is characteristic of most forms of dementia; they typically cause a slow, insidious, and irreversible deterioration of function.

There are a few reversible forms of dementia. In these, the dementia improves when the underlying medical condition is treated. Toxins, including mercury and aluminum poisoning, alcohol use, heart disease, low blood pressure, thyroid disease, and B_{12} deficiency can all cause reversible dementia. Depression can also cause a reversible dementia (known as pseudodementia) in the elderly. It is sometimes missed because the physician assumes that the dementia represents Alzheimer's disease and that the depression is a result of the disease, rather than the symptoms being the result of the depression.

Alzheimer's disease is by far the most common cause of dementia, with nearly two-thirds of all dementia thought to be related to Alzheimer's and over 15 percent of women over the age of sixty-five having Alzheimer's disease. The cause of Alzheimer's disease is unknown, although scientists are investigating a number of intriguing possibilities. These include abnormal protein (amyloid) deposits, dysfunctions of programmed cell death, and genetic susceptibility, among others.

Vascular dementia, or multi-infarct dementia, is the second most common cause of dementia in the elderly. It is often the result of prolonged high blood pressure or hardening of the arteries (atherosclerosis). Both conditions are irreversible.

Treatment

The treatment of reversible dementia consists of removing the cause of the symptoms. For the irreversible dementias, the goal of treatment is to slow the progression of the disease and to improve functioning. Several medications have been found to be helpful, including drugs that improve functioning of key messenger chemical systems, such as acetylcholine.

Tacrine (THA or Cognex) inhibits the breakdown of acetylcholine and increases the amounts of acetylcholine available. Tacrine has only recently been released, so experience is limited, but it appears to improve brain function and to slow memory loss. The side effects of tacrine therapy are numerous and include liver problems, nausea, vomiting, diarrhea, dizziness, and chills. These frequently are so severe that the woman must discontinue treatment. Hydergine is another drug that has been reported to be helpful to patients with Alzheimer's disease. The mechanism of action of this drug is unknown, but it appears to increase arousal and thereby improve brain functioning. Several other drugs are under investigation currently, although none has been shown to be helpful to the majority of patients participating in their controlled trials.

Alzheimer's disease is frequently complicated by depression and by anxiety. Treatment of these secondary conditions may improve the patient's life more noticeably than does treatment of the primary condition, particularly if the depression is causing further impairment of the woman's cognitive abilities. One of the primary therapeutic interventions for a patient with dementia is to ensure her safety, sometimes by setting strict limits on activities (for example, suspending her driver's license) and at other times, by prescribing a companion or placing her in a nursing home. Too often in the past, the patient's dementia would be denied until she had been harmed in some way, so now physicians tend to intercede earlier rather than later in the course of the illness. Supportive therapy is helpful both to the patient suffering from the dementia and to her family members.

Summary

The disorders that cause disturbances in cognition are the most serious and debilitating of all the psychiatric disorders. The treatments for the chronic psychotic disorders, such as schizophrenia and schizoaffective disorder, are only partially effective and carry the risk of serious side effects. In Alzheimer's disease, there isn't yet a proven, effective treatment.

On the other hand, in all of these disorders, reversible causes sometimes exist, and these will respond to treatment. Careful evaluation is essential to ensure that appropriate treatment is provided if the psychosis or dementia is reversible.

Even for the chronic disorders, there is hope—hope that more effective treatments will soon be developed and hope that the cure is right around the corner.

Resources

Psychotic Disorders

National Alliance for Research in Schizophrenia and Depression (NARSAD)
60 Cutter Mill Road
Great Neck, New York 11021
800–829–8289 or 516–829–0091

National Alliance for the Mentally Ill
200 North Glebe Road, Suite 1015
Arlington, Virginia 22203
800–950–NAMI

National Mental Health Association
1021 Prince Street
Alexandria, Virginia 22314–2971
703–684–7722

National Mental Health Consumers Association Self-Help Clearinghouse
1211 Chestnut Street
Philadelphia, Pennsylvania 19107
800–553–4539

Further Reading

Backlar, Patricia. *The Family Face of Schizophrenia*. New York: Jeremy
    Tarcher–Putnam Book, 1994.
Keefe, Richard S., and Philip D. Harvey. *Understanding Schizophrenia: A*
    Guide to the New Research on Causes and Treatment. New York: Free
    Press, 1994.
Mueser, Kim T., and S. Gingerich. *Coping with Schizophrenia: A Guide for*
    Families. Oakland, CA: New Harbinger Publications, 1994.
Torrey, E. Fuller. *Surviving Schizophrenia: A Manual for Families, Consumers,*
    and Providers. 3rd ed. New York: HarperPerennial, 1995.

Alzheimer's Disease and Dementia

Alzheimer's Disease and Related Disorders Association
70 East Lake Street, Suite 600
Chicago, Illinois 60601
312–853–3060

Further Reading

Aronson, Miriam, ed. *Understanding Alzheimer's Disease: What It Is, How to*
    Cope with It, Future Directions. New York: Charles Scribner's Sons, 1988.

Cohen, Donna, and Carl Eisdorfer. *The Loss of Self: A Family Resource for the Care of Alzheimer's Disease and Related Disorders*. New York: W. W. Norton, 1986.

Mace, Nancy L., and Peter V. Rabins. *The Thirty-six-Hour Day: A Family Guide to Caring for Persons with Alzheimer's Disease, Related Dementing Illnesses, and Memory Loss in Later Life*. Baltimore: Johns Hopkins University Press, 1991.

CHAPTER 12

Worries, Fears, Phobias, and
Panic

Although Julia had always been a "worrier," she hadn't always had a fear of tunnels. That fear had started when she was eight years old and her family got stuck in the Holland Tunnel. They were at a standstill for over three hours, in the middle of heavy traffic and without a clue as to why they were stopped. Julia could sense that her parents were more afraid than they would admit, and as time passed, her fears also grew. She saw a damp spot on one of the walls and worried that it meant a leak had developed and that they would all drown. She worried that the tunnel would collapse; after all, it was under tons and tons of water and didn't look that strong. This worry intensified when her brother whispered, "The contractor who built this tunnel got arrested last year for using bad materials. The experts don't know when it will cave in, but it could be any day or any minute." Julia took her brother's teasing seriously and cowered between the seats, hoping that the collapse would come tomorrow instead of today. As she sat there, she began to feel sick, and she worried that they were being poisoned by the buildup of exhaust fumes (it was awfully smelly in there!). On top of it all, she had to go to the bathroom, and she was desperately afraid that she would have an accident in her pants.

Ever since that episode, Julia has had a fear of tunnels and has avoided them whenever possible. She knows that her fear is groundless, but she gets so uncomfortable when she tries to confront the phobia that she has given up trying. It's better just to avoid tunnels. When she travels, she takes the long way around cities instead of using the bypass tunnels, and she never visits the mountains, where tunnels might be unavoidable. She has planned her commute to work so that she uses only the portions of the public transit system that are above ground, and she pays extra for valet parking at her apartment so that she can avoid the underground parking garage. With these minor concessions, she has been able to cope nicely. In fact, she frequently forgets that she has a problem with tunnels.

Julia had reason to remember her fears recently, however, when she was downtown with a group of friends and they decided to go out to the suburbs for dinner. Before she knew it, the group was heading into the subway station to take the westbound train. When she recalled that the westbound traveled underground for over a mile, Julia began to feel very anxious and light-headed. She knew that she wouldn't be able to stand going through the tunnel, yet she was too embarrassed to admit that she couldn't ride the subway because of an irrational fear.

Julia quickly became so anxious that she was pale and sweaty; she was breathing quickly, and she felt like she was going to faint. She looked just as awful as she felt, so her friends believed her when she said, "I'm feeling really sick. I think I'll just go home." As soon as she got out of the station, she began to feel better. Her head cleared, her pulse slowed, and her anxiety faded. As she recovered, Julia wondered what had happened to her. How had her fears caused such a strong physical reaction? And why was she still afraid of something that had happened over twenty years ago?

Temperament and Biology: The Basis for Anxiety Disorders

Every mother almost instinctively knows what kind of child she has and what his or her needs are. Some children do well when they are dropped off the first day of nursery school with a warm kiss, a pat, and a "See you at lunchtime"; others sob hysterically as they are pried away from their mother's legs. Still others can't separate at all; they are the ones whose hysterics can't be quieted and about whom the kindergarten teachers eventually say, "Maybe we should wait until next year and try again. Meanwhile, try leaving her with a baby-sitter occasionally." Even as toddlers, children are clearly different from one another: some are introverted, shy, and have difficulty separating; others are extroverted, outgoing, and have an easy time leaving their parents. These patterns continue throughout life. Some people are introverts, and some are extroverts. Some women avoid all risks, and others actively seek out risky situations. Some are shy and anxious, while others seemingly have no fears or worries. Our temperament appears to influence our behavior in every social situation. For example, people who go to amusement parks can be divided into those who will ride the roller coaster and those who won't, and of course, there are those who wouldn't even dream of going to the amusement park in the first place.

Although there is still debate about the development and meaning of temperament, there is beginning to be agreement that temperament is an innate characteristic. We appear to be born with a certain temperament that serves as a framework for determining how we view ourselves and how we interact with others. Dr. Jerome Kagan has studied temperament extensively at the Harvard Infant Study Laboratory. In one stress-inducing experiment, he presented toddlers with a novel stimulus (a totally new situation or object) and noticed that children could be separated into two groups: those who were shy and fearful (behaviorally inhibited) and those who were more sociable and bold (behaviorally uninhibited). When he later questioned the parents about the children's behavior at home, he was told that it was quite similar and had been since early in infancy. Those who were inhibited in the laboratory were also cautious and quiet at home. These children went on to be shy, introverted children when they reached school age. In contrast, the group of children who had been uninhibited in the laboratory were found to be much more gregarious and bold when they grew older.

Dr. Kagan and his colleagues proposed that shyness and sociability are enduring temperamental traits that have a biological basis.[1] They proved this by demonstrating that the shy children also differed from the outgoing children in their physical (biological) responses to new situations. The shy, inhibited children seemed to have a much higher heart rate at baseline and more rapid increase in their pulse in response to the stress than did the outgoing, sociable children. This suggested that they had an overly active stress response.

If these biological differences were long-lasting, then the shy children might be more vulnerable (and the outgoing children relatively immune) to developing anxiety disorders and stress-related illnesses. Drs. Biederman and Rosenbaum followed up on Dr. Kagan's pioneering work and demonstrated that this theory was correct.[2] They found that children of parents with an anxiety disorder were more likely to be shy and inhibited than were children born to parents without anxiety disorders; more important, they found that many of the shy children went on to develop anxiety disorders. There was no way that the anxiety of the parents could have "taught" the children's nervous system to be behaviorally inhibited. It appears that anxiety disorders are biologically and genetically determined.

If there is a biological link between shyness and anxiety disorders, what does this mean for the shy, inhibited girl? Is she destined to suffer from an anxiety disorder? The answer is perhaps, but not necessarily. The odds would suggest "perhaps," as women make up the vast majority (over 80 percent) of patients with anxiety disorders (and the vast majority of shy, inhibited children). In addition, the anxiety disorders appear most frequently during young adulthood, a time of maximal life stress (see Chapter Three), which suggests that environmental stressors impact on the biologically vulnerable individual and cause anxiety disorders.

On the other hand, behavioral inhibition in childhood does not necessarily lead to an anxiety disorder in adulthood. As with all inborn vulnerabilities, environmental factors can dramatically influence outcome. For example, a girl with behavioral inhibition might be coddled by her parents and allowed to retreat from new or stressful situations. In order to protect her from her anxiety, she is allowed to stay home from school "sick" on the day of her oral book report, or to come home from a camping trip when she gets lonely, or to drop out of the band right before the big concert so that she won't have to play in front of an audience. The only problem with this is that she will become a little more anxious each time she is asked to break free from her protective cocoon and she refuses (like Julia and her tunnel avoidance).

Another girl, with the same shy, introverted temperament, is encouraged to try new things and is *supported* in doing so. Her parents help her to practice the book report and give her tips on overcoming stage fright, but they require her to perform; or they might tuck a special token of their love into her suitcase on the camping trip but won't come get her right away when she calls to say that she might be homesick. Her parents are providing her with opportunities to learn more effective means of dealing with stress and anxiety. The young girl learns to conquer her fear; in so doing, she learns that the anxiety subsides fairly quickly and that eventually there is no longer any anxiety.

This notion of supported risk taking has become a mainstay of several effective treatments for the anxiety disorders: patients are provided with opportunities to confront their fears in a controlled manner, and they are supported as they do so. Once the fear has been confronted and mastered, the anxiety disorder disappears. Recent evidence obtained from brain-imaging studies demonstrates that biochemical changes occur in association with this behavior therapy; this research suggests that even those treatments that are considered to be psychological, rather than medical, are affecting the biology of these disorders.

There are four main types of anxiety disorders: generalized anxiety disorder, phobias, social phobia, and panic disorder. We will describe the symptoms and clinical course of each of these types of disorder separately, and then we will combine them for the discussion of treatment options.

Generalized Anxiety Disorder

Nellie earned her nickname as a little girl growing up in Georgia because she was always such a "nervous Nellie." She worried about everything— her appearance, her health, her parents' health, her grades, her brother's grades, her performance in the school play and that of the kids down the block. Her parents would offer her reassurance for these worries, and this would satisfy her for a few moments, but then she would have a new worry and require additional comforting. When her parents grew frustrated with her concerns and refused to reply to her questions of "Are you sure it's all right that . . . ?," Nellie would burst into tears and retreat to the safety of her bed. She would often miss school the next day because her distress had made her sick.

Somehow, Nellie managed to leave home and graduate from college, earning her degree in math and secondary education. As a young teacher, she remained nervous and tense, but she used her anxiety to become the best teacher in the school. Her handouts were letter perfect, her lesson plans were always prepared well in advance, and her classroom setup was a model of organization and efficiency. If she developed a worry about a student's performance, she couldn't ask him for reassurance, so she would expend extra effort to ensure that he really learned the material; consequently all her students did better than expected on their standardized tests. Her career was going well, but her social life had been destroyed by her anxiety.

Nellie had not had a date since she left college, and even then, she had gone out only a few times. It was just too uncomfortable for her. Not only did she have to worry about how she looked and how she was going to act and how the evening would go but she always carried along the nagging fear that her date might insist on driving drunk or that she might be a victim of date rape. After the dates, she had to worry about what she had said and what she had done—Was it all right? Had she embarrassed herself? Would he call again? So she protected herself from the anxiety by withdrawing and adopting a "stay-away-from-me" attitude. It worked, and she stopped being asked out. But that led to its own set of worries: Was she the one deciding that she didn't want to go out, or was it just that men were not attracted to her? Maybe she was ugly? Did she smell bad? Or was she really a lesbian at heart? That thought made her so scared that she picked a fight with her best friend and broke up their relationship. But this didn't seem to help her anxiety, and now she was all alone—and totally miserable.

Nellie might still be alone if she hadn't seen an ad in the newspaper for a meeting of the local chapter of the Anxiety Disorders Association. The advertisement invited people with "unexplained worries and fears" to attend a support group session the following morning. Nellie went to the meeting and was surprised to find the room filled to capacity—and with normal-looking people, too. Could they all have problems with excessive anxiety and worries? The morning's speaker was a psychiatrist from the local mental health center. He talked about problems that sounded identical to Nellie's and described them as biologically based anxiety disorders. Then he presented an update on the new antianxiety medications and reminded the audience about the effectiveness of psychological treatments for these disorders. Nellie was dumbfounded; not only were there other people in the room who had the same problems as she did but there were doctors who were willing and able to treat it. Right after the meeting, she ran to the pay phone to call the number that the doctor had provided.

Nellie did well with her treatment—a combination of medications, individual psychotherapy, and group therapy. The medications provided almost immediate relief to her "free-floating anxiety," and the psychotherapy helped with her fears and worries. She also found the group therapy to be extremely helpful because it allowed her to relearn how to interact with people. With that base of support, she made a number of new girlfriends and started dating again. Best of all, her new friends call her by her real name: Annette.

Generalized anxiety disorder is, as its name implies, an anxiety disorder without a specific focus. The disorder is a chronic condition that by definition lasts for at least six months. Often it has been present since childhood. These are the children from Dr. Kagan's study who are described as worriers when they are young and who continue to be worriers as adults. The worries are excessive for the circumstances (for example, a mother who fears that her child's slight build is a symptom of malnutrition) or unrealistic (a financially secure woman who fears poverty). Frequently, the woman with generalized anxiety disorder will have multiple fears and worries that change over time. In addition, according to the *DSM-IV*, she must have at least three of the following symptoms:

1. Restlessness or feeling keyed up or on edge
2. Easily fatigued
3. Difficulty concentrating or mind going blank
4. Irritability
5. Muscle tension
6. Insomnia and/or restless, unsatisfying sleep.

The worries and fears may increase to the point where they produce a "fight-or-flee" stress response (the body's way of preparing to fight an enemy or flee from a stressful situation, as described in Chapter Three). This response is characterized by symptoms related to excessive nervous system stimulation. The symptoms of the fight-or-flee response include:

1. Increased nervous system activity; hyperarousal
   a. Shortness of breath or smothering sensations
   b. Palpitations or accelerated heart rate
   c. Sweating or cold clammy hands
   d. Dry mouth
   e. Dizziness or light-headedness
   f. Nausea, diarrhea, or other gastrointestinal complaints
   g. Hot flashes or chills
   h. Frequent urination
   i. Trouble swallowing or a "lump in throat"
2. Being on guard
   a. Feeling keyed up or on edge
   b. Exaggerated startle response
   c. Difficulty concentrating
   d. Irritability

3. Muscle tension
   a. Trembling, twitching, or feeling shaky
   b. Muscle tension, leading to muscle aches or soreness
   c. Restlessness.

Unlike panic disorder, the fight-or-flee episodes (or anxiety attacks) are somewhat predictable in generalized anxiety disorder. The woman will start to worry about something relatively minor; then her worries will increase, and she will become more and more anxious. Eventually, the anxiety will build to the point where the fight-or-flee response is triggered and she will have an anxiety attack. In panic disorder, the same symptoms occur, but they come without warning or provocation.

What Could It Be If It's Not Generalized Anxiety Disorder?

Normal Anxiety. A certain amount of anxiety is actually a normal part of life. It's hard to imagine a woman who wouldn't worry if her child wasn't home by curfew, or if she missed a mortgage payment, or if someone she cared about was severely ill. Anxious feelings arrive frequently during the day but remain only momentarily. For example, if you get to work late and realize that you have to prepare a memorandum for discussion at a luncheon meeting, you might have a brief feeling of anxiety, as you think, "What if I don't have time to get this done?" and "What if I can't do it at all? Maybe it's too difficult for me to do alone, and now it's too late to ask for help." This normal anxiety often acts as fuel for getting a job done, pumping up your adrenaline level enough to help you function at peak capacity. (Note, however, that even normal anxiety can be problematic if it causes excessive stress, as described in Chapter Three).

Excessive Anxiety. Excessive anxiety is worrying about something far more than what would seem to be normal and appropriate. For example, if your memo was completed on time and the meeting went well, but you continued to agonize over the fact that there had been three typos, that would be excessive worrying. Excessive anxiety may be annoying and even somewhat distressing, but it should not cause noticeable impairments. It should not interfere with your ability to function.

Stress Reactions. Stress can cause anxiety, and anxiety can cause stress. The spiral rises quickly, and stress reactions often lead to anxiety disorders. However, the two can be distinguished by examining the underlying cause of the symptoms, as described in detail in Chapter Three.

Medical Conditions. A complete list of medical conditions causing generalized anxiety disorder is included in Chapter Five. Before the diagnosis of generalized anxiety disorder is made, it is particularly important to ensure that the woman doesn't have hyperthyroidism or excessive stimulant intake (caffeine, over-the-counter diet pills, decongestants, or amphetamines). Although these medical conditions don't typically cause excessive worrying, they can lead to symptoms similar to the fight-or-flee response.

Specific Phobias

Louise had just finished her annual physical with Dr. Adams, her favorite physician at the HMO. She really liked the doctor and especially the rapport that they had developed. Dr. Adams made it so easy to confide in her that Louise felt comfortable telling her about her most personal concerns and worries. But Louise had never told the doctor about her fear of blood and needles. It was too embarrassing and babyish. She couldn't admit her silly fears to Dr. Adams, not even when the physician said, "Let's get some blood work on you today, Louise. We haven't had any for a couple of years."

Almost immediately, Louise felt her heart jump and her breathing quicken. She managed a weak smile and an "OK" before Dr. Adams walked out of the room. But as soon as she was left alone, Louise began to feel nauseated and dizzy, and then everything started to go black. She collapsed onto the floor, just as the nurse came in to draw her blood. The nurse called for Dr. Adams, and the pair were able to revive Louise easily with some smelling salts and cold compresses.

When Louise had recovered enough to sit up, she somewhat sheepishly explained that she was desperately afraid of having her blood drawn. She admitted that she had always had a terrible fear of needles; it seemed to have started when she got a particularly painful vaccination before entering kindergarten. Plus, she hated the sight of blood; it disgusted and frightened her. Over the years, her fears had gotten worse and so had her reactions: whereas she used to just get pale and shaky, a few years ago she had started having fainting spells. Now, just anticipating having a blood test was enough to make her faint.

Dr. Adams reassured Louise that her reaction to the blood test was quite common and was called a vasovagal response. Her fear was so strong that it made her heart race out of control—the vasovagal response stopped this by resetting her heart rate, but that made her feel dizzy and faint. Dr. Adams went on to explain that vasovagal responses are just one of several well-described examples of how profoundly the mind can affect the body: the brain causes such an intense stress reaction in response to the fear and anxiety that the body spins out of control and has to be reset by the vasovagal response. Dr. Adams continued by explaining that the reactions are not only treatable, they are preventable. Several things could be done to make the experience easier for Louise, such as drawing the blood while she is lying down, helping her to do relaxation exercises during the procedure, and making sure that Louise doesn't see the needle or the blood. The doctor also recommended a new topical anesthetic cream that makes the procedure totally painless (if the cream is applied to the site one hour beforehand). Dr. Adams explained that the anesthetic cream doesn't completely take away the fear of the blood draw, but by eliminating the pain, it helps to make the behavioral techniques more effective and vasovagal response less likely.

Phobias or excessive and irrational fears are quite common. It is estimated that as many as one in ten women have suffered from a phobia at some time in their life, and many more have excessive fears of specific objects or situations. The line between fear and phobia is drawn by determining whether or not the woman is suffering significant distress and interference in response to her fear. Phobias are characterized by intense and persistent fear of a certain circumstance, object, or situation. Common phobias include fear of animals, mice, thunderstorms, heights, blood, tunnels, bridges, planes, or enclosed spaces. Coming in contact with the feared circumstance provokes anxiety (which may be so dramatic that it causes a panic-like attack), so the woman avoids the feared situation or object.

Often phobias run in families. This is particularly true for phobias concerning blood, needles, accidents, and medical procedures. If one family member is affected, chances are that several family members will be. With other phobias, the general class might be the same (for example, fear of animals), but each family member will have a slightly different phobia (one fears horses, another fears dogs, and another, insects). No one knows for sure how phobias might be transmitted from one family member to another. Modeling might explain some cases; for example, the behavior of a needle-phobic mother who can't handle her child's vaccinations might "teach" her child to be excessively anxious (and eventually, phobic) about the procedure.

Genetics or biological causes might also explain the family patterns. We recently cared for a twelve-year-old boy with a lightning phobia. He had such a profound fear of thunderstorms that he was unable to play ball with his friends for fear that a storm might come up unexpectedly and he would be struck by lightning. When there was a thunderstorm, he would have to hide in his closet. His grandmother also had a phobia about lightning. She too had hidden in the closet during every thunderstorm for her entire life. But there was no way that our patient could have "learned" his fear from her, as she lived abroad and had not visited since he was quite young.

Phobias tend to have their onset early, beginning in childhood or by the time a woman is in her midtwenties. A traumatic event is sometimes linked to the development of a phobia: a dog bite might lead to a phobia about dogs, a choking episode to a fear of eating in public, and a fall (or near fall) could trigger a fear of heights. The phobias usually develop without a specific trigger, however. If there was a clear trigger for the phobia, the response should be out of proportion to the degree of the threat; for example, a person might get a minor bee sting and then develop a fear of all flying insects. This is why phobias are known as *irrational* fears; they have no basis in fact. One of the most frustrating things about having a phobia is that the woman recognizes that the fear is excessive and irrational, but she is powerless to overcome it. This is at least in part a reflection of the biological basis for this disorder; the reaction exceeds the reality of the threat.

Phobias cause anxiety, and in severe cases like Louise's, physical reactions, including vasovagal responses. Because the phobic response is so unpleasant, affected individuals learn to avoid situations that might expose them to their feared object. People with insect phobias will refuse to attend their company picnic, while those with a fear of eating in public would refuse the picnic as well as invitations to dinner at a nice restaurant. Sometimes the avoidance rituals have become so exaggerated and complex that it is difficult to determine the nature of the primary phobia. For example, Louise's fear of blood and needles was the obvious cause of her avoidance of doctor's offices, the Red Cross blood drive, and so on. But she also refused to eat in public restaurants and to attend sporting events. Why? For fear that someone at a nearby table might order a rare steak or bloody prime rib; and because one of her son's friends had once had a soccer ball kicked into his face and had gotten a bloody nose, and she worried that it might happen again. The phobia is contagious; it spreads by direct extension, and once a place is contaminated, it stays contaminated and must be avoided. Avoidance is one of the key symptoms targeted during treatment of specific phobias, as it frequently causes the most distress and impairment.

Social Phobia

Christine had worked very hard to get to her current position. She had started as a secretary in the front office, and through hard work and perseverance, she had advanced into the position of administrative assistant and, eventually, to the position of assistant manager. As proud as Christine was of her accomplishments, she knew that she would have been made a manager by now if only she weren't so terribly shy.

Christine had always been shy. In fact, as a child, she had been so inhibited that she hadn't spoken to anyone outside her immediate family. Her grandparents and her aunts and uncles were pleased with the hugs that she would give them but offended by the fact that she wouldn't say please or thank you at the dinner table. She was too shy to speak to the other children at school or to her teachers, and she spent the first few years of grade school in special education classes. The embarrassment made her shyness even worse, for being in these classes meant that she was a "dummy" as well as a wallflower.

Eventually, Christine outgrew the problem of not being able to speak, but she remained painfully shy and withdrawn. She was able to reply to her teacher's questions with short answers, but she couldn't raise her hand in class and risk drawing attention to herself. To this day, she can still remember the frustration of having the right answer and of not being able to tell someone about it. In fact, she continues to experience that same feeling; she had it today at work as she sat in the team meeting with a great idea but too much fear to share it with the others. It was this continued fear of drawing attention to herself that was ruining her career.

Christine's social life, on the other hand, had been ruined by her fear of doing something embarrassing. Her shyness made it very difficult for her to make friends. And if one of her friends was the least bit loud or inappropriate, Christine couldn't be seen with her again. She hated to eat in restaurants for fear that she might spill something or have a bit of lettuce on her tooth and embarrass herself. She avoided clothing stores with public fitting rooms because she couldn't be seen in her underwear; and after a department store's salesclerk opened the door of her dressing room to ask, "Is there anything I can get for you?," Christine shopped only through catalogs. Of course she didn't date. She was afraid that she might do something stupid or that she would act too silly or too naive or too sexy. The thought of kissing a man was overwhelmingly scary to her—there were far too many opportunities to embarrass herself in that interaction!

Christine might have gone on indefinitely this way if not for her minister, Reverend Michaels, who asked her to read the Scripture on Laity Sunday and refused to take "No!" for an answer. After all, she was going to be in church that morning, and there was no such thing as "too shy" in his church—this was the Lord's work. Christine hoped and prayed that he was right. She practiced the reading over and over again in her bedroom until she knew it cold. She slept poorly on Saturday night, and when Sunday morning came, she felt horrible. She was pale and sweaty, she felt sick to her stomach, and her heart was racing a thousand miles a minute. But she knew that Reverend Michaels would accept no excuses, so she dressed and drove to the church. She took a seat in the front pew and nervously waited for her turn. When it finally came, she walked to the podium and was surprised to find that she wasn't worrying about her reading as she walked. Instead she was worrying that her slip might be showing, or that her zipper was unzipped, or that in some other way she was embarrassing herself. When she reached the podium, she didn't dare to look up at the congregation; she knew that would make her even more terrified. She quickly opened the Bible and turned to the page she had marked; she opened her mouth and tried to speak, but nothing came out. Christine was mute again.

The experience was so humiliating and so painful that Christine decided she couldn't go through it ever again. She had to get some help. She stayed home from work the next morning so that she could see her family doctor. Fortunately, Dr. Jones had taken care of her for such a long time that she felt comfortable enough with him to be able to speak. She told him that she needed help with her shyness and her fears, and he reassured her that such help was available. Dr. Jones told her that she most likely was suffering from social phobia and that she needed to see a psychiatrist for a complete evaluation; she might need an antianxiety medication and/or behavior therapy.

Christine started therapy later that week and now, several months later, she is greatly improved. She is happier, more relaxed, and more at *ease in social situations. Although she hasn't started to date yet, she has made several new girlfriends and has gone out to dinner with them twice. Her performance at work has improved too, in part because one of her behavior therapy homework assignments is to speak up at least once at each team meeting. Her boss was so impressed with her idea last week that he came by her office specifically to compliment her. Christine hopes that her improvement continues until she's completely comfortable in social settings. But even if it doesn't, she's happy just to have a public voice again.*

Women with social phobia have a persistent fear of situations in which they might be exposed to scrutiny by others and/or a fear of doing something that will bring them humiliation or embarrassment. Because the fear is so intense, it produces uncomfortable levels of anxiety and can lead to attacks of "stage fright" (with physical symptoms similar to anxiety attacks or panic attacks). Rather than expose herself to this discomfort, the woman with social phobia will avoid all threatening social situations. The avoidance may so restrict her social activity that it causes interference with her career and her social life, as happened in Christine's case.

Social phobia is a chronic condition that affects women more commonly then men; two-thirds to three-fourths of all patients with social phobia are female. The characteristics of social phobia appear to be present quite early in childhood, as was discussed earlier in this chapter. Some recent work with the childhood disorder of selective mutism suggests that this may be the childhood counterpart of social phobia. Selective mutism is the inability to speak in public, often because of fears similar to those experienced in social phobia—the children are afraid (or embarrassed) to have others hear their voice. The children have normal speech and language at home but consistently do not speak in social situations, including the classroom, school playground, and restaurants. As in Christine's case, this can lead to the misdiagnosis of a developmental delay and inappropriate educational placements for the younger child, social isolation in the older child, and sometimes, social phobia in adults.

Social phobia is divided into two types: generalized social phobia, in which the woman fears *all* social situations in which she might be observed; and specific social phobias, in which the fear is directed at a specific circumstance or situation. The *Diagnostic and Statistical Manual of Mental Disorders (DSM-IV)* lists the following specific situations:

1. Being unable to continue talking while dining in public
2. Saying something foolish or embarrassing
3. Choking on food when eating in front of others
4. Being unable to urinate in a public lavatory
5. Having one's hand tremble when writing in front of others
6. Not being able to answer questions.

Thus, some women with social phobia are not able to use public rest rooms, and others are not able to eat in public, talk on the phone, or speak to strangers. An activity that most people might take for granted, such as asking for directions, writing a check, or eating lunch at McDonald's, might be impossible for the woman with social phobia.

In social phobia, anxiety is directly related to exposure to the feared situation. For example, the woman with social phobia and a specific fear of eating in public will feel little or no anxiety when she is sitting at her breakfast table, but she will experience a great deal of anxiety when she is sitting at a table in a restaurant. This direct relationship between the feared circumstance and the production of anxiety distinguishes social phobia from panic disorder. Panic attacks aren't linked directly to a specific situation; they can occur anywhere, at any time.

Despite this key difference between social phobia and panic disorder, it can sometimes be difficult to separate the two (particularly if the panic disorder is accompanied by agoraphobia), as the avoidance patterns might be indistinguishable. For example, by now you know that women with social phobia often avoid restaurants. Women with panic attacks and agoraphobia also avoid eating dinner in restaurants, but the avoidance typically arises from a fear of being trapped in the restaurant during the panic attack, rather than a direct fear of being humiliated or embarrassed. In severely affected patients, the fears may have generalized to the point that the primary fear is no longer distinguishable; in those instances, the woman might receive both diagnoses.

Panic Disorder

The music of Beethoven washed over the audience like ocean waves. Pat and her husband, Ralph, were thoroughly enjoying their evening at the concert. Suddenly, Pat's heart began to race, beads of perspiration formed on her forehead, and the tips of her fingers began to tingle. It felt as if a heavy weight had landed in the middle of her chest and was about to smother her.

"Ralph," she whispered, "we have to go!"

Ralph, who was transfixed by the music, turned to her with an annoyed look on his face. The annoyance quickly turned to concern as he noticed Pat's desperate, startled appearance. The couple got up quickly and, as quietly as possible, exited the row and headed up the aisle. Outside the concert hall, Pat soon recovered. She no longer felt as if her heart was pounding out of her chest, and her breathing slowed to its normal rate.

As they sat together, Pat looked sheepishly at Ralph and said, "Honey, I'm sorry I ruined the concert for you. I don't know what came over me." She sighed, and then said, "One minute I was taken up by the music, and the next I was overcome by this suffocating feeling. You know, like I couldn't breathe . . . and my heart was pounding so hard. . . . I just had to get out of there. The weird thing was that I kept thinking to myself, 'I'm only thirty-eight years old—how can I be having a heart attack?' I feel perfectly fine now, though."

Several weeks passed before the same awful feeling swept over Pat once again. This time, she was at the shopping mall looking for a pair of shoes to go with her new spring suit. Just as before, a weight seemed to settle on her chest, she started to sweat and tremble, and her breathing became faster and deeper. She was so dizzy, and the pins and needles had returned to her fingers. "Oh, please, God, don't let me die!" she prayed. She made her way out of the shoe store and sat down heavily on a bench in the middle of the mall. A few seconds passed, which seemed like an eternity to Pat. Then, as quickly as it started, it was over. The dreadful feeling of impending doom lifted, and she could finally catch her breath. Convinced this time that she had had a heart attack, Pat got in her car and drove to the hospital.

"I was having terrible chest pains," she said to the clerk behind the desk in the emergency room. Pat was immediately whisked to a cubicle behind a faded tan curtain and was hooked up to a heart monitor. Eventually, a physician came in and took a brief history and listened to her heart and lungs. He then examined the EKG tracing and told her that she was going to have some blood tests done. Several hours later, as she crossed the hospital parking lot back to her car, she replayed the doctor's words in her mind: "I can't find anything wrong with you, so I'm discharging you. Your EKG is fine, the lab tests have all come back normal, and your physical exam is fine."

"Well, if I'm so fine," she thought, "why did I feel like I was going to die?"

Over the following weeks, she had several more episodes—at work, in the grocery store, and while driving. Pat began to think that there was something terribly wrong with her; either she was losing her mind, or she was really sick. Both alternatives were equally terrifying, but they were only half as bad as her constant fears of having another attack.

"Pat, let's go to that new restaurant Courtney and Chandler were raving about the other day," said Ralph.

"I'd rather not," replied Pat casually. "There are some leftovers in the fridge that we should finish up." Meanwhile, she was thinking, "If I go out, I might have another attack! What if I couldn't get out of the restaurant in time? I'd be so embarrassed if any of my friends saw me like that and so afraid that the paramedics wouldn't be able to reach me in time. If I stay home, I'll be safer. The attacks never seem to happen here." So they didn't go out that night nor any other night that month.

Pat's world suddenly became a much smaller place. She begged off the family vacation to the beach with the excuse that she had to work. But she was a little miffed that her family didn't cancel their plans and stay home with her. How could she be expected to travel? What if she had an attack on the causeway? Or on the road to the shore? Or on the beach?

The first few days that her family was away, she managed to get to work, but it was so difficult to leave home that she would linger in the foyer, on the front porch, and in her car in the driveway. After a few days, she couldn't stand to leave the house at all, so she called the office with an excuse of "I'm sick today" or "A pipe sprung a leak in our basement—I have to stay home and wait for the plumber."

By the time Pat's family returned, she was out of food and milk, but she still hadn't left the house. "Our home is safe," she explained to Ralph. "If I have an attack at home, I'll be OK. If I'm out somewhere, heaven only knows what will happen to me." Ralph was so concerned about the change in his wife that he immediately put her in the car and took her to the emergency room. This time, he spoke to the doctor and convinced him that the attacks were serious and that Pat was in terrible anguish.

When the cardiac workup was once again normal, a consulting psychiatrist was called, who diagnosed Pat as having panic disorder with agoraphobia. He recommended an antianxiety medication and behavior therapy. The treatments were somewhat successful, particularly for her agoraphobia. Pat was able to leave her house with a companion after six sessions, and after several months, she could go shopping alone and eat in restaurants again. The medications prevented her from having another attack, but she continued to fear the possibility for the next several years.

The Mind-Brain Connection: Psychiatric Disorders   245

The attacks had started without warning, and she feared that they could return again just as capriciously.

Panic disorder is defined by a history of having had at least four separate panic attacks or having had one panic attack that was followed by a persistent (lasting longer than a month) fear of having another attack. Panic attacks come on a person out of the blue and are characterized by feelings of intense fear or discomfort. Unlike the anxiety reactions seen in social phobia, panic attacks are usually unexpected and are not triggered by situations in which the person is under social scrutiny. Sometimes, the first panic attack is linked to a certain phobic situation, such as crossing over a bridge or riding on a subway train, but these attacks subsequently take on a life of their own and can come at any time, in any place, and without warning. Because they come so unexpectedly and they are so unpleasant, the person is always on guard against the attacks and is constantly anticipating their arrival. This type of anticipatory anxiety (tension about a possible future occurrence) is the hallmark of panic disorder and is frequently more debilitating than the panic attacks themselves.

Panic disorder is somewhat different from the other anxiety disorders because the panic attacks so closely mimic a medical illness. As listed in the *DJM-IV*, the characteristic symptoms of a panic attack include:

1. Shortness of breath or smothering sensations
2. Dizziness, unsteady feelings, or faintness
3. Palpitations or accelerated heart rate
4. Trembling or shaking
5. Sweating
6. Choking
7. Nausea or abdominal distress
8. Numbness or tingling sensations
9. Hot flashes or chills
10. Chest pain or discomfort
11. Sense of being unreal or not feeling like yourself
12. Fear of dying
13. Fear of going crazy or of doing something uncontrolled.

Ten of these thirteen symptoms are related to physical complaints. Given the nature of the symptoms (chest pain, tingling sensations, shortness of breath, accelerated heart rate, and sweating), it is not surprising that people with panic attacks often end up in the emergency room for cardiac (heart) evaluations. Many men with panic disorder have been ad-mitted to intensive care units to rule out a heart attack (or myocardial infarction). Unfortunately, when they are found not to have a heart problem, they are discharged without receiving appropriate psychiatric care for their panic disorder.

As you might expect—given the bias that women's problems are "all in their heads"—women have the opposite problem. They are rarely mistakenly diagnosed with heart disease when they are suffering from a panic disorder; instead, all too frequently, women with heart attacks are told that they are "fine" or "just having a panic attack" and are sent home without a complete cardiac evaluation. Even if the correct diag-nosis is panic disorder, the woman should receive a complete cardiac examination, including a physical examination, an electrocardiogram (an ECG or EKG), and laboratory studies.

The Association Between Panic Disorder and Mitral Valve Prolapse

One of the reasons that it is so important for women with panic symp-toms to have a complete diagnostic workup for heart problems is that *mitral valve prolapse* is much more common among women with panic disorder than in the general population. Mitral valve prolapse is a flop-piness of the valve between the chambers of the left side of the heart. It is important to make the diagnosis of mitral valve prolapse as early as possible, because the defect makes the woman more vulnerable to bac-terial infection (so that she should receive antibiotics for dental work and certain surgeries), and also more susceptible to irregularities of the heart rhythm, including palpitations and double heartbeats.

Some scientists believe that the association between panic disorder and mitral valve prolapse is mere coincidence; both disorders appear to have a genetic basis, and the genes might be located closely enough to-gether so that they are inherited together. Others think that mitral valve prolapse contributes to the development of panic disorder. The mitral valve prolapse can cause palpitations and other heart rate irregularities that cause a physiological stress response. In people who have an in-creased vulnerability to developing anxiety disorders, this physiological stress could lead to the development of panic disorder.

Physical Symptoms of Panic Disorder

The symptom of shortness of breath is one of the most common experi-enced by patients with panic disorder. During a panic attack, sufferers will often say, "I'm having trouble breathing" or "I can't get enough air." They may feel like they are smothering or suffocating. A natural response to this sensation is to breathe faster and harder (hyperventilate) in order to make sure that one gets enough air. This hyperventilation (excessive breathing) makes the condition worse, because the person blows off too much carbon dioxide. This leads to changes in the pH balance of the blood and can cause numbness and tingling in the hands and legs, light-headedness, dizziness, and the feeling that one is going to faint (all of which are also symptoms of a panic attack). One quick fix for hyperventilation is to have the woman breathe into a paper bag. This causes her to rebreathe her own air and quickly brings the carbon dioxide concentrations back to normal levels, alleviating the woman's symptoms.

It is not uncommon for a woman with panic disorder to feel that her heart is racing and that she is having "extra" heartbeats. Often, she actually is having tachycardia (rapid heartbeat) or doubled heartbeats (extra beats caused by dysfunction of the heart's regulatory system). Once she notices the irregularity, the woman may begin to wonder if this is a life-threatening condition, and this causes her to become even more anxious. The anxiety further increases the heart rate and the chances of having an irregular heart rhythm, making the situation even worse. One way to slow down a fast heart rate is to use "the dive reflex"—holding one's breath while putting ice or cold water on the mouth, face, or throat. Alternatively, putting firm pressure on the carotid arteries (located at the front sides of the neck) or on the woman's closed eyes may also slow a runaway heart rate.

The dizziness and light-headedness associated with panic attacks may be a reflection of hyperventilation, as just described, or it may arise directly from the anxiety. Both can lead to fainting. When the person suffering from a panic attack says, "I feel as if I'm about to faint," she isn't just seeking attention—she needs assistance, and quickly.

Sometimes panic attacks are also characterized by a feeling of choking. Patients with this symptom have told us that it feels as if their throat has tightened up for no apparent reason. They never know when this might happen, and they avoid eating in public because they are so fearful that their airway could get blocked suddenly.

Other symptoms include nausea or abdominal pain, facial flushing, sweating, hot flashes and chills, and numbness and tingling. The numbness and tingling usually occur in the arms, hands, feet, or around the face and neck. Sometimes this may lead the woman to think that she has some devastating neurological illness, and once again, this increases her anxiety and compounds the problem.

Psychological Symptoms of Panic Disorder

There are three psychological symptoms of panic attacks: (1) feelings of depersonalization and derealization, (2) a fear of dying, and (3) a fear of going crazy or doing something uncontrolled. Depersonalization is the sensation of being outside of, or detached from, your own body and mind, as if somehow you are looking at yourself from a distance. You might also feel disconnected from your feelings and emotions or from your thought processes. Derealization is the sensation of being in an alien environment. Even though the situation may be as familiar as your own bedroom, it feels strange and unreal. Sizes or colors might be distorted so that the person feels like Alice did as she nibbled on the mushrooms and biscuits in Wonderland. In other instances, the person feels as if she is somehow detached from her surroundings. A fog or an invisible barrier stands between her and the tangible objects about her. The feelings are so real and so unexplained that the person fears she is going crazy. Fear of going crazy and fear of dying are both natural results of the strange physical symptoms caused by panic attacks.

One of the hallmarks of panic disorder is what is called "endogenous anxiety." The word *endogenous* comes from the Greek word meaning "to be born or produced from within," and this is exactly what people with panic disorder describe: a welling up of an intense feeling of anxiety and dread, without apparent trigger or cause. This is what separates panic disorder from the other anxiety disorders. It is also what makes panic attacks so frightening. There is no way to prevent them because there is no way to know why they occur. Because there is also no means of guessing when or where they will occur, agoraphobia is a natural result: "The panicky feelings might start in the middle of the movie theater; if it's crowded, I won't be able to get help. I'd better stay home."

What Could It Be If It's Not Panic Disorder?

Heart Attack. Heart attacks are the most obvious mimic of a panic attack. As discussed earlier, panic attacks have at least ten symptoms in common with heart attacks, so the first time a woman has symptoms of a panic attack, she must receive a complete medical evaluation. Even if the woman has had previous panic attacks, she should seek medical attention any time her physical symptoms differ from previous episodes or when they persist for longer than a few moments. Because early intervention saves lives in heart attacks, this is one instance where it is truly "better to be safe than sorry."

Normal Response to Panic-Inducing Situations. As with anxiety, almost everyone has had symptoms of a panic "attack" at some point in his or her life. You might have awakened in the middle of the night and feared that an intruder was in your home, or your car might have gotten stuck on the railroad tracks with a freight train approaching, or you might have just heard, "We are experiencing some mechanical difficulty with our aircraft. Please assume the crash position." You panic, certain that you're about to die. Suddenly your heart is racing, you're breathing quickly, and you're sweaty and sick. But this is not a panic attack, because it was triggered by an external event. The anxiety is *exogenous* (caused by something outside yourself), not endogenous.

Phobias. Persons with phobias can experience similar levels of panic when confronted with their feared object or situation. These panic reactions are also triggered by an external stimulus, so they aren't called panic attacks. However, repeated panic reactions can serve as the basis of panic disorder, or the person may develop a prolonged fear of having another attack and suffer symptoms similar to panic disorder because of this.

Medical Conditions. Many medical illnesses mimic panic disorder, as described earlier in this chapter and in Chapter Five. Two medical conditions are particularly common and should always be eliminated as possibilities before the diagnosis of panic disorder is made. The first, hyperthyroidism (excess thyroid hormone), can cause many of the physical symptoms associated with panic disorder and can also cause feelings of anxiety and dread. The other common medical cause of panic symptoms is an excess intake of stimulants, such as caffeine, amphetamines, and other medications that stimulate the central nervous system, including decongestants and over-the-counter appetite suppressants.

Agoraphobia

Although the name *agoraphobia* implies that this disorder is a fear of open spaces, it is defined clinically as the fear of being in places or situations from which escape may be difficult or embarrassing or in which help may not be available in the event of a panic attack. Agoraphobia is intimately related to panic disorder, and the two frequently occur together. In fact, the relationship is so close that until recently, the diagnosis of agoraphobia could not be made if the woman didn't also have panic disorder. Agoraphobia may involve a fear of leaving the house alone (because doing so puts the person at risk of being unable to get help for or being embarrassed by a panic attack), but it is not restricted to this. Other agoraphobic situations include being in a crowd or standing in line, being on a bridge, riding in a bus or a train or traveling as a passenger in a car, riding in the subway, or flying in an airplane. Situations from which escape is more difficult, such as being underground in a tunnel or aloft in an airplane, are particularly distressing.

The degree to which agoraphobia impacts a person's life depends on the situations that trigger the anxiety responses and the severity of the agoraphobia. Some people can live a relatively normal life; they are able to drive to work, to go out to the movies (if someone else buys the tickets and they sit in an aisle seat near the exit), or shop in a grocery store with manageable amounts of anxiety. However, they can't stand to be in crowds or airplanes. Usually, though, they can avoid those circumstances without causing interference in their life. Sometimes, such "closet agoraphobics" come up with creative solutions to avoid uncomfortable circumstances. For example, if they live in the area of Washington, D.C., and Baltimore, they might still plan a vacation in Ocean City, Maryland, but they will take the long route to get there (nearly doubling the travel time). The thought of getting stuck on the six-mile-long bridge across the Chesapeake Bay is absolutely intolerable to them.

Persons with agoraphobia may be very reluctant to enter an elevator in a skyscraper, or go for a drive in the country, or fly in a commercial airplane. If these things are necessary for them to get to work or to accomplish their jobs, they cannot be avoided and will cause distress (in the form of anxiety) and/or interference (because of an inability to accomplish the necessary tasks). Most people who are suffering from agoraphobia will have both distress and interference. Some are so impaired that they are unable to leave their homes or even their beds because of the overwhelming distress associated with leaving their safe havens.

Treatment of the Anxiety Disorders

The term "the worried well" is a pejorative designation used by insurance companies and HMOs to deny payment for treatment of patients with anxiety disorders. The implication is that these patients are actually not ill but merely enjoy sharing their problems with a therapist once a week. As you have already seen in this chapter, that charge simply isn't true; the anxiety disorders are real and cause both distress and impairment. The patients are suffering, and they deserve effective treatment.

Symptomatic treatments were quite popular in the past. In this approach, therapists targeted treatment at each of the patient's symptoms. The woman might receive a sleeping pill for her insomnia, a tranquilizer for her anxiety, and a muscle relaxant for her jitteriness and muscle pain. As we have seen in Chapter Five, such drug combinations can be dangerous and are usually not effective. Indeed, symptomatic treatment has fallen out of favor as we have learned more about the anxiety disorders.

Currently, there are three mainstays of treatment for the anxiety disorders: psychotherapy, behavior therapy, and medications. Each of the anxiety disorders responds to all three types of therapy, but to varying degrees. For example, generalized anxiety disorder is treated more effectively by medications than by behavior therapy, while for specific phobias, behavioral techniques are the first choice.

Psychotherapy

Psychotherapy, which is also known as dynamic psychotherapy or insight-oriented psychotherapy, is a useful treatment for generalized anxiety disorder and social phobia and, to a lesser extent, for agoraphobia. The purpose of this therapy is to help the woman understand the nature of her anxiety and to help her regain control over her excessive worries. The therapist guides the woman's self-examination toward an understanding that her current behaviors and feelings arise out of behavior patterns that she has practiced throughout her life. Armed with this knowledge, she can then adopt new means of coping with anxiety-producing situations in order to avoid setting off an anxiety response.

Cognitive-behavioral psychotherapy is used to improve self-esteem and coping skills. The patient learns to identify her negative and self-defeating thoughts (such as "I'm not good enough" or "Nobody likes me because I can't play basketball") and to replace those thoughts with positive ones (such as "I'm good enough" and "People like me for who I am, not what I can do"). She monitors the positive impact those thoughts have on her experience, behavior, and feelings and then uses this new source of strength to cope with her anxieties and worries.

Cognitive-behavior therapy can also be directed at specific worries. For example, "I can't go into that tunnel, I'm afraid" is replaced with "I can go into that tunnel, there is nothing there for me to fear." The specific fear or phobia is considered to be a learned (conditioned) response that can be replaced by a more positive response. The old negative responses are reframed as positive responses, and these are practiced until they become as automatic as the phobias had been previously.

Behavior Therapy

There are several different behavioral techniques. They appear to be most helpful for treating phobias—specific phobias, general phobia, social phobia, and agoraphobia—but they can also be beneficial to patients with generalized anxiety disorder. The principle underlying behavior therapy is similar to that for cognitive therapy: the phobias are learned responses that must be "unlearned" and replaced with appropriate responses. In the case of phobias, the learned response is to fear (or avoid) a particular object or situation. The negative response must be blocked and replaced with a positive (or neutral) response.

Systematic desensitization is one type of behavior therapy. As its name implies, it is a slow, step-by-step approach to learning a new response to the fear. It often starts with imagined exposure to the feared object, in order to control the level of anxiety that is produced in response. The woman is first asked to imagine the feared object at a distance and then to imagine bringing it closer to herself. Once she is able to imagine holding or touching the feared object, then the exposure starts with the real object or situation. To treat Louise's fear of blood tests, she would first imagine entering a hospital and walking past a laboratory where the technicians were drawing blood samples; then, she might imagine walking into the laboratory and looking around; then, sitting in the blood-drawing chair for fifteen seconds; and so forth. The series would continue until she was able to imagine having her blood drawn and holding the vial of blood in her hand. Once she was able to do that, then the series would start over with real exposures of gradually increasing intensity. Systematic desensitization is also helpful for patients with social phobia; the woman learns to be comfortable eating or speaking in public by breaking the experience down into manageable units.

The *flooding* technique is exactly as the word implies: it consists of a large, intense dose of exposure to the feared object. Rather than proceeding slowly and gradually, as in systematic desensitization, the woman is confronted with her real feared situation almost immediately. Flooding has the advantage of being effective much more rapidly, but it is intolerable to many patients because of the intensity of the anxiety produced. Relaxation techniques are usually used with the flooding technique, and in some cases, antianxiety medications are used to block the anxiety response.

Exposure with response prevention is a behavioral technique that has gained rapid acceptance, in part because it is effective for such a wide range of symptoms. As with systematic desensitization, the person is deliberately exposed to her feared object or situation in ever-increasing doses. But exposure with response prevention adds another dimension: response prevention, which refers to the practice of voluntarily stopping the behavioral response. Exposure with response prevention is particularly useful for patients who have specific responses to feared situations or who have learned to avoid their feared object or situation (like Julia's strategies to avoid being exposed to tunnels). Another advantage of exposure with response prevention is that much of the work can be done at home. The therapist and the patient design the exposure schedule together and then agree on homework assignments, which the patient must complete before her next session. Relaxation techniques are used as aids to the therapy, but antianxiety medications are typically not prescribed so that the patient understands that her improvement was a result of the behavioral techniques and not the medication.

Relaxation therapy is a useful addition to systematic desensitization and the other behavioral techniques because it serves to disconnect the physical and psychological reactions. Relaxation therapy is usually composed of muscle relaxation and controlled breathing techniques that block a physical fight-or-flee response and keep it from contributing to the psychological experience. In a phobic reaction, the woman's body has learned to associate the feared situation with a stress response. When confronted with her phobic stimulus (a mouse, a tube of blood, or a needle), she feels her pulse and breathing quicken, she begins to sweat, and she may feel nauseated or shaky. This is a conditioned (learned) response, so it happens automatically. The anxiety is totally outside her voluntary control (and may be disconnected from the primary stress-producing experience, just as Julia's reaction to the subway station came twenty years after she was stuck in the tunnel), but because it is a conditioned response, it can be reconditioned (relearned) through relaxation therapy combined with one of the behavioral techniques.

Medications

Antianxiety medications, or anxiolytics, may play a primary or secondary role in the treatment of each of the anxiety disorders. In generalized anxiety disorder and panic disorder, they play a primary role and are effective in decreasing symptoms to acceptable levels in over 80 percent of the patients. For phobic disorders, including social phobia, they might be used as primary agents in time-limited situations (for example, a person who fears flying might take an antianxiety medication to help her tolerate an airplane flight) or as secondary agents to help manage anxiety during behavior therapy or cognitive therapy. Several medications have proved to be effective in decreasing anxiety and blocking panic attacks.

Buspirone (Buspar) is an antianxiety drug that is now frequently chosen as first-line therapy for women with mild to moderately severe anxiety disorders. Because it takes up to a month to start working, it is not appropriate for severely ill patients nor for the short-term management of anxiety. Buspirone differs from other antianxiety medications in several important ways. It is stimulating, rather than sedating, which may explain why it is not helpful for panic disorders (actually, buspirone has been reported to worsen panic attacks in some patients). It may cause slight agitation and jitteriness, but in general, it has few side effects. It doesn't cause physical dependency, so it doesn't raise concerns of addiction. Further, it can be stopped abruptly without causing withdrawal symptoms.

Benzodiazepines, commonly known as tranquilizers or sedatives, have been used to treat anxiety for over thirty years and are still the most widely prescribed antianxiety drugs. They are very effective in blocking panic attacks, and they help over three-quarters of the women who take them for panic symptoms. There are two classes of benzodiazepines: short-acting drugs such as alprazolam (Xanax), oxazepam (Serax), and lorazepam (Ativan); and long-acting drugs, including diazepam (Valium), chlordiazepoxide (Librium), clonazepam (Klonipin), clorazepate (Tranxene), flurazepam (Dalmane), and prazepam (Centrax). You might recognize some of the names of these frequently prescribed medications and realize that the drugs are used to treat both anxiety disorders and sleep disorders (see Chapter Seven).

The short-acting benzodiazepines are metabolized very quickly and eliminated from the body in just a few hours. This is an advantage to the woman who is taking the benzodiazepine occasionally for phobic disorders or at nighttime for insomnia. The medication will help her to fall asleep at night, but she will be alert and fully awake in the morning. The short duration of action may be a disadvantage to the woman who is taking the benzodiazepine for treatment of an anxiety disorder, as she may experience withdrawal symptoms between doses. In such cases, she will have good relief of her anxiety for two to three hours, and then she may experience increasing anxiety, difficulties with concentration and "fuzzy" thinking, muscle cramps, jitteriness, and tingling in her fingers or toes. In contrast, the long-acting benzodiazepines do not have problems with between-dose withdrawal symptoms, but they frequently leave the woman feeling groggy and sedated during the daytime hours, even when she has taken her dose at bedtime the evening before.

The benzodiazepines are commonly assumed to be addictive drugs. Typically they are not, however, as there is no true psychological dependency; the drugs don't produce a chemical "high," so the woman doesn't get "hooked." However, they do produce physical dependency, which means that the woman's body adjusts to the medications, and soon their presence is required for her to feel normal. If the benzodiazepine is stopped abruptly, the woman will experience withdrawal symptoms similar to those described earlier. In cases where the treatment has been prolonged for several months, abrupt discontinuation can cause very serious withdrawal symptoms. Thus, a gradual decrease in dosage is indicated; the drug may need to be weaned away over several weeks' time. In the case of short-acting benzodiazepines, withdrawal symptoms may be prevented by dividing the total daily dose into small portions and taking the medication more frequently throughout the day.

Physical dependency can lead to tolerance so that the woman may feel that she requires increasing doses of benzodiazepines for adequate symptom relief. This is not advisable and is one of several reasons why benzodiazepine treatment should be closely monitored by an experienced physician.

The choice of a slow-acting benzodiazepine versus a long-acting benzodiazepine has to be an individual one. Each patient reacts to the benzodiazepines differently, and each woman has different needs. One may prefer to avoid the increased anxiety associated with between-dose withdrawal and choose a long-acting drug like Valium, while another might wish to avoid feeling groggy and choose a short-acting drug, such as Xanax. Sedation is the most common side effect associated with use of the benzodiazepines. It can have serious consequences, as it interferes with concentration and can increase the chance of motor vehicle accidents. Other side effects are less common but include confusion, forgetfulness, and dizziness.

Benzodiazepines are also associated with a rare side effect known as behavioral disinhibition. Behavioral disinhibition is characterized by a sudden change in behavior; the woman might act in inappropriate ways, or she might become impulsive, loud, or rude. Behavioral disinhibition is a serious side effect and usually necessitates discontinuation of the benzodiazepine medication.

Finally, one has to be careful drinking alcohol while taking a benzodiazapene, as the two drugs have similar effects and their combined use can cause the woman to be very sleepy or confused or to black out.

Beta-blockers, such as propranolol (Inderal), are very effective at blocking the physical symptoms associated with acute anxiety and social phobia ("stage fright"). The beta-blockers do not have any effect on the anxiety, but they are very effective in preventing the fight-or-flee response and its accompanying dry mouth, racing heart, and feelings of light-headedness or faintness. The beta-blockers might be considered to be the chemical equivalent of relaxation therapy, as they disconnect the physical symptoms of anxiety from the emotional response.

Tricyclic antidepressants, such as imipramine (Tofranil), nortriptyline (Aventyl or Pamelor), and clomipramine (Anafranil), are effective antianxiety drugs; they are even more effective in combating panic. Imipramine was shown to be effective for treatment of panic disorder in the early 1960s and has continued to be used with good success since then. In fact, it remains the gold standard by which other medications are judged. However, the side effects of tricyclic treatment can be troublesome. These side effects include sedation, dry mouth, dizziness, and weight gain.

Selective serotonin reuptake inhibiting drugs (SSRIs), such as fluoxetine (Prozac), sertraline (Zoloft), paroxetine (Paxil), and fluvoxamine (Luvox), offer the same benefits for the treatment of anxiety disorders and panic as do the tricyclic antidepressants. (Chapter Nine contains a complete discussion of both SSRIs and tricyclic antidepressants.) The SSRIs have an additional advantage in that they have fewer side effects. But note that the serotonin reuptake inhibiting drugs cause stimulation, rather than sedation, and sometimes they can actually increase anxiety for a short time after the therapy is started. Fluvoxamine (Luvox) has been found recently to be effective for panic disorder; this offers a new treatment option for patients who have undesirable side effects with imipramine treatment. Further, the combination of fluvoxamine and behavior therapy appears to be more effective than either treatment alone.

Summary

The anxiety disorders—phobias, generalized anxiety disorder, social phobia, and panic disorder—are characterized by the presence of excessive or inappropriate anxiety. Targeted therapies, such as anxiolytic medications, behavior therapy, and cognitive-behavior therapy, can reduce the anxiety to a manageable level, or, in some cases, eradicate it completely. If you have been "suffering in silence," then break the silence by asking your doctor for a referral to a well-qualified mental health professional.

Resources

Anxiety Disorders Association of America
6000 Executive Boulevard, Suite 513
Rockville, Maryland 20852
301–231–9350

Office of Scientific Information
National Institute of Mental Health
5600 Fishers Lane, Room 7C–02
Rockville, Maryland 20857
301–443–4513

The NIMH has recently launched a national campaign to promote awareness of panic disorder and will provide free information on request.

Further Reading

Beck, Aaron T., and Gary Emery. *Anxiety Disorders and Phobias: A Cognitive Perspective.* New York: Basic Books, 1985.
Dowling, Colette. *You Mean I Don't Have to Feel This Way? New Help for Depression, Anxiety, and Addiction.* New York: Scribner, 1991.
Kernodle, William D. *Panic Disorder: What You Don't Know May Be Danger-*

ous to Your Health. 2nd ed. Richmond, VA: William Byrd Press, 1993.

Klerman, Gerald L., and other members of the World Psychiatric Association. *Panic, Anxiety, and Its Treatment.* Washington, DC: American Psychiatric Press, 1993.

Marshall, John R. *Social Phobia: From Shyness to Stage Fright.* New York: Basic Books, 1994.

Ross, Jerilyn. *Triumph over Fear: A Book of Help and Hope for People with Anxiety, Panic Attacks, and Phobias.* New York: Bantam Books, 1994.

Sheehan, David. *The Anxiety Disease.* New York: Bantam Books, 1983.

Notes

1. Jerome Kagan, J. S. Resnick, and N. Snidman, "Biological Bases of Childhood Shyness," *Science* 240 (1988): 167.
2. Joseph Biederman, Jerrold Rosenbaum, and colleagues. *Child and Adolescent Psychiatric Clinics of North America,* vol. 2, no. 4 (Philadelphia: W. B. Saunders, 1993), 667–84.

CHAPTER 13

Excessively Compulsive, or Obsessive-Compulsive Disorder?

Rebecca raced to the car with her half-open briefcase in one hand, her change of shoes and her coffee cup in the other, knowing that she hadn't a minute to spare to get to work on time. Once inside the car, she wondered, "Did I turn off the coffeemaker? Did I lock the front door?" Because she was late and had to leave immediately, she tried to reason with herself, "I always turn off the coffeemaker. I'm sure I must have locked the door." Then began the struggle. "I know there's less than a one in a million chance that I didn't, but if I don't check, the house might burn down or we'll be robbed." The more she tried to resist the urge to check, the more anxious she became.

Rebecca finally gave in to her obsessive worries and returned to the house. Arriving at the front door, she found it locked—just as she had expected. She quickly unlocked it and ran into the kitchen. She checked the electric coffeemaker—it too was just as she had left it. She stared at it and knew that it was turned off, yet she kept looking. Three, four, five times she checked, as if she couldn't quite trust what her eyes were seeing. Then she checked the stove and the toaster oven and went upstairs to make sure that her curling iron was unplugged. Feeling angry at herself for giving in to her worries yet again, she went through her exit ritual one more time and ran to her car, promising herself that tomorrow she wouldn't repeat this foolish ritual. But she would, just as she had each morning for the past six years.

Each and every evening Rebecca had to perform a similar checking ritual before she could leave her office. Her rational self knew that nothing bad would happen if the pencils weren't lined up "just so," or the file cabinet locked, or her mug carefully washed and placed in the exact center of her desktop, but she became so anxious if she didn't check that it ruined her entire evening. So she would make up an excuse to leave her friends at the elevator and run back to perform her checking ritual. Some evenings she would be stuck at her desk for over two hours; other times, she could feel satisfied in as little as five minutes. Stress and worry in her life seemed to make the rituals more intense, but they were never gone, because Rebecca has obsessive-compulsive disorder.

Obsessive-compulsive disorder (OCD) is a neuropsychiatric illness characterized by the presence of obsessions (distressing or intrusive thoughts) and compulsions (repetitive, ritualized behaviors). In the last few years, OCD has become a household term, as television talk shows, morning news programs, and weekly tabloids have told the stories of people who have hidden their obsessive-compulsive behaviors for decades but are now coming out of the closet and receiving help.

The recent interest in OCD doesn't mean that this is a new disorder. In fact, descriptions of obsessions and compulsions have been around for as long as there has been the written word. Early religious texts instructed priests and rabbis on the proper procedure for treating morality obsessions or religious scrupulosity (excessive concern about sin and wrongdoing). Women with scrupulosity struggled to achieve religious perfection, so they constantly confessed to and begged forgiveness for the slightest transgressions. If the cleric recognized her religious obsessions, he offered a cleansing ritual designed to relieve all anxiety about any accidental transgressions. Sometimes this was enough, but usually the reassurance wasn't sufficient. After all, how did the woman with OCD know for sure that the priest had performed the ceremony correctly? And even if he had, how long would she be protected? How would she know if she wasn't? Maybe it was already invalid?

Perhaps the most famous historical example of OCD is found in the guilty obsessions and ritualized hand washing of Shakespeare's Lady Macbeth. Lady Macbeth washed for hours into the night, and despite the invisibility of the "damned spot," she could not be reassured. In the modern era, Howard Hughes's extreme preoccupation with germs and contaminants is considered to be classic for severe OCD. He protected himself from contamination by sealing windows, placing tissues over the furniture and floors, and giving detailed instructions about the sterile preparation of his food. As with many OCD patients, the more he avoided possible sources of contamination, the more his fears became entrenched and the worse his illness became. Eventually, his rituals around bathing and grooming himself were so incapacitating that he began to avoid these activities completely. He stopped bathing and would no longer cut his hair or fingernails—so despite his obsessive fear of contamination and dirt, he became filthy and slovenly. Such paradoxes are not at all uncommon in OCD; in fact, avoidance is a key symptom of the disorder. One rock star's rituals to avoid contamination became a nationwide fad: millions of teens emulated him by wearing a single glove and leaving their shoelaces untied.

Obsessive-compulsive disorder is not unique to the rich and famous, however. People from all walks of life can be affected. An accountant with severe checking rituals might spend sixteen hours each day, seven days a week, at her desk, checking the same column of numbers over and over again or adding and re-adding a client's bill to make absolutely certain that she hasn't overcharged him. A housewife might spend ten hours a day cleaning and recleaning her apartment, while across town, a beautician with repeating rituals loses her job because she had to cut each hair five times "perfectly," and in order to do so, she kept cutting and recutting a client's hair until the woman was almost bald. Another woman was forced to quit her nursing position because she had such overwhelming obsessive fears about harm coming to her children that she had to park outside her children's school all day in order to keep them safe.

Even when women don't lose their jobs or become prisoners at their desks or in their homes, OCD can have an impact on their work and home life by making even the simplest of tasks take hours to perform. For example, getting dressed in the morning could take two hours or more when each piece of clothing has to be perfectly clean, so it has to be removed and replaced if it touches something dirty. Or writing a letter might be impossible because of the necessity of forming each letter perfectly. The excess time required to perform a ritual and the disruption caused by the rituals and the obsessive thoughts contribute to the disorder's interference with one's life.

Interference and *distress* are what determine whether or not a woman is suffering from OCD. Distress arises in response to the frightening content of the obsessions, recognition of the irrationality of the obsessions and the futility of the compulsions, and also from the inescapable presence of the OCD. Some women have mild obsessive worries and brief checking rituals but are not distressed by them, nor do these rituals interfere in their lives. These women don't have OCD.

Do You Have Obsessive-Compulsive Disorder?

Before deciding whether or not you might have OCD, it is important to know what the disorder is and what it is not. Obsessive-compulsive disorder is *not* excessive compulsiveness. It is not merely being extra careful or extra neat or extra thorough. Obsessive-compulsive disorder is a neuropsychiatric disorder characterized by the presence of obsessions and compulsions.

Obsessions are unwanted thoughts that keep coming back over and over again. They are distressing in content or so persistent that they interfere with your ability to pay attention. When you try to ignore or suppress an obsession, it makes you feel nervous or anxious inside, despite the fact that the thoughts are clearly senseless and irrational. If you have obsessive fears about germs and contamination, for example, you might worry that you caught AIDS while using the movie theater's rest room. Despite knowing that you can't *really* get AIDS from touching a doorknob, the obsessive thought, "But what if . . . ?" returns over and over again. Your anxiety builds until you give in and compulsively wash away the (nonexistent) AIDS germs. The washing brings immediate relief, but soon the "what-ifs" return: "What if the water wasn't hot enough to kill the virus? What if the faucet handle still had AIDS germs on it, and now they're back on my hands? What if the virus already got into my body? Maybe I should have a blood test just to make certain I'm OK." But there is no end to the uncertainty.

The French identified OCD as *folie de doute*, or the "doubting disease," because of these feelings of uncertainty and the persistent "what-ifs." The term "doubting disease" captures the essence of the uncertainty accompanying the obsessions; the slightest doubt is intolerable. Our patients have told us that it is like the "one-in-a-million-chance center in my head goes crazy and starts dominating my life. The rest of my brain is screaming, 'Shut up! Shut up!' as loud as it can, but the OCD part just won't listen."

In other cases, obsessional thoughts might be limited to repeated nonsensical words or snatches of music. Such thoughts become distressing when they are present constantly or are distracting enough to prevent you from conversing coherently or reading simple sentences. Other obsessions are distressing because of their content. Some obsessions are violent mental images so terrible that they make the OCD sufferer cringe in horror—for example, scenes from the Nazi death camps or the sight of a child being struck by a train as you stand helplessly nearby. Unlike psychotic thoughts, obsessions are almost always recognized as senseless and irrational ("crazy") and as coming from inside one's own head. Common obsessions include:

- Fear that harm will come to you or others
- Violent or horrific mental images
- Fear of dirt, germs, or environmental contaminants
- Fear of contamination by people, animals, insects, or others
- Fear that you will do something embarrassing, illegal, or dangerous
- Fear of blasphemy or excessive concerns about morality
- Need to hoard or save things
- Need for symmetry or exactness
- Intrusive sounds, thoughts, or music.

Compulsions are rituals and behaviors that are carried out in response to an obsessive thought. Compulsions are *not* the same as excessive compulsiveness. Excessive compulsiveness is the careful attention to details and procedure, while compulsions are useless, repetitive behaviors. Compulsions are performed according to certain rules and are designed to dispel the anxiety that accompanies an obsession. Sometimes the rules governing a compulsive ritual become so complex that it is impossible to perform the ritual perfectly; then the OCD sufferer never feels relief. In severe cases, even when she can perform the ritual correctly, the compulsion is only able to decrease the obsessive anxiety for a brief moment, so it must be repeated over and over again. Because compulsions are designed to neutralize the bad feelings that accompany an obsession, they frequently involve washing and checking. Common compulsions include:

- Ritualized hand washing, bathing, or showering
- Ritualized cleaning or removal of contaminants
- Checking that you haven't harmed someone else or yourself
- Checking for danger or to make sure that something terrible hasn't happened
- Repeating routine activities, such as rereading or rewriting
- Counting compulsions and other mental rituals
- Hoarding or saving compulsions
- Confessing, asking for reassurance, or questioning repeatedly
- Ritualized eating behaviors.

As stated earlier, OCD is more than merely having obsessive thoughts or performing compulsive rituals. It is diagnosed only when the symptoms are distressing and interfere in the woman's personal and work life. If you find that you have obsessive worries or ritualized behaviors that are upsetting and interfere with your life, then you should seek evaluation and treatment.

If You Don't Have OCD, What Could It Be?

Subclinical OCD

When Rebecca (the young woman with OCD whom you met at the beginning of the chapter) was in high school, she had repeating compulsions that caused her to have to do things three times in a row. She brushed her teeth three times, washed her hands three times, took three sips of milk before setting her glass down, traced over the figures on her geometry test three times, and so forth. The repetitions weren't very upsetting to her because they were easy to do and didn't waste much of her time. At that point, she had subclinical OCD. As her symptoms worsened, however, she spent more than an hour each day doing her rituals, and she began to have distress and interference. At that point, she no longer had subclinical symptoms—she had full-blown OCD.

If you have obsessive thoughts or compulsive rituals similar to those listed earlier, but they are not particularly time-consuming or distressing, then you might have subclinical OCD. Subclinical OCD refers to patients with symptoms that are too mild to meet diagnostic criteria but that are still of concern. Many times, therapy is not required; when it is, treatments that are helpful for OCD (such as behavior therapy or serotonin reuptake inhibiting medications) are also helpful for subclinical OCD.

In addition, if you have a depression and subclinical OCD, you may get more relief from an antidepressant medication that also has anti-OCD properties than from other medications. It is important to tell your doctor about any obsessions or compulsions that might be bothering you, even if they're "crazy" or embarrassing. Chances are, your doctor has heard similar complaints from other patients and will be able to help you.

Normal Habits, Superstitions, and Excessive Compulsiveness

Ramona has always been superstitious, ever since she was a little girl who carefully avoided stepping on the cracks in the sidewalk. She really believes that she can have a good day if she picks up a dropped penny or that she can prevent bad luck by knocking on wood or throwing spilled salt over her shoulder. Ramona also has a ritual for everything, from getting up in the morning and making her bed right away to having a very particular order for brushing her teeth, putting on her pajamas, and applying her face cream at night.

On the other hand, if Ramona is staying at a hotel and forgets her night cream, she can go to bed without experiencing any anxiety or concern. None of the rituals is disturbing to her; in fact, she thinks that most are both sensible and necessary. She feels that she is more efficient when she organizes her life this way. She has chosen to perform certain rituals because they are comforting and provide order to her life, not because she's trying to protect herself from an obsessional fear.

Nearly everyone has a few rituals and superstitions. We may even be "excessively compulsive"—taking extra care to ensure that a job is done perfectly or that our home is neat and tidy. New parents are often compulsive about their babies, checking (and rechecking) that the child is safe and warm at night or avoiding crowds for fear that the baby will catch something. Having such "compulsive" rituals can be productive when they keep your life under control and help you cope with the demands of modern life. This excessive compulsiveness doesn't cause distress or waste time, so it does not qualify as OCD. Unless it is of concern to you, excessive compulsiveness doesn't require evaluation or treatment.

Obsessive-Compulsive Personality Disorder

Rachel strode purposefully to the car with her neatly packed briefcase in one hand and her coffee cup in the other. Once in the driver's seat, she mentally checked off her house-exiting list: "Did I turn off the coffeemaker? Did I lock the front door? Do I have everything I need for the day?" As she went through the list, she discovered that she didn't have her personal journal and returned to the house to reclaim it, quite annoyed that her carelessness had upset the day's carefully planned schedule. For Rachel believed in schedules and in sticking to them, no matter what the circumstances.

Rachel also believed in organization, lists, and attention to details. Sometimes, this excessive concern with minor details prevented her from getting the job done or from even getting started; for example, there was the time when a major project had to be done in only two days and Rachel spent the first day and a half deciding on the type font and layout for the write-up. Rachel makes endless lists and writes dozens of notes — again, sometimes to the exclusion of completing the primary project. That is, if she can decide on a primary project. She frequently is indecisive to the point of being paralyzed; she is also inflexible and stubborn, particularly about moral issues. She may have difficulty throwing things away, even though they have no sentimental value, and she is stingy with both her money and her time. Rachel is often impatient with others because they aren't as perfectionistic as she is. Because she is so rigid, others perceive her as emotionally unavailable and think that she must lead a miserable, lonely existence, yet it doesn't seem that way to her.

Obsessive-compulsive personality disorder is distinguished from OCD by the absence of obsessive thoughts and compulsive rituals. Unlike excessive compulsiveness, however, it *is* a disorder and may require treatment because the personality traits have the potential to cause interference and impairment. For example, hoarding (defined as the inability to throw out *anything*, including outdated newspapers, old clothes, even food wrappers and other trash) is often a feature of obsessive-compulsive personality disorder. It might require treatment if it is so excessive that it causes health risks or interferes with normal functioning.

The medications used to treat OCD may be helpful for some women with obsessive-compulsive personality disorder. Several research studies, including one done by our group, suggest that in some cases, the obsessive-compulsive personality traits are a coping response to early OCD. This might explain why the anti-OCD medications are effective. The medicines don't change the woman's basic personality, but they do decrease the compulsive attention to detail and the indecisiveness. Often, the best treatment for obsessive-compulsive personality disorder is a combination of medication and psychotherapy. Obviously, in order to receive treatment, the woman with obsessive-compulsive personality disorder must want help; this means that she must be at least somewhat distressed by her personality traits.

Ruminations

Ruminations are worries or guilty thoughts that, like obsessions, keep coming back over and over again. Unlike obsessions, however, they are not perceived as senseless, and they do not lead to compulsive rituals. Frequently, they concern real (but uncontrollable) problems, events that have gone poorly, or worries about upcoming situations. For example, a woman with ruminations might lie in bed at night and worry about what she did at work that day. She knows she must get to sleep, yet she keeps returning to the thought, "If only I had done this instead of that . . ." Other times, she finds herself ruminating about her husband's poor health or their mounting bills. Another woman, whose boyfriend left her precipitously, might replay their last date over and over, preoccupied with what she could have done differently.

Each of the ruminative worries is rational, but they are excessive and pointless. Because of this, it is sometimes difficult to distinguish ruminations from obsessions, and the distinction may be made only after the underlying disorder has been identified. Ruminations often result from major depression and sometimes from severe emotional stress. A careful diagnostic evaluation will reveal the nature of the recurrent worries and suggest the appropriate treatment.

Hypochondriasis

Hypochondriasis is a chronic psychiatric condition that is similar in many ways to OCD. It is characterized by the persistent fear of having a disease (or the belief that one has a disease), despite medical evidence that you are healthy. This obsession with one's health leads to the compulsion of seeking medical reassurance. A hypochondriacal woman will go from doctor to doctor, looking for the one physician who will understand her symptoms and find the illness that she is convinced is there.

She requires constant reassurance that her symptoms haven't progressed, and even when the lab tests (that *she* insists on having) come back normal, she can't believe the results. That is one of the differences between hypochondriasis and OCD. Women with hypochondriasis are typically convinced of the truth of their concerns; OCD sufferers recognize that their obsessions are senseless and irrational (at least until they are severely ill). Further, while OCD patients usually have several obsessive concerns, patients with hypochondriasis have only one symptom: fear of having a serious disease. The specific disease may change over time, but other obsessive concerns do not develop. The treatment of hypochondriasis requires a complex combination of psychotherapy, cognitive therapy, and medications, including those used to treat OCD.

Hypochondriasis is a rare disorder that should be distinguished from the more common condition of "being a hypochondriac." Psychiatrists use the terms *somatization disorder* and *somatoform disorder* to describe this condition. Somatization disorder is a chronic condition that begins before the woman turns thirty and continues throughout her life. Somatoform disorder doesn't last as long and can begin at any time. Women with these disorders have multiple physical complaints, which result in excessive use of the medical system. They are unable to tolerate normal aches and pains because they worry that the discomforts might represent a more serious illness. They also worry excessively about menstrual cramps, irregular menstrual bleeding, and other gynecological complaints and about digestive difficulties such as heartburn, bloating, constipation, and diarrhea. Often, women with somatization disorders will have had several different workups to find the cause of their pain, digestive difficulties, menstrual irregularities, and/or neurological symptoms, such as dizziness, numbness, difficulty swallowing, or weakness.

Doctors may become frustrated with the woman's inability to accept reassurance, and the woman is equally frustrated by the doctors' inability to find the cause of her discomfort. Often, she will "doctor shop" in the hope that she will find a more competent, sympathetic physician. She may undergo surgery, particularly gynecologic surgeries such as a D and C (dilation and curettage) or hysterectomy, in an effort to relieve her suffering, but the procedure doesn't help and recovery is often difficult. Women with somatization disorder frequently don't recover fully; they develop pain at the incision site or in the internal organs surrounding the operation.

Women with somatization disorder and somatoform disorder are the ones who are most likely to be told that their symptoms are "all in your head"—but they're not. Both disorders appear to have a biological basis deserving of accurate diagnosis and treatment. Combination therapy appears to be most effective for the somatization disorders, and many physicians recommend a comprehensive treatment plan consisting of behavior therapy, medication (antidepressants such as the SSRIs and antianxiety medications), and psychotherapy.

Psychotic Disorders

When patients are severely ill with OCD, they lose perspective on their obsessions and may no longer be able to view their obsessive fears as senseless and irrational. In such cases, it is difficult to separate OCD from the psychotic disorders, in which a person can't distinguish fears from facts. In the past, this led to the misdiagnosis of OCD as schizophrenia, and countless numbers of OCD patients spent years on the back wards of state psychiatric hospitals. Now, however, psychiatrists will examine the content of the thoughts and note that they resemble obsessions rather than psychotic symptoms, or they may call on the family members to provide evidence that the patient initially recognized the senselessness of the obsessions and compulsions. In most patients, the course of the symptoms can clarify the nature of the disorder, but in some cases, a medication trial is necessary to sort out the primary diagnosis. Obsessive-compulsive symptoms will respond to treatment with anti-OCD medications such as serotonin reuptake blockers, but they will not respond to antipsychotics; for psychotic symptoms, the opposite is true.

Medical Disorders That May Masquerade as OCD

Irritable Bowel Disorder

Irritable bowel disorder is a medical condition in which the patient suffers from abdominal pain and alternating bouts of diarrhea and constipation. It may be confused with OCD because the patients frequently become obsessed with their bowel function and compulsive about maintaining a healthy lifestyle. In addition, irritable bowel disorder may be accompanied by symptoms of depression and anxiety, as is OCD. Another similarity is that stress contributes to symptom flare-ups in both irritable bowel disorder and OCD.

A careful history should be sufficient to distinguish between OCD and irritable bowel disorder. While an OCD patient may worry excessively about bowel function, she has normal stools; those of a patient with irritable bowel disorder, on the other hand, are rarely normal. Interestingly, anti-OCD medications and antidepressants often help irritable bowel disorder because they can decrease bowel motility and irritability and also decrease excessive worrying.

Cushing's Disease

Cushing's disease is a rare disorder caused by excessive production of the hormone cortisol—a steroid hormone that affects many different systems in the body, including the kidneys and immune system, and plays a key role in metabolism, particularly of sugars, fats, and protein. The symptoms of Cushing's disease include obesity, high blood pressure, fatigue, weakness, loss of menstrual periods, increased facial hair growth, and purplish stretch marks on the abdomen. The chemical changes associated with Cushing's disease may also cause obsessive-compulsive symptoms in addition. Typically, the patient will have obvious physical symptoms by the time she develops OCD. If she has a complete physical examination as part of her workup for OCD, it should lead the physician to order the appropriate laboratory studies and diagnose Cushing's disease. If the OCD symptoms of Cushing's disease are problematic, the standard drug and behavioral therapies prescribed for OCD are often helpful. Cushing's disease is treated with drugs that block the effects of the excess cortisol and/or by surgery to remove the malfunctioning portions of the adrenal glands. Once the Cushing's disease has been effectively treated, the obsessive-compulsive symptoms will also resolve.

Tourette's Syndrome

Tourette's syndrome is also rare but is frequently missed, especially in women. Tourette's syndrome is a neurological condition characterized by the presence of involuntary vocalizations (such as coughs, grunts, throat clearing, sighing, humming, sniffing, singing, or swearing) and episodic motor tics and twitches (ranging from simple eye blinks, grimaces, and shoulder shrugs to complicated touching, tapping, and stepping patterns). The tics begin during childhood and often disappear during adolescence. When they do not improve with age, they can be quite embarrassing and may interfere with the young woman's ability to socialize or obtain employment.

Because the tics of Tourette's syndrome can be quite complex and may follow a "compulsive" urge, they can be difficult to distinguish from the compulsive behaviors of OCD. However, the "compulsive urge" of Tourette's syndrome differs from a true obsession, and typically, in Tourette's, there are no obsessive thoughts. It is important to make the distinction between compulsions and tics, as tics are not helped by antiobsessional medications or behavior therapies. In fact, tics are best treated by low doses of the major tranquilizers (dopamine-blocking agents such as pimozide, haloperidol, and others).

Encephalitis, Strokes, and Other Neurological Conditions

Shortly after World War I, there were nationwide epidemics of influenza (flu) and encephalitis (brain infections). Many people who had this kind of encephalitis developed OCD, particularly during the recovery phase. Other infections, including viruses and bacteria, have also been reported to cause OCD. Despite the frequency with which OCD patients worry about AIDS, it is not known to cause obsessive-compulsive symptoms.

There have been several reports of strokes, anaphylactic shock (severe allergic shock), and other brain injuries causing OCD. Such brain injuries are extremely rare, but if someone were to develop OCD suddenly, "out of the blue," a neurological cause should be suspected. Since some of these neurological conditions can be helped by medication or physical therapy, it is important to look for a brain injury. In other cases—for example, strokes located in the basal ganglia—the neurological damage is permanent and the only recourse is to try to treat the secondary symptoms, including OCD, with appropriate medications.

Autoimmune OCD

Recent research has suggested that certain autoimmune diseases may cause OCD. Autoimmune diseases are those in which antibodies (infection-fighting cells) turn against the body and try to destroy it. Examples of autoimmune diseases include rheumatoid arthritis (the antibodies attack the joints), lupus (the antibodies attack the skin, kidneys, and brain), and rheumatic fever (the antibodies attack the heart, joints, skin, or brain). Rheumatic fever is slightly different from other autoimmune diseases because it affects children only, and the antibodies that attack the child's tissues begin as "good" antibodies produced to fight off a strep throat infection. Rheumatic fever is an example of an autoimmune disorder that can cause OCD when the antibodies cause inflammation in certain parts of the brain. Lupus may also cause OCD if antibrain antibodies are produced. OCD that is caused by an auto-immune disorder would respond best to treatment of the underlying immunological problem. A careful medical history and physical examination are essential for all newly diagnosed cases of OCD.

Treatment of OCD

Obsessive-compulsive disorder can be very effectively treated with medication, behavior therapy, or a combination of the two. Psychotherapy may be helpful for some of the issues related to the OCD, but it is not effective for the treatment of the obsessions and compulsions themselves. For example, when OCD symptoms are effectively treated with medications or behavior therapy, some patients who have suffered for long periods of time may find that psychotherapy can help put their lives back together. Similarly, group therapy might be indicated for those patients whose symptoms were so severe that they never had a chance to learn essential social skills.

Drug Treatment: The SRIs

The recent development of a new family of medications, the serotonin reuptake inhibitors, or SRIs, was a revolutionary breakthrough in the treatment of OCD. The SRIs appear to correct the chemical dysfunction of OCD by readjusting the balance in the serotonin system, one of the brain's chemical messenger systems. The SRIs useful for OCD include clomipramine (Anafranil), fluoxetine (Prozac), sertraline (Zoloft), paroxetine (Paxil), and fluvoxamine (Luvox).

Clomipramine differs from the other SRIs in that it is a tricyclic antidepressant (see Chapter Nine for more information about tricyclics). The other SRIs are grouped together as SSRIs: selective serotonin reuptake inhibitors. Any drug that inhibits serotonin reuptake can cause serotonergic side effects, such as headache, body aches, nausea, abdominal discomfort, diarrhea or constipation, and appetite changes resulting in weight loss (20 percent of patients) or weight gain (15 percent of patients).

The SRIs offer symptom relief to over three-quarters of the patients with OCD. They appear to work directly on the obsessive-compulsive symptoms, suggesting that OCD is the result of a defect in the serotonin system. Anti-OCD drugs can't help everyone, however, and usually they don't completely eliminate the obsessive-compulsive symptoms; rather, they diminish the intensity of the obsessions to the point where they can be ignored or suppressed. In addition, although side effects may develop immediately, the anti-OCD drugs may not have a noticeable benefit for three weeks or longer and often don't reach maximum effectiveness for up to three months.

At present, there is no way to predict which patients will respond to SRI treatment nor to guess which of the SRIs will be the most helpful. A patient might need to try several SRIs before finding one that is both helpful and has tolerable side effects. Although the side effects of the SRIs are much less than those of the traditional antidepressants, they still may be problematic for some patients. The individual SRIs differ in their side-effect profiles, so if one causes problems, it is worth trying another. Striking the balance between a positive clinical response and negative side effects requires teamwork on the part of the patient and her physician.

For most people, the anti-OCD medication will need to be continued for the rest of their life in order to maintain symptom control, although often the dosage can be lowered after the symptoms have subsided. The SRIs typically offer treatment, not a cure, of the OCD. It has been reported that one in seven patients with OCD may have a spontaneous remission, so your psychiatrist might advise you to take a drug holiday in order to determine whether or not the medication is still needed. If the OCD symptoms recur as the medication is tapered, the drug dosage can be increased and will regain effectiveness. (Unlike the situation with mood-stabilizing drugs and bipolar disorder, stopping and restarting SRI therapy in OCD does not seem to be associated with a loss of therapeutic benefit.) Such drug holidays can be tried every year or so to determine whether the medication is still necessary.

Behavior Therapy: Exposure with Response Prevention

The best psychological treatment of OCD is a behavior therapy technique known as exposure with response prevention. Behavior therapy appears to work as well as medications for the treatment of OCD in patients who can comply with the requirements of the therapy. As its name implies, "exposure" involves deliberately coming into contact with the thing that the person fears—for example, touching a dirty toilet seat. "Response prevention" means that the person doesn't do what she normally would do to relieve the anxiety—such as wash her hands.

Sometimes the behavior therapy uses imagined scenes instead of real exposures. For example, if Jane's obsession was that she would become contaminated by AIDS, it would be too frightening to her to ask her to hold a vial containing the AIDS virus and then not wash her hands. Rather, she and her therapist would devise a treatment schedule that would utilize a series of increasingly difficult exposures. Each day, she would spend at least one hour practicing the imagined or real exposures and preventing herself from washing afterward. She might first just imagine herself going into a public rest room, using the toilet, and leaving without washing her hands. Despite the dirty feelings this imagined scene would evoke, she wouldn't allow herself to wash, and over a relatively short period, the anxiety would fade and she would be ready to move on to the next degree of anxiety-producing exposure. She would keep progressing until new exposures didn't evoke anxiety or compulsions, at which point the obsessions typically have been brought under control.

Behavior therapy requires a motivated patient who chooses to fight her OCD actively. Most behavior therapy centers find that only about 40 percent of the OCD patients who inquire about behavior therapy actually enter and complete treatment. Some can't imagine that this technique could really work; others can't stand the thought of increasing their anxiety levels even momentarily. Other patients are too demoralized by their symptoms to be able to cooperate with the therapy. Still others have only obsessive thoughts and no compulsive behaviors, and it is very difficult to develop a behavior therapy plan for them utilizing exposure and response prevention.

For those patients who complete a course of behavior therapy, the improvement is generally equivalent to that of drug therapy. Effective behavior therapy offers one advantage over drug treatment: the patients tend to remain in remission over the long term, requiring only occasional refresher sessions to keep their symptoms under control.

Medications Versus Behavior Therapy: Which to Choose?

With two such different treatments available, how does one choose between the two? Some people do not want to take medications, so they choose to make the commitment to behavior therapy. Others prefer drug therapy because the few mild side effects they experience are far outweighed by the quick benefits of decreased obsessive-compulsive symptoms. Still others use both medication and behavior therapy, or they choose to start with an SRI in order to gain control over their OCD and then use behavior therapy to obtain long-term symptom relief. The bottom line is that *both* medications and behavior therapy work for the majority of patients with OCD. The choice between them is an individual one that must be made in consultation with your physician.

Rebecca (the young woman with OCD whom you met at the beginning of the chapter) sought help recently from a psychiatrist experienced in treating anxiety disorders. The psychiatrist took a careful history, spoke to Rebecca's internist about her physical examination, ordered some laboratory studies, and asked Rebecca to return to discuss treatment options. At the next appointment, they discussed the advantages and disadvantages of behavior therapy and the serotonin reuptake blocking medications before deciding together that Rebecca would try clomipramine (Anafranil) first. She noticed that the medicine made her mouth dry, but otherwise she had no problems with side effects. After three weeks, Rebecca found that her obsessive worries weren't as strong and that she sometimes could resist the urge to carry out her checking rituals. After six weeks of medication treatment, she was able to leave the house in the morning and drive directly to work, without having to return to the house to recheck. Soon she could leave work in the evening with her coworkers because she didn't need to return to check.

Rebecca felt cured, but she wasn't. When her dosage of clomipramine was decreased a few months later, her symptoms returned. This time she knew that she was ready to try behavior therapy. She remained at the lower medication dose so that she continued to have some obsessive fears and compulsive rituals and began an intensive course of therapy using exposure with response prevention. The behavior therapist acted as her guide and coach, but Rebecca did the hard work of forcing herself not to check and waiting out the waves of anxiety that followed. After a few weeks, she no longer felt the obsessive anxiety, and she was able to leave places without checking even once. Eventually, she had only faint twinges of the checking urge left, and she was able to stop her medication completely. When the obsessions and compulsions didn't return, Rebecca knew that she was finally free of her OCD.

Summary

Obsessive compulsive disorder is characterized by the presence of obsessions (unwanted thoughts) and compulsions (ritualized behaviors). The obsessions and compulsions are biologically based and respond to treatment with serotonin-reuptake inhibiting drugs and behavioral therapies, particularly exposure with response prevention. Obsessive compulsive disorder is another disorder in which there is no longer any reason to "suffer in silence." If you are troubled by symptoms of OCD, ask your doctor for referral to a psychiatrist experienced in the disorder.

Resources

The Obsessive Compulsive Foundation
P. O. Box 70
Milford, Connecticut 06460
203–878–5669

Tourette Syndrome Association
42–40 Bell Boulevard
Bayside, New York 11361
718–224–2999

Patient Information Center

The Obsessive Compulsive Information Center
Dean Foundation for Health, Research, and Education
8000 Excelsior Drive, Suite 302
Madison, Wisconsin 53717–1914
608–836–8070

Further Reading

Baer, Lee. *Getting Control: Overcoming Your Obsessions and Compulsions.* Boston: Little Brown, 1991.

Foa, Edna B. *Stop Obsessing! How to Overcome Your Obsessions and Compulsions.* New York: Bantam Books, 1991.

Rapoport, Judith L. *The Boy Who Couldn't Stop Washing.* New York: E. P. Dutton, 1989.

CHAPTER 14

You Can Never Be Too Thin or Too Beautiful—or Can You?

"Tina, you're so thin—you look fabulous!"

"I wish I were a size two like Tina, don't you, girls?"

"How much weight have you lost, Tina? You look pretty skinny."

After weeks of dieting, Tina was finally getting the compliments she had always longed to hear. The first few pounds had been really hard to lose, but then she had seemed to find the secret and the next fifteen came off easily. Tina began really to focus on her diet, avoiding all fats and limiting herself to 650 calories a day—and she exercised. Oh, boy, did she exercise! An hour run in the morning, a brisk walk at noontime instead of eating lunch, and then an aerobics class at the gym each evening. Before she climbed into bed, she would do an extra one hundred sit-ups and fifty push-ups "just for good measure."

Tina can't tell you when she lost control of her dieting. Maybe it was when she decided to lose an extra ten pounds, or when she found a size-four dress that fit, or maybe it was when she stepped on the scale and realized that she had lost forty pounds in less than three months—but at some point the diet took on a life of its own. She could never allow herself to eat a complete meal anymore, and she had to restrict her calorie intake to only 500 per day. Sometimes, if she thought she had taken in a few extra calories, she would excuse herself and go off to the bathroom to vomit. Tina hated throwing up—it tasted gross and hurt her throat—but it was worth it to get rid of those nasty calories.

When Tina's weight dipped below a hundred pounds, her parents became concerned. After all, she was five feet six inches tall and not particularly fine-boned. Tina's parents suggested that she stop dieting, cut back on her exercise program, and enjoy her new body. But Tina couldn't enjoy her new body—her thighs were much too fat, her hips much too wide, and her abdomen had an unpleasant mound at its base—so she kept right on dieting and exercising.

Tina came to medical attention after she passed out at work one morning. When she was admitted to the emergency room of her local hospital, her weight was recorded at eighty-eight pounds. The doctor immediately diagnosed her as having anorexia nervosa and spoke with her sternly about her restriction dieting. Tina blithely lied when she answered him, telling him that she knew she had had a problem but that it was all right now; she had cut back on her exercising and increased her calorie intake. She hadn't, and in fact, she did an extra hour of aerobics that evening to make up for the calories she had received in the IV fluids.

Tina might have died from her self-imposed starvation if her mother hadn't happened to pass by her partially opened door; she caught a glimpse of her daughter's emaciated body and, frightened by the sight, immediately called their family physician and asked for help. The doctor recommended a psychiatrist who specialized in eating disorders and arranged for Tina to be seen that afternoon. At first, Tina refused to go, insisting that she didn't "need to see a shrink to tell me what I already know—I'm fine—just leave me alone." But Mrs. Graham insisted and drove her over to the psychiatrist's office. Dr. Thomas took a careful history from Tina and her mother, noted Tina's emaciated state, and recommended immediate hospitalization. Again Tina protested and initially refused to go. But Mrs. Graham and Dr. Thomas won out, and Tina was admitted to the eating disorders unit at the local hospital.

Despite Tina's protestations, she felt relieved to be in the hospital. Somewhere deep inside her, she knew that there was something dangerous about the dieting and exercising and something wrong with her constant worries about being too fat. On the other hand, when she looked in the mirror, she still saw fat places. They were real; she could see them and she knew that she had to get rid of them. She couldn't stop now; she was too close to achieving her goal—just a few more pounds and she'd finally be thin.

Tina was momentarily surprised when the hospital scale registered eighty-four pounds; that was low, even for her. But she immediately dispelled her concerns by remembering that this was an eating disorders unit and that the nurses would have rebalanced the scale so that they could trick her into eating more. Actually, she wasn't going to have a choice about how many calories she took in. Because her weight was so low, the psychiatrist had ordered a feeding tube for Tina. Tina did not want to be force-fed but also refused to eat, so putting a feeding tube in place was a major but necessary ordeal for both Tina and for the nurses. When it was finally secured, Tina seemed to give in, and she allowed them to infuse the nutritional supplements.

In fact, Tina hadn't given up at all. She had decided that they might succeed in forcing her to take in the extra calories, but they wouldn't succeed in making her gain weight; she would simply burn off the calories by exercising more. So she ran in place in the bathroom, did isometric exercises whenever possible, and sneaked in as many jumping jacks and push-ups as she could by her bedside. The staff members saw what was happening and began to address the issue in group therapy. Other anorexic women were asked to share their stories, and they all had a similar theme: the nurses and doctors are trying to save you from yourself, Tina; give in and let go; gaining weight is the only way to get out of here and, more important, the only way to stay alive. Tina fought against these concepts almost as hard as she had fought against the feeding tube, but gradually she began to participate in the group therapy sessions and to share her own thoughts and feelings. She was starting to get well.

Through her private sessions with Dr. Thomas, Tina was beginning to understand some of the reasons for her self-destructive behavior; armed with this understanding, she started the hard work of controlling her anorexia and bulimia. She was discharged from the hospital when her weight reached 103 pounds, but she continued in therapy. Rather than living at home with her parents, Tina moved into an apartment with a girlfriend. The two prepared and ate their evening meal together, talking and laughing as they did so. Eventually, Tina became less fearful of the calories she was consuming and could almost enjoy the dinners with her friend. But she still feared being fat and knew that she might never be completely cured of her anorexia. She has control of her disorder now, though, and remains hopeful that she will never have to give in to self-starvation again.

Anorexia Nervosa and Bulimia

Anorexia nervosa (commonly called anorexia) is characterized by:

1. Refusal to maintain "normal" body weight ("normal" is defined as no more than 15 percent underweight)
2. Intense fear of gaining weight or of becoming fat
3. A distorted view of one's body.

Tina suffered from each of these symptoms. She refused to keep her weight at a healthy level and was so fearful of gaining weight that she fought against the nurses and doctors who were trying to help her. When Tina looked in the mirror, she didn't see an emaciated skeleton but rather a young woman with too much fat on her thighs, hips, and buttocks. This pattern of self-criticism is typical of patients with anorexia nervosa. When anorexic women draw life-size pictures of themselves, they add an extra three or four inches onto their hips and thighs. Even when confronted by an actual tracing of themselves overlaid onto the line drawing, they are unable to comprehend the discrepancy. Many doctors think that this irrational body image is the most difficult aspect of anorexia to treat. It is certainly the most dangerous, as it drives the women's continued attempts at weight loss.

Anorexia nervosa is divided into two types: restricting type, in which calorie intake is dramatically decreased and exercise is increased; and binge-eating/purging type, in which the woman might gorge herself and then vomit or use laxatives to purge the excess calories. Some women have binge eating and purging, fasting, or excessive exercise; they are said to have bulimia nervosa or bulimia.

Bulimia is characterized by:

1. Recurrent episodes of binge eating
2. A feeling of lack of control over these eating binges
3. The regular use of excessive exercise, fasting, and self-induced vomiting, laxatives, or diuretics as purgatives.

Bulimics will have frequent eating binges in which they consume a large amount of food in a short period of time, and then this "pigging out" will be followed by self-induced vomiting, excessive exercise, use of laxatives or diuretics, or even a self-induced fast. Women with bulimia also have a persistent overconcern with body shape and weight, so they use the purging to keep their weight at a desirable level.

While fewer than one woman in a hundred has (or has had) anorexia, another ten to fifteen have had excessive weight loss and/or body image distortions at some point in their life. Bulimia is also common, and up to 5 to 10 percent of young women have used purging to control their weight (although they may not have out-of-control eating binges, so they don't have true bulimia).

Society has often been blamed for the fact that the eating disorders are so common. Some believe that the American preoccupation with physical beauty has distorted our view of ourselves and that women with anorexia are merely the most visible, extreme end of a large spectrum of women suffering from eating disorders. Others think that the families, especially the parents, are to blame; they describe the anorexic patients' mothers as dominating and their fathers as passive. Still others conceptualize anorexia as an individual problem reflecting unresolved developmental issues, such as achieving independence and becoming sexually mature. By starving herself, the young woman prevents menstruation and (symbolically, at least) postpones moving into womanhood and dealing with her sexuality. Biological psychiatrists continue to search for a hormonal or chemical basis for anorexia, theorizing that the physical changes are so extreme that the disorder must have a biological basis. Unfortunately, starvation leads to so many physiological changes that it is impossible to tease apart cause and effect. So at present, the cause of anorexia and of bulimia is unknown.

If You Don't Have Anorexia or Bulimia, What Might You Have?

Other Eating Disorders

Anorexia and bulimia are the most severe forms of a spectrum of eating disorders that includes excessive dieting, binge eating, laxative abuse, and purging. The psychiatric disorders are diagnosed when the woman loses control of the situation and, in the case of anorexia, when her weight is dangerously low and her body image distorted. However, even before a woman meets these diagnostic criteria, she may have unhealthy symptoms:

1. Excessive concern with being thin
2. Chronic dieting to maintain a weight below expected for height (Sometimes the weight loss is occupationally required, as with models and ballet dancers. Anorexia is far more common among these groups than among other occupations. It is thought that chronic self-starvation may eventually lead to the development of anorexia, by changing the levels of the brain's messenger chemicals.)
3. Excessive exercise (For example, male anorexics—only one in twenty anorexics is male—frequently have been avid long-distance runners before they become ill; as with self-starvation, the excessive exercise may induce changes in the brain chemicals that increase the chances of becoming anorexic.)

4. Binge eating, particularly when it occurs during the premenstrual period or when binges follow emotional disappointments

5. Self-induced vomiting (In one survey of female college students, one in four had used vomiting to purge after a particularly big meal or to achieve rapid weight loss. Chronic vomiting erodes the teeth and can cause metabolic disturbances or ulcers of the esophagus.)

6. Use of laxatives to purge (Laxative abuse can cause long-term changes in bowel function. Dependency develops quickly so that ever-increasing doses of laxatives are needed to move the bowels.)

7. Use of appetite suppressants, diet pills, or prescription medications to help lose weight (The drugs circumvent the hunger-satiety center and may cause the woman to be unable to recognize hunger and fullness.)

If you have one or more of the symptoms listed here and you are concerned that you might have an eating disorder, then you should probably get help. Cognitive behavior therapy (discussed later in this chapter) is particularly helpful for the treatment of purging and binge eating disorder. It may not be necessary to see a psychiatrist or psychologist if your symptoms aren't severe, as there are several self-help groups available, including local chapters of Overeaters Anonymous. Some weight-loss groups, such as Weight Watchers and Take Off Pounds Sensibly (TOPS), focus on changing both eating habits and self-image. These groups may be sufficient for mild symptoms. For more serious or chronic problems, it is important to seek professional help. Eating disorder units, mental health clinics, or the local psychiatric society can provide referrals.

Other Psychiatric Disorders

Anorexia is rarely confused with other psychiatric disorders or medical conditions because the symptoms of the disorder are so distinctive. Depressive disorders can be accompanied by a lack of interest in food, decreased appetite, and weight loss, but there is no fear of eating or of gaining weight nor any disturbance in the self-image. Patients with obsessive-compulsive disorder may also become very thin, because they are exercising compulsively or avoiding "contaminated" foods, but they do not have a disturbance in their body image and don't fear getting fat.

Physical Illness

Physical illnesses can also cause marked dietary restriction and weight loss. In particular, some cancers and serious infections (such as hepatitis or tuberculosis) can cause the patient to lose her appetite or even to avoid certain foods because they now "taste funny." Sometimes weight loss and decreased appetite are the first symptoms of these disorders. But again, because there are no body image distortions, the patient's condition should not be confused with that of anorexia nervosa.

Treatment of Anorexia and Bulimia

Both anorexia and bulimia can be quite difficult to treat. Multiple therapies are frequently combined, as in the case described at the beginning of the chapter, and treatment usually continues for many months, if not years. For severely underweight patients, hospitalization and tube feedings may be required. But for less ill patients outpatient treatment is more common and may be more effective in the long term. There are many clinics and inpatient units across the United States that specialize in the treatment of eating disorders. Even if the woman's symptoms are not severe enough to require inpatient therapy, such units might provide a good starting point for treatment or a source of referrals. Similarly, medical schools and local psychiatric societies can provide referrals for specialists in eating disorders.

Psychotherapy and Family Therapy

Psychotherapy remains an important treatment for anorexia and bulimia. Individual and group sessions have proved to be effective in helping the patient overcome her fears and see her body in a way that more closely resembles its true shape and size. The long-term goal of psychotherapy is to improve self-esteem and self-control so that thinness and weight loss aren't necessary as external markers of self-worth and control. Psychoanalytic psychotherapy may be useful in dealing with these issues, as it can help the anorexic woman to master key developmental tasks, including accepting her sexuality and becoming an independent adult.

Family therapy often plays a crucial role in the treatment of adolescents with anorexia and may be essential for the treatment of young adult women, as well. Studies have shown that adolescents receiving traditional psychotherapy plus family therapy were much more likely to recover than those teens who received only psychotherapy. Usually, the goal of family therapy is to reinforce the patient's recovery rather than to root out any family pathology that may be contributing to the eating disorder.

Cognitive-Behavior Therapy

As the name implies, cognitive-behavior therapy utilizes two techniques, cognitive therapy and behavior therapy. Sometimes the two are used sequentially, but usually they are conducted simultaneously. Cognitive therapy starts with education about the anorexic and bulimic symptoms and then attempts to normalize the woman's eating patterns, before progressing to issues of self-esteem, stress management, and control. In behavior therapy, maladaptive responses to environmental cues (for example, eating three hot fudge sundaes because you walk by an ice cream parlor) are replaced with positive, healthy responses (eating a small ice cream cone or abstaining from the ice cream altogether because it's almost time for lunch). The combination of cognitive and behavioral therapy means that the anorexic woman learns the appropriate responses to various environmental cues, practices them, incorporates them into her life, and in so doing, comes to believe that they are true.

Cognitive-behavior therapy appears to be particularly useful for bulimia and for the binge/purge type of anorexia, perhaps because the target behaviors (that is, binge eating, vomiting, and laxative use) are easier to identify and prevent. For example, one of the first steps in cognitive-behavior therapy of a binge/purging-type anorexic might be to require the patient to eat each bite of a sensible meal and to sit at the table for a specified period of time following the meal to prevent purging. During the after-meal period, a staff member might review the nutritional contents of the meal or focus the patient's attention on her feeling of fullness and satiety. Of note, most studies have shown that although cognitive-behavior therapy is quite effective in decreasing the severity of anorexia and bulimia, it is rarely effective in eradicating all the symptoms of the eating disorders.

Medications

Until recently, medications appeared to have limited utility in the treatment of anorexia and bulimia. In various controlled studies, major tranquilizers (such as chlorpromazine, pimozide, and haloperidol); minor tranquilizers (such as Valium and others); amitriptyline (Elavil, an antidepressant drug); and appetite-enhancing medications (such as cyproheptadine—Periactin) were of no more benefit than a placebo (sugar pill). Recently, however, fluoxetine (Prozac) has been shown to be useful for anorexia and several antidepressant medications, including desipramine (Norpramin), trazodone (Desyrel), and fluoxetine (Prozac), have been shown to be superior to placebo therapy in a number of controlled trials for bulimia. Fluoxetine appears to be particularly effective for bulimia, perhaps because of its ability to block serotonin reuptake; this changes the brain's response to food intake, allowing the woman to recognize her hunger and fullness, and also dampens the compulsive urge to binge and purge. The effectiveness of fluoxetine and the other serotonin reuptake blocking medications is not surprising since their antiobsessional effects have been demonstrated, and both anorexia and bulimia have symptoms in common with obsessive-compulsive disorder (see Chapter Thirteen).

Body Dysmorphic Disorder

Eve is a very pretty young woman. With big blue eyes, freckles sprinkled across her perfectly shaped nose, and lustrous jet-black hair pulled back into a ponytail, she looks like she should be a college cheerleader. Except that she is preoccupied and withdrawn, rather than being enthusiastic and outgoing. Even though you smile at her, she shrinks from your gaze and that of the other patrons in the restaurant. As you continue to watch her for a few minutes, you notice that Eve constantly checks her reflection in a compact mirror. She compares the right side of her face with the left and then the left with the right, over and over again. She frowns as she does so and seems to become more upset each time she looks. Suddenly, she closes the compact and puts it into her purse, pushing it to the bottom, as if she can't stand to look at it anymore. But a few minutes later, she pulls it back out and starts the whole process over again.

Eve has body dysmorphic disorder. She is consumed with worry about her appearance because she is convinced that the left side of her face is bigger than the right side. Although she once knew that her worries don't make sense, they have been going on for so long and occupy so much of her attention that she now believes that she is a freak of nature, an ugly hag whose disfigurement is obvious to all who gaze at her. She has measured her face so many times that she knows there is but an infinitesimal fraction of an inch difference in size—yet the overpowering feeling of ugliness persists. It affects every aspect of her life: Eve has few friends and no social life; she passed up a big promotion because it would have required her to meet new people; and she spends hours each evening in front of the bathroom mirror, crying with frustration as she checks her appearance yet one more time.

A *few weeks ago, Eve went to see a plastic surgeon, Dr. Kelly. She asked the doctor to make her look "normal" and showed him how her left cheek jutted out over her jaw more than the right side did. Dr. Kelly misunderstood her description and thought that she wanted to have more prominent cheekbones and a less prominent jaw. He told her that the surgery was possible and would be effective but that it was quite expensive. Further, he required all of his patients to have a psychological evaluation before being scheduled for surgery.*

The psychologist quickly determined that Eve was expecting more from the surgery than Dr. Kelly could deliver. Concerned that she might have body dysmorphic disorder, he referred her to a psychiatrist, Dr. Daniels. Dr. Daniels found that Eve's symptoms were so severe that she was no longer able to tell him that they didn't make sense. She attributed most of her unhappiness to the fact that her face was grossly crooked and said that the defect was ruining her life.

Dr. Daniels recommended treatment with a serotonin reuptake blocking medication, fluvoxamine (Luvox). He told Eve that she might experience some side effects initially but that they should improve over the first few days of taking the medication. As Dr. Daniels had predicted, Eve felt a little queasy and tired for a few days, but she soon noticed that she was starting to get better. After a couple of weeks of treatment, she realized that she wasn't as upset about her appearance as she had been and that she was checking her face in the mirror less frequently. She could push the irrational worries away if she tried really hard, and she could occasionally return a stranger's smile as they passed on the street.

Eve's recovery was not without setbacks. There were times when Eve would still burst into tears over her perceived ugliness, or she would feel compelled to touch first the right and then the left side of her face until she could convince herself that her face was OK. But over the next few weeks, her symptoms slowly faded away, and she was able to participate in behavior therapy. The combination of medication and behavior therapy totally eradicated her symptoms, and Eve is finally able to look in the mirror and see what others see: a beautiful, happy young woman.

Body dysmorphic disorder (BDD) is characterized by an intense preoccupation with some imagined or slight defect in appearance. Women with BDD believe that there is something physically wrong with the way they look or that a real but slight physical defect is having a powerful, negative effect on their lives. As in Eve's case, the preoccupation can sometimes take on the characteristics of an irrational delusion because the person becomes completely convinced that she is ugly or defective. In other cases, a person might become irrationally preoccupied with the effect that the physical defect has had on her life. For example, a woman whose nose is slightly enlarged might become convinced that she didn't get a job promotion because her nose made her look too ethnic.

Evelyn blamed her lack of cleavage for the fact that she has never had a serious boyfriend. Convinced that her love life would improve if she could only fill a B cup, she went to a plastic surgeon for breast augmentation. Evelyn was initially pleased with her new bustline, but when nothing about her life changed, she became convinced that she really should have increased to a C cup. When the second surgery still didn't improve her social life, she switched her attention to her thin, "unsexy" lips.

A woman with body dysmorphic disorder will often have multiple plastic surgeries — breast augmentations, collagen infusions, nose jobs, face lifts, tummy tucks, buttock lifts, and/or liposuction. Each time she has a surgery, she believes that fixing the perceived physical defect will improve some (unrelated) aspect of her life. But because the surgery can't remove the underlying problem, it doesn't even come close.

How to Know If You Have Body Dysmorphic Disorder

As with many psychiatric disorders, body dysmorphic disorder is diagnosed when the symptoms cause distress and interference. Usually, unless they have lost perspective, women who suffer from BDD know that their fears are irrational and senseless. Despite this knowledge, they are unable to overcome the preoccupation.

The distress that accompanies BDD allows us to separate it from a normal, healthy concern about one's appearance. Because we place so much emphasis on having the perfect haircut, flawless skin, and a beautiful figure, a woman without BDD may spend as much time looking in a mirror as does a woman with BDD. However, when the healthy woman looks, she is satisfied with her appearance. Women with BDD can never enjoy peace about the way they look.

Treatment

Treatment of body dysmorphic disorder includes medications and behavior therapy, particularly exposure with response prevention (see Chapters Twelve and Thirteen for complete descriptions of behavior therapy). The behavioral therapies have not been systematically tested for BDD but appear to be useful. In each of these treatments, the patient is challenged to expose herself to avoided social situations and resist the urge to ritualize in response, for example, not checking her defect in a compact mirror or picking at her skin. In addition, she is encouraged to remove any camouflaging makeup. This is often quite difficult, so it is done in a series of steps with a therapist's help. Not only does the therapist provide support during the anxiety-producing exercises but he also provides feedback about the irrational nature of the fears.

Medications that appear to be useful for body dysmorphic disorder include the serotonin reuptake blocking drugs, such as fluoxetine (Prozac), sertraline (Zoloft), fluvoxamine (Luvox), and paroxetine (Paxil). Clomipramine (Anafranil) is a serotonin reuptake blocking tricyclic antidepressant that is quite useful for obsessive-compulsive disorder and may be effective for body dysmorphic disorder as well. The serotonin reuptake blocking medications appear first to decrease the intensity of the preoccupation and eventually to extinguish it completely.

In some cases, the serotonin reuptake blocking drugs are not sufficient to treat the symptoms, and neuroleptic medications, such as pimozide (Orap) or haloperidol (Haldol), might be prescribed in addition. The neuroleptics appear to boost the effectiveness of the serotonin reuptake blocking drugs, but they are not very helpful on their own.

The best treatment for BDD may be a combination of medication and behavior therapy. Patients treated with this combination appear to have a better chance of complete recovery.

Summary

The eating disorders and body dysmorphic disorder share features in common with both obsessive compulsive disorder and the psychotic disorders. In anorexia and bulimia, women are "obsessed" with dieting and exercising and often have a compulsive urge to binge or purge; they also have an irrational, almost-delusional distortion of their body image—they see themselves as fat when they are completely emaciated. Similarly, in body dysmorphic disorder, women are obsessed with a particular defect in their appearance, and have an irrational view of its importance—often, they become convinced that every failure in their life is a result of the perceived defect. Treatment of these disorders is often difficult because of the complexity of the symptom patterns, but combination therapy (medication plus cognitive-behavior therapy and/or psychotherapy) has been found to be helpful to many women.

Resources

Anorexia and Bulimia

American Anorexia/Bulimia Association, Inc. (AABA)
418 East 76th Street
New York, New York 10021
212–734–1114

Anorexia Nervosa and Related Eating Disorders, Inc. (ANRED)
P. O. Box 5102
Eugene, Oregon 97405
503–344–1144

Bulimia Anorexia Self-Help, Inc. (BASH)
6125 Clayton Avenue, Suite 215
Saint Louis, Missouri 63139
314–567–4080

National Association of Anorexia Nervosa and Associated Disorders (ANAD)
P. O. Box 7
Highland Park, Illinois 60035
708–831–3438

Overeaters Anonymous
P. O. Box 92870
Los Angeles, California 90009
310–618–8835

Body Dysmorphic Disorder

There are no specific patient support groups for BDD, although some patients
have found the Obsessive Compulsive Foundation (Chapter Thirteen) to
be helpful.

Contact your own physician or the psychiatric association in your area to obtain referrals.

Further Reading

Bruch, Hilde. *The Golden Cage: The Enigma of Anorexia Nervosa.* New York:
Vintage Books, 1978.

Callaway, C. Wayne. *The Callaway Diet: Successful Permanent Weight Control
for Starvers, Stuffers, and Skippers.* New York: Bantam Books, 1990.

Chernin, Kim. *The Obsession: Reflections on the Tyranny of Slenderness.* New
York: Harper & Row, 1981.

Levenkron, Steven. *Treating and Overcoming Anorexia Nervosa*. New York: Warner Books, 1982.

Roth, Geneen. *Feeding the Hungry Heart: The Experiences of Compulsive Eating*. New York: Bobbs-Merrill, 1982.

Siegel, Michele, Judith Brisman, and Margot Weinshel. *Surviving an Eating Disorder: New Perspectives and Strategies for Family and Friends*. New York: Harper & Row, 1988.

CHAPTER 15

Irresistible Impulses

This chapter is divided into two parts: the addictive disorders of drug and alcohol abuse; and the impulse control disorders such as kleptomania, compulsive gambling, compulsive shopping, and trichotillomania (compulsive hair pulling). Although these disorders are quite different from one another, we have included all of them in a single chapter because they have in common the person's inability to resist self-destructive impulses. Scientists are now discovering that these irresistible impulses are biologically based; this means that the failure to resist the urge is not merely a lack of willpower but rather indicates a biological disorder requiring diagnosis and treatment.

Addictive Disorders: Drug and Alcohol Abuse

Hi, my name is Linda, and I'm an alcoholic. This is my story.

When I was a teenager growing up in the suburbs, the only thing to do on the weekends was to hang out and have a few beers. In college, fraternity "keggers" were the mainstay of campus social life. I would have a couple of beers, and it would make me feel relaxed and sociable enough to talk to the really cute guys. But pretty soon, I had to have a drink in order to feel good about myself, and not a single weekend went by without my partying on Friday and Saturday nights and spending all day Sunday hung over and sick. I never drank during the week though, so I didn't even think about being a problem drinker. Now, as I look back, I realize that I was already an alcoholic. I really needed those drinks on the weekends, and my drinking interfered with my studies and my friendships.

Over the years, my drinking pattern changed. After I had my kids, there was no opportunity to go out and party on the weekends, so I starting drinking during the week. At first, it was just a beer or a glass of wine in the evening to relax and unwind, but soon that wasn't enough. My husband was having trouble with his job and the kids were increasingly demanding, so there was always a reason to have a drink "to calm my nerves." I got to the point where I needed to have that drink whether there was anything stressful going on or not. I would have a couple of glasses of wine in the afternoon while I watched the soaps, a cocktail when my husband got home from work, more wine with dinner, and of course the obligatory nightcap. I was soon having five, six, or seven drinks a day. I even had a little morning pick-me-up, because if I hadn't had a drink by lunchtime, my hands would start to shake and I would feel queasy and uncomfortable.

I was never drunk, though. My body was so tolerant of alcohol that I rarely even got a buzz. I just became miserable if I didn't drink, so I kept on drinking. Then the blackouts began, and my friends would talk about things that I had said to them the night before that I couldn't remember—I wouldn't even remember having gone out with them. I made a real fool of myself sometimes, but I didn't really admit that I had a problem even then; my denial was just too strong. I might still be drinking if the alcohol hadn't eaten away the walls of my stomach and given me a bleeding ulcer. One wintry night, I threw up a whole bucketful of blood, and the doctor in the emergency room told me that I could die if it happened again. That really scared me, so I swore off alcohol.

I tried stopping cold turkey and quickly discovered how badly I was hooked. I couldn't go even three hours without starting to get shaky and sick. I was so scared—I would die if I didn't stop drinking and let my stomach heal, but surely I would die without a drink too. My doctor suggested that I dry out in a drug and alcohol rehabilitation center, but my insurance wouldn't pay for the twenty-one-day program unless I had failed outpatient therapy, and we couldn't afford to pay out of pocket, so I decided that I would do it on my own.

Over the next few weeks, I was able to cut back to the point where I only had two or three drinks a day. I began to convince myself that I could drink in moderation, and I did OK with this for a few months, but then one day something happened and I went on a binge that lasted for a week. I don't even know what happened during that week—maybe it's good that I don't—all I know is I really hit bottom. I finally realized that

I had to get sober and that I couldn't do it by myself. I checked into the treatment center, and it was terrible to dry out, even from my "controlled" level of drinking. At first, I tried to find all the reasons that I was different from everyone else. The Higher Power part was hard for me to accept at first, too. Finally, I let go and accepted that I was powerless over alcohol and that my life had become unmanageable. With His help, I took it one step at a time and finally sobered up.

It has been five years since my last drink. I still come to AA meetings every day, because every single day I still want and need to have a drink. I know that if I were to stop coming to the meetings, the dishonesty would sneak back into my life and the illness would make me think that I could have just one drink. But I can't have just one drink. I'm an alcoholic and I will never be cured. With the strength of the fellowship, though, I'm recovering—one day at a time.

Hundreds of thousands of women like Linda are alcoholics or have an addiction disorder. Whether it is alcohol, prescription medications, or street drugs, the addictions have in common a physical dependency on a chemical substance. In some cases, the chemical is so powerful that it almost immediately causes physical dependency (nicotine and cocaine, for example). Some alcoholics also report that they felt the physical addiction with the very first drink. The woman's body craves the chemical in order to feel right, and she seems to be incapable of saying no to it. The woman's own body chemistry may be responsible for her addiction. Although the process isn't well understood, laboratory studies have shown that certain animals can never become addicted to morphine or alcohol while others become addicted with their first exposure. These genetic differences are thought to explain the differences in susceptibility that some women have to addiction with drugs, alcohol, and prescription medications.

Although medical science hasn't yet found a cure for alcoholism and drug abuse, some recent reports from the National Institute of Drug Abuse suggest that a cure for cocaine abuse may be available within the next few years. Great progress has been made in our understanding of the causes of alcoholism too, and treatments are increasingly effective. At present, however, the best that can be hoped for is control of the addiction. Through effective behavioral treatment programs, an addict can stay drug-free, and an alcoholic can stay sober.

How Do You Know If You Have a Drug or Alcohol Addiction?

Unfortunately, since denial is often central to addiction and alcoholism, many women who could most benefit from this chapter will either refuse to read it or won't recognize themselves when they do. In some cases, however, women can recognize their need for help, or friends might be effective in getting an alcoholic into treatment, so it is useful to know the warning signs of alcohol abuse. The signs of alcoholism and problem drinking include:

1. Having to have a drink in order to function or to cope
2. Regular pattern of excessive drinking
3. Frequently drinking until intoxicated (drunk)
4. Going to work or driving a car while intoxicated
5. Experiencing blackouts—that is, spells of unconsciousness or memory lapses
6. Sustaining an injury as a result of being intoxicated
7. Doing something while under the influence of alcohol or drugs that you wouldn't do without those substances
8. Difficulty refusing a drink or failing at attempts to stop drinking
9. Withdrawal symptoms when alcohol intake is stopped or cut back.

Other warning signs of alcohol abuse include frequent drinking binges, a steady increase in the amount of alcohol consumed, and drinking in the morning, especially before going to work. Blackout spells are a particularly frightening symptom of alcohol abuse. A blackout can be either a period of true unconsciousness or the inability to remember periods of time while drinking; this is a sign of serious neurological impairment and a signal that your alcohol intake is excessive. Another hallmark sign of alcohol abuse or alcohol dependency is the recognition that you can no longer control your own alcohol intake. You may want to quit but are unable to do so, or you may even have had unsuccessful attempts to cut down or control your use of alcohol. The lack of control leads to feelings of helplessness, which in turn can cause increased drinking and/or depression.

Drug dependency and drug addiction/abuse can range from the excessive use of prescription or over-the-counter medications to the use of illicit drugs such as LSD, cocaine, and heroin. Nicotine dependency (cigarette smoking) should also be included in the addictive disorders. Former Surgeon General C. Everett Koop said that nicotine was among the most addictive substances known to humans and should be considered a major threat to the health of the American public (in the same category as heroin and cocaine). Many would agree with Dr. Koop, but equal numbers might disagree. We don't have adequate space to discuss the pros and cons of this issue, but suffice it to say that nicotine addiction is medically indistinguishable from other addictions, both psychologically and physically.

Drug abuse and *addiction* are terms that are often used interchangeably, although addiction implies physical dependency—that is, both your body and your mind are "hooked" on the substance while abuse means excessive or inappropriate use without dependency. Thus, although marijuana may be a drug of abuse, it is unlikely to cause addiction because it doesn't make you physically dependent. On the other hand, psychological dependency (addiction) can occur with marijuana, and it can cause occupational and social dysfunction.

Both physical and psychological addiction can be caused by over-the-counter medications, such as diet pills, nighttime cough preparations containing large amounts of alcohol, cough medicines containing the narcotic-based cough suppressant dextromethorphan (such as Robitussin DM, Nyquil, and others), stimulant drugs (such as NoDoz, Vivarin, and others), or sleeping pills (such as Nytol, Sleep-Eze, and Sominex). Each of these medicines contains substances that have the potential for physical dependency and psychological addiction; therefore, they are addictive drugs. By examining carefully the degree to which you feel dependent on these medications, you may be able to determine whether or not they are a problem for you. If you aren't certain, consult with your physician, a mental health professional, or drug treatment center.

If You Have a Drug or Alcohol Addiction, What Should You Do?

If you suspect that you have a drug or alcohol problem, you probably *do* have a drug or alcohol problem, and you should seek treatment. It is often difficult to find a physician who feels comfortable treating addictive disorders, so you may need to seek out a drug rehabilitation clinic or a center specializing in the treatment of alcoholism and addictive disorders. Even if you don't need inpatient treatment, such centers are frequently the best source of physicians skilled in recognizing the subtleties of drug and alcohol addiction and in effectively treating them.

The mainstay of treatment of addictive disorders is psychological and group treatment. Often that group treatment is in the form of a twelve-step program, such as Narcotics Anonymous (NA) and Alcoholics

Anonymous (AA). Both groups provide sponsors to incoming members and utilize a buddy system to avoid relapses. The twelve-step programs presume that complete recovery is not possible but rather that members will learn to control their addictions through group support and acceptance of the twelve steps:[1]

1. We admitted that we were powerless over alcohol (or our addiction) and that our lives had become unmanageable.
2. Came to believe that a Power greater than ourselves could restore us to sanity.
3. Made a decision to turn our will and our lives over to the care of God as we understood Him.
4. Made a searching and fearless moral inventory of ourselves.
5. Admitted to God, to ourselves, and to another human being the exact nature of our wrongs.
6. Were entirely ready to have God remove all these defects of character.
7. Humbly asked Him to remove our shortcomings.
8. Made a list of all persons we had harmed and became willing to make amends to them all.
9. Made direct amends to such people wherever possible, except when to do so would injure them or others.
10. Continued to take personal inventory, and when we were wrong, promptly admitted it.
11. Sought through prayer and meditation to improve our conscious contact with God as we understood Him, praying only for knowledge of His will for us and the power to carry that out.
12. Having had a spiritual awakening as a result of these steps, we tried to carry this message to alcoholics (addicts) and to practice these principles in all our affairs.

As with any treatment, the use of a twelve-step program must be individually prescribed. Twelve-step programs have helped countless numbers of women, but they aren't for everyone. Some women are unwilling to accept the religious nature of the AA and NA programs, while others prefer individual treatment to these group therapies. Recently, moderation management (MM) has been proposed as a means of controlling alcoholism without complete abstinence (see Audrey Kishline's book, *Moderate Drinking*, listed under "Resources" at the end of this chapter). The technique is both new and controversial; it hasn't yet been proved effective by time or experience, but if you have problems with alcohol and AA isn't appealing to you, MM may be the answer. Whichever form of therapy you choose, it is vital that the you stick with it once you start. Relapses are common for the addictive disorders, and the best prevention of relapse is continued treatment.

Medication as an Aid to Recovery from Addictive Disorders

Whether or not prescription medications can aid in the recovery from an addiction depends on the nature of the abused substance. For example, marijuana can be stopped "cold turkey" without medical intervention, although psychological treatments may be helpful, including supportive therapies or group programs. Nicotine and alcohol are both associated with strong physical dependency, and withdrawal symptoms may occur rapidly when the cigarettes or alcohol are discontinued. Nicotine patches can be helpful, as they allow a woman to stop smoking abruptly but avoid withdrawal symptoms by gradually decreasing the amount of nicotine in her system. Stopping alcohol intake abruptly can lead to seizures and other life-threatening medical problems. It is for this reason that many alcohol treatment programs utilize inpatient withdrawal periods. Prescription medications can be used to block the unpleasant and dangerous side effects of withdrawal and prepare the woman for outpatient therapy of the psychological and physical addiction to alcohol.

Several medications are available that appear to help prevent relapse in recovering alcoholics. Antibuse (disulfiram) is a medication that causes unpleasant effects—such as facial flushing, headache, lightheadedness, nausea, vomiting, and abdominal cramping—when the woman has taken it and then drinks alcohol. The theory is that if drinking alcohol makes you sick, then it will be easier to avoid drinking. The use of Antibuse is somewhat controversial, as the physical symptoms caused by the combination of Antibuse and alcohol can be quite severe. For many women, however, it offers a helpful reminder of their need for sobriety.

Medications that block the craving for alcohol or drugs might be more helpful in preventing relapse. Although no medication has yet been found that completely blocks the craving for alcohol, bromocriptine and naltrexone appear to help decrease the intensity of the alcohol cravings. Naltrexone, an opioid-blocking medication, blocks the "high" associated with both narcotics and alcohol and also decreases cravings.

Some scientists have suggested that by blocking the pleasant effects associated with alcohol or drug use, the desire decreases. Others theorize that the naltrexone occupies the same site in the brain as the alcohol does, so it decreases the withdrawal symptoms of abstinence by providing similar feelings of relaxation and satiety.

Naltrexone is also used to treat addictions to heroin, morphine, or other narcotic drugs. In fact, it is primarily thought of as an antinarcotic drug. Naltrexone clearly occupies the opioid (narcotic) receptors and decreases the physical cravings for narcotics. To a lesser extent, it helps reduce psychological cravings as well. When addicts are treated with naltrexone, they appear to suffer fewer relapses and remain drug-free longer.

Methadone has a similar effect. Methadone is actually a narcotic, but it does not give the rush associated with the other narcotic drugs and does not induce psychological dependency. Because methadone acts as a narcotic, it forestalls the cravings that result from the physical withdrawal symptoms.

Impulse Control Disorders

The impulse control disorders include compulsive shopping (or buying) disorder, kleptomania (compulsive stealing), pathological gambling, and trichotillomania (compulsive hair pulling). Each of these disorders is characterized by the presence of a compulsive urge (or irresistible impulse) to spend, steal, gamble, or pull hair, which is accompanied by a sense of tension or anxiety. The anxiety increases proportionately to the length of time elapsing before the urge is satisfied, and it increases dramatically when the woman actively resists the urge. Relief and pleasure are associated with giving in to the urge. This relief is often so intense as to be described as "orgasmic," but it is short-lived, and the compulsive urge quickly returns. A vicious cycle is established: the compulsive urge leads to feelings of tension and anxiety; these feelings are relieved only by performing the self-destructive behavior; and the relief is perceived as pleasurable. Each time, the urge is stronger, the anxiety worse, and the need to perform the behavior is even greater.

The impulse control disorders all share this pattern, but the individual disorders differ in their clinical presentation and in the negative consequences of the behavior. For example, women with compulsive shopping disorder face mounting credit card bills and bankruptcy, while those with kleptomania may be jailed for shoplifting. The disorders are important enough in their own right that we will describe each fully before discussing common treatment strategies.

Compulsive Shopping

Barbara used to love to shop, but now she has to shop. If a particularly pretty jacket catches her eye or she sees a pair of shoes on sale, she'll say, "I must have it." But she doesn't buy just one pair of shoes or a single jacket. She buys a dozen pairs of shoes at a time or eight jackets—in different sizes and colors—and takes them home to be put in her closet with the other never-worn clothes. Actually, there isn't enough room left in her closet for the latest purchases, because every time Barbara shops, she shops to excess. The TV shopping network is particularly difficult for Barbara because each time she flips to the channel, she dials the 800 number and orders whatever is on the screen. Her home is filled with boxes and boxes of crystal, jewelry, and porcelain figurines. It happens almost before she realizes it—but even when she recognizes that she doesn't really want to buy the Austrian crystal necklace, she can't stop herself.

Barbara has compulsive shopping disorder. It is so severe that all her credit cards are charged to the limit, and she will soon have to declare bankruptcy. Barbara recognizes the excessiveness of her behavior and tries to resist the urge to buy, but in the end, she is powerless against the compulsive urge.

It is hard for women who do not have compulsive shopping disorder to realize how painful this impulse control disorder can be. After all, each of us has had a spending spree at one time or another, and usually they were fun, even exhilarating. We may even have used shopping as a remedy for PMS, a failed relationship, or a disappointment at work or school. Compulsive shopping is similar to these "normal" spending sprees in that it often occurs after the woman has suffered a loss or disappointment. Initially, the shopping and buying make her feel better, but then these urges take on a life of their own. The urge to buy becomes overwhelmingly strong and provokes anxiety when denied. Often the anxiety is relieved only if the woman buys "exactly" the right thing, so she'll buy eight jackets to make sure that she gets just the right color and style. The urge to shop may increase each time the woman gives into it; buying six pairs of shoes may be sufficient in January, but by June, the urge is satisfied only by purchasing a dozen pairs.

Kleptomania

Maggie shivered with excitement as she left the store with a silk scarf and an expensive negligee tucked into her handbag. The alarms hadn't gone off, the security guard hadn't budged—she was going to get away with it! Each time, it seemed that she had to take a little bigger risk in order to satisfy the ever-increasing urge to steal. At first, she had gotten pleasure from taking a package of mints or a candy bar; just the act of stealing was enough. Then she began to be compelled to steal things of value, especially items with theft-deterrent devices. She had stolen hundreds of dollars' worth of merchandise and had been arrested twice. Fortunately, the stores hadn't carried through on their threat to "prosecute to the full extent of the law," and the charges had been dropped. But the arrests were frightening enough that Maggie decided that she had to quit stealing. She knew that she wasn't strong enough to resist the urge to steal, so she attempted to control her symptoms by avoiding all tempting situations.

After Maggie had been "clean" for six months, she began to think that she had conquered her problem, and she accepted a friend's invitation to go to dinner and a movie at the local shopping mall. As luck would have it, they ended up having extra time before the show, and Maggie's friend suggested that they spend it browsing at the Gap. Maggie was too ashamed to admit her problem, and she couldn't come up with a reasonable excuse to avoid the store, so they went in together. Almost immediately, the familiar urge returned: Maggie had to steal something. She tried to resist the urge, but it was too strong; in fact, the tension she was feeling was so strong that it was making her sweaty and nauseous, and she gave in. With her friend as an unwitting decoy, she was able to swipe a pair of socks without being caught. That theft reopened the floodgates, and Maggie had been stealing several times a day since then. Until this last time . . .

Just as she was enjoying the flood of relief that always followed a theft, Maggie felt a hand on her shoulder and heard the dreaded words, "You're under arrest for shoplifting." The security cameras had caught her in the act of stealing both the scarf and the negligee, and after calling the police, the security guard had taken his station at the front door to avoid tipping her off and to make sure that he knew which way she went on leaving the store. Maggie knew that this time the charges wouldn't be dropped and that she would be going to jail. Fortunately, in her state, a psychological assessment is required of each incoming prisoner, and Maggie was able to tell the prison psychologist about her problem. He diagnosed her as having kleptomania, arranged for her to be released on probation, and referred her to a psychiatrist specializing in impulse control disorders. The psychiatrist prescribed a serotonin reuptake blocking medication and group therapy. The combination was so effective that within a few weeks, Maggie's compulsive stealing was truly under control.

Kleptomania, or compulsive stealing, is characterized by a sense of increasing tension preceding the theft and a sense of relief following the theft. Resisting the urge to steal causes the woman with kleptomania discomfort and anxiety, just as the woman with compulsive shopping feels discomfort when she resists the urge to buy or a woman with obsessive-compulsive disorder feels uncomfortable when she refuses to perform a compulsive ritual. The stealing is not committed to express anger or vengeance, and it feels uncontrollable to the person who suffers from the disorder. As you might suspect, it is sometimes difficult to differentiate kleptomania from ordinary theft, and therapists use established patterns of behavior to separate the two.

Pathological Gambling

Pathological gambling is just what its name implies: gambling that is excessive, has negative consequences, or is out of the woman's control. A woman with pathological gambling may be preoccupied with gambling or with obtaining the money to gamble. She feels a sense of discomfort if prevented from gambling, so she gambles ever more frequently. Often the pathological gambler will have lost large sums of money, and she may have made repeated efforts to stop gambling. The gambling becomes problematic when it interferes with social, occupational, or recreational activities or when it continues despite the woman's inability to pay the mounting debts.

Trichotillomania

Tracy was thirty-one years old when she first sought treatment for her hair pulling. For over seventeen years, she had plucked out her eyebrows and eyelashes and pulled the hair on her head, arms, legs, and pubic area. Tracy knew that her hair pulling was self-destructive; she hated wearing a wig to cover the huge bald spot on her head, and she resented wasting time applying false eyelashes and penciling in eyebrows. She had tried to stop pulling her hair so many times that she had lost count, and she had always failed. Relaxation therapy hadn't worked, neither did hypnosis, nor wearing gloves, or keeping busy, or meditating. At one point, she had become so desperate to quit that she cut the tips of her fingers with a razor blade in the hope that the pain would keep her from plucking out her hair, but she had just put Band-Aids on the wounds, gritted her teeth against the pain, and continued pulling.

That was just one of many unpleasant memories associated with her hair pulling. Tracy could still remember the first time she had pulled her hair. She had been sitting in Ms. Abram's second-period class when she felt a hair that didn't seem as soft and smooth as the others. She plucked it out and spent the rest of the class period running her fingers through her hair to make sure that there were no other rogues. That night (and countless others to follow), she spent a long time in front of the mirror, carefully examining her hair and plucking out any hairs that were different in color or texture. When she finished, there was a small pile of hairs on the counter in front of her and a tiny bald spot over her left ear.

Over the next few years, the hair pulling increased, and by the time Tracy was in high school, she had a noticeable bald spot on her left temple. When her mother asked her about it, Tracy said she didn't know what was causing it. Her mother took her to a dermatologist, who diagnosed her baldness as alopecia areata (a not-uncommon scalp condition that causes bald patches to appear) and prescribed a steroid cream. The cream did nothing, but Tracy stopped pulling in that spot and her hair regrew. Both the dermatologist and Tracy's mother were so pleased with her progress that neither noticed the new bald patch at the base of her scalp.

Tracy's hair pulling improved dramatically during her freshman year in college, but it returned at full force early in her sophomore year. Tracy spent her remaining college years in isolation. She didn't have a roommate so she could pull in privacy; she didn't go swimming or ride in a convertible for fear that her wig might be dislodged; she didn't date because she was afraid that if a young man got too close, he might notice her bald spots or her false eyelashes and pencilled-in eyebrows. Tracy so wished that she could have those years back; she mourned the social life she had missed, the hours she had wasted while stuck in front of a mirror pulling her hair, and her lost beauty. Now when Tracy looked in the mirror, she saw an anxious, bald, ugly woman staring back at her. It was time to get help.

The therapist whom Tracy consulted told her that her hair pulling had a name—trichotillomania—and that it wasn't a failure of willpower but rather a biological disorder. The doctor prescribed clomipramine (Anaf-

ranil), which Tracy found quickly suppressed the urge to pull. Tracy also practiced the fist-clenching exercises her therapist had suggested and soon was able to resist the hair-pulling urge successfully. Within a few months, her hair had regrown, and she was starting to catch up on all the things she had missed—like dating, and swimming, and riding in a convertible.

The diagnosis of trichotillomania is correctly made when it is determined that the patient feels a compulsive urge to pull her hair and responds to it in order to relieve the accompanying anxiety. *Habitual* hair pulling is not considered to be trichotillomania because there is no preceding anxiety or compulsive urge; it happens almost unconsciously, and raising awareness of the habit is often sufficient to prevent the hair pulling. Other related disorders include pathological nail biting (that which results from an irresistible urge to bite or pick at the nails) and face picking (or pimple picking—again, this is considered to be an impulse control disorder only if the picking occurs in response to an overwhelming urge and is accompanied by preceding anxiety and subsequent relief). Trichotillomania and pathological nail biting and face picking are all disorders of impulse control.

Common Elements of Impulse Control Disorders

What the impulse control disorders have in common is that the impulse to perform the behavior is stronger than the woman's ability to resist it. Medical researchers are currently trying to determine whether pathological gambling, kleptomania, compulsive shopping, and trichotillomania are related to obsessive-compulsive disorder or to the addictive disorders. Each of these disorders has features in common with obsessive-compulsive disorder (see Chapter Thirteen) in that there is a sense of tension or urgency prior to performing the behavior and a sense of relief following it. However, they also have features in common with the addictive disorders in that each of them is associated with a pleasurable sensation. In pathological gambling, it is the "rush" associated with the possibility of having won the bet; with kleptomania, it is the thrill of getting away with it; and with compulsive shopping, it is the pleasure associated with acquisition. The pleasurable sensation is more tactile in trichotillomania, but it can be equally strong; some women have even described an orgasmic feeling associated with hair pulling. Because of the unique nature of the disorders, they are grouped together as impulse control disorders.

If You Have an Impulse Control Disorder, What Should You Do?

One of the first places to turn if you suspect that you have an impulse control disorder is to your local mental health clinic. The clinics have the range of mental health professionals needed to deal with the complex psychosocial problems created by the impulse control disorders. If you seek treatment in a clinic, you can expect to have an intake interview by a social worker or counselor. It is important to be honest about the extent of your disability and the problems that it is causing. (There is one exception to this rule: women with trichotillomania may not be ready to show the intake worker the extent of their baldness, and they should not be required to do so.) For example, if you have been arrested for kleptomania or need to declare bankruptcy because of your compulsive buying problems, you should tell the intake worker so that supportive services can be arranged. The intake worker will then assign your case to the appropriate professional. In some cases, psychological treatments such as behavior therapy are the most appropriate. In others, medications might be tried.

Behavior therapy of the impulse control disorders varies. For some, a technique known as *aversive therapy* appears effective (aversive therapy utilizes negative reinforcements to help stop the problem behavior—for example, snapping a rubberband against your wrist each time you find yourself touching or pulling your hair), while for others, cognitive-behavioral techniques have been found to be useful. For trichotillomania, a technique developed by Drs. Azrin and Nunn appears to be most effective (see the "Resources" section at the end of this chapter). In this technique, the woman learns to substitute another behavior, usually fist-clenching, for the hair-pulling. She practices the fist-clenching several times each day, and when she feels the urge to pull, she makes a fist and prevents herself from pulling. Habit reversal also employs awareness training and several other techniques to achieve maximal effectiveness.

Group therapy is widely used for compulsive shopping, kleptomania, and pathological gambling. Recently, it has been shown to be helpful for trichotillomania as well. The group therapy sessions have some features in common with those used for the addictive disorders; in fact, Gamblers Anonymous is based on the twelve-step program of Alcoholics Anonymous. Even those that don't utilize the twelve-step program emphasize group support and the concept that the whole is greater than the sum of its parts. Therefore, the woman isn't alone; she has friends within the group to offer help and support and a special buddy who helps prevent her from relapsing. A buddy system is utilized frequently for compulsive shoppers, pathological gamblers, and women with kleptomania. For trichotillomania, group therapy sessions may be directed at learning the habit-reversal techniques, with buddies assigned to check on each other's compliance with homework assignments.

The serotonin reuptake blockers, such as fluoxetine (Prozac), clomipramine (Anafranil), fluvoxamine (Luvox), sertraline (Zoloft), and paroxetine (Paxil), are the most effective medications for treating the impulse control disorders. These medications are discussed in detail in Chapter Thirteen and will not be described further here. The serotonin reuptake blocking drugs appear to decrease the anxiety associated with the impulse control disorders; they also decrease the intensity of the compulsive urge. For these reasons, the medications help the woman to resist the negative impulse effectively. Effective resistance is the basis of behavior therapy, and one way in which the medications might work is by allowing the woman to do her own behavior therapy.

Summary

Addictive disorders, such as alcoholism and drug abuse, and the impulse control disorders of kleptomania, pathological gambling, trichotillomania, and compulsive shopping, are not the result of poor willpower but rather result from an abnormal, biological compulsion. Researchers are now beginning to unravel the mysterious causes of these impulse control disorders and new treatments offer help to women trying to free themselves from these compulsive urges. Medications, psychotherapy, and cognitive-behavioral techniques can all play an active role in recovery.

Resources

Support Groups

Twelve-step programs, such as Alcoholics Anonymous, Narcotics Anonymous, and Gamblers Anonymous, are found in most communities. Local newspapers and telephone books will contain contact phone numbers and meeting times.

Dean Foundation
Obsessive Compulsive Information Center
8000 Excelsior Drive, Suite 302
Madison, Wisconsin 53717–1914
608–836–8070

The National Council on Problem Gambling, Inc.
445 West 59th Street
New York, New York 10019
212–765–3833 or 800–522–4700

Obsessive-Compulsive Disorder Foundation
P. O. Box 70
Milford, Connecticut 06460
203–878–5669

Trichotillomania Learning Center
1215 Mission Street, Suite 2
Santa Cruz, California 95060
408–457–1004

Further Reading

Alcohol and Addictive Disorders

Twelve Steps and Twelve Traditions. New York: Alcoholics Anonymous World
    Services, 1980.
Goodwin, Donald. *Alcoholism: The Facts.* 2nd ed. New York: Oxford Univer-
    sity Press, 1994.
Kishline, Audrey. *Moderate Drinking: The New Option for Problem Drinkers.*
    Tucson, AZ: See Sharp Press, 1994.

Pathological Gambling

Estes, Ken, and Mike Brubaker. *Deadly Odds: Recovery from Compulsive
    Gambling.* New York: Parkside Publishing, 1994.

Trichotillomania

Anders, Jeffrey, and James W. Jefferson. *Trichotillomania: A Guide.* Booklet
    available from the Dean Foundation at address listed above.
Azrin, N. H., and R. G. Nunn. *Habit Control in a Day.* New York: Simon &
    Schuster, 1978.

Notes

1. *Twelve Steps and Twelve Traditions.* New York: Alcoholics Anonymous
    World Services, 1980.

Index

Imitrex, 60
Immune system problems, 53–54; suppression, 96–97
Imipramine. See Tofranil
Impulse control disorders, 300–307
Impulsivity, 119–20
Increased appetite, 161
Inderal, 61
Infectious diseases, 56, 93–94, 166; infectious mononucleosis, 56, 183
Insomnia, 143–44
Interference: OCD and, 264; as treatment hallmark, 36–37
Interpersonal psychotherapy, 187
Irritability, 160–61, 165
Irritable bowel disorder, 271–72
Isocom. See Midrin
Isometheptene mucate combinations. See Midrin
Isoptin, 61. See also Calcium channel blockers

Jamais vu, 102
Jamison, Kay Redfield, 148
Jet lag, 141

Kagan, Jerome, 231, 235
Kindling phenomenon, 150
Kleptomania, 302–3
Klonopin, 152, 255. See also Benzodiazepines

Lark, Susan, 51
Laxative abuse, 284
Life stress scale, 50–51
Light therapy (phototherapy), 139, · 167–69
Lithium, 40–41, 150–51
Living of Charlotte Perkins Gilman, The (Gilman), 16
Lopressor, 61. See also Beta-blockers
Lorazepam. See Ativan
Ludiomil, 189
Lupus. See Collagen vascular diseases; Systemic lupus erythematosus
Luvox, 204, 274, 290, 307
Lyme disease, 56, 94

Mania (manic episode), 148. See also Bipolar disorder

Manning, Martha, 191
Maprotiline. See Ludiomil
Masochism, 12–13
Medical conditions: autoimmune disorders and, 101; causing generalized anxiety disorder, 327; infectious diseases and, 93–94; masquerading as psychiatric disorders, 85–91; metabolic disorders and, 91–93; neurological disorders and, 101–5; psychosis due to, 212–13; toxins and, 105–6; that accompany depression, 184–85; that mimic ADD, 124–25; that mimic anorexia, 284; that mimic depression, 85–87, 180–85; that mimic panic disorder, 249–50; that mimic PTSD, 200–201; that mimic SAD, 166
Medications: antianxiety, 255–58; antipsychotics, 40, 151–52, 216–18; for BDD, 290; causing psychiatric symptoms, 106–9; for cyclic mood disorder treatment, 150–52; depression as side-effect of, 107–8, 185; for eating disorders, 286–87; for obsessive-compulsive personality, 268–69; physical impact of over-the-counter, 85; for prevention of migraine headaches, 60; for psychiatric disorders, 40–43; psychosis due to, 212–13; for PTSD treatment, 203–4; for recovery of addictive disorders, 299–300; side-effects masquerading as ADD, 124; sleep disorders caused by, 143; stimulant (for ADD), 126–31; used for CFS treatment, 98–100; used for depression, 189–91; used for PMS/PMDD, 71–72; used in SAD treatment, 169; vs. therapy for OCD, 276–77; that induce panic, 250. See also Antidepressants
Melancholia, 175–76
Memory loss, 52, 200. See also Alzheimer's disease; Dementia; Post-traumatic stress disorder
Menopause, 79–81
Menstrual cycle, 69

DEC 27 1996